C000304024

Flowers in Honiton Lace

Flowers in Honiton Lace

Elsie Luxton and Yusai Fukuyama

B.T. Batsford Ltd · London

Patterns 1–28
Designed by Elsie Luxton
Worked by Elsie Luxton

Patterns 29–48
Designed by Yusai Fukuyama
Worked by Saikoh Takano

First published 1992

Typeset by Lasertext, Stretford, Manchester, UK

Printed and bound in Great Britain by BPCC Hazells Ltd
Member of BPCC Ltd

Published by
B.T. Batsford Ltd
4 Fitzhardinge Street
London W1H 0AH

A catalogue record for this book is available from the British Library

ISBN 0 7134 6314 7

Contents

Acknowledgements 6
Preface 7
The visual approach 9
A technical note 10
How to use this book 12
Finished pieces (actual size) 15
The patterns 27
Appendix I: Fillings 108
Appendix II: Working threads from one section to another 121
Appendix III: Book suppliers 122
Appendix IV: Equipment suppliers 123
Appendix V: Sources of information 125
Further reading 125

Acknowledgements

Translations by Puck Smelter-Hoekstra (Dutch); Brigitte Wichlei (German); and Margarete Wenzel (French). Fillings section abbreviated for translation by Lesley Thomas. Illustrations by Yusai Fukuyama, except for fillings diagrams 1a–17a, which were drawn by Graham Searle (from original diagrams by Lesley Thomas). Photographs by Yusai Fukuyama. Technical Note written by Elsie Luxton.

Preface

This, my fifth book, has been planned to appeal to the more advanced lacemaker. My own designs are mostly raised and rolled work, and this time the fillings at the end of the book are only those that are used in the patterns. Other Honiton fillings appear in previous publications. As in *Honiton Lace – The Visual Approach* the photographs show both the right and the wrong side of the lace, as students have found this to be a great help.

I have enjoyed designing and making 28 of the patterns in this book, and I hope students will be able to follow the diagrams with ease. My grateful thanks go to Yusai for doing all the photography and artwork, and to my Dutch student Marieke Bellinga who has worked the Cowslip so beautifully for this book.

As I near my retirement, I should like to thank all my past and present students in the lace world for their friendship and patience over the years. I hope I have helped to keep this Devon heritage craft alive, and I know it will continue to flourish in the future.

Elsie Luxton

It is a great honour to produce this book in collaboration with Mrs Elsie Luxton MBE, and I thank Elsie sincerely for the opportunity. I hope this book will help and encourage all lacemakers, and give as much pleasure to those making the designs as Elsie and I had in producing them.

Yusai Fukuyama

The visual approach

People admire the art of Honiton lace and believe it to be one of the most elegant and beautiful laces in the world. Yet many think it is a lace which is too difficult for them to make themselves; some think their eyesight is not good enough to see the fine threads, whilst others believe the techniques are too difficult for them to understand.

This book has been planned so that a lacemaker who has a basic knowledge of bobbin lacemaking can easily understand the patterns by studying the diagrams and photographs. As there is very little written description with the patterns, it is anticipated that language will not be a barrier and hence the book may be used by lacemakers in any country, irrespective of the language they use.

When making Honiton lace, the lacemaker is looking at the wrong side of the work, so every design in this book has a photograph of the right and wrong side of the lace – so the lacemakers do not need to reverse the usual photograph of the lace in their minds.

The authors have tried to show that Honiton lacemaking may be easily understood from the illustrations. The working order is shown by the arrows.

Yusai Fukuyama

A technical note

Many of Elsie Luxton's designs in this book are raised and rolled work and so are intended for the advanced student. As students often ask what is meant by raised and rolled work, here is a brief description of the method of working.

First the rib, or 10 stick, is worked along one side of the outline of a chosen section of the pattern and, at the top of the section, the pillow and bobbins are turned to fill this part with either whole or half stitch. The pin holes are then worked on one side in the normal way, but at the rib side, the runner is sewn into the pin hole of the completed rib, i.e. in either the top or bottom loop of the pin hole – not into the actual pin hole, as this is a flat sewing. At the end of the section move the pairs around, to be in a position to roll or rib along the completed section (*see* Appendix II). After the two pairs of runners have been sewn at the bottom, put the centre pairs between one pair of sewn runners and use this pair to roll around these centre bobbins until the roll is long enough to reach the next section to be worked. Sew the pair, making the roll into the top of the completed section in a position for the next row of pin holes. The other sewn pair of runners left at the bottom is used to attach the roll to the completed section: i.e. sew into each hole, taking one thread under the roll and one over, and tie once. If a worked rib is preferred, this is worked instead of the roll. In this case, sewings are made into the completed section as the rib is worked. Apart from the desired three-dimensional effect, it is a great advantage and much neater to be able to continue working many sections without taking the bobbins off and re-starting, as is necessary in flat work. The rib may, if desired, be made around a whole section as in the centre petal of the bell flowers (Pattern 25). In this case, pairs should be laid in and put aside at the top of the section, and used to fill this part when the rib has been carried forward ready for the next section to be worked.

Elsie Luxton

Technische Erläuterung

Elsie Luxton's Entwürfe zu diesem Buch sind vorwiegend 'raised' (erhabene) und 'rolled' (gerollte) Arbeiten und für fortgeschrittene KlöppLerinnen gedacht. Da häufig die Frage gestellt wird, was 'erhabene' und 'gerollte' Arbeiten sind, wird eine kurze Erläuterung gegeben.

Zürst wird die Rippe (oder '10 stick' = 10 Kloeppel bzw. 5 Paare) entlang dem Aussenrand eines gewählten Musterteils geklöppelt; an der Spitze dieses Teils wird das Kissen gedreht, um diesen Teil mit Leinen-oder Halbschlag zu füllen.

Die Nadellöcher werden an einer Seite wie gewohnt gearbeitet, an der Seite der Rippe wird das Laufpaar an einen Nadelpunkt der fertigen Rippe gehäkelt, entweder an den oberen oder unteren Steg, keinesfalls in das eigentliche Loch wie bei der flachen Arbeit.

Am Ende dieses Teils die Paare so arbeiten, daß sie bereitliegen, um eine Rolle oder Rippe entlang des fertigen Teils zu machen (s. Anhang II). Nachdem die beiden Laufpaare unten eingehäkelt wurden, legt man die mittleren Paare zwischen ein Paar der angehäkelten Läufer. Mit diesem Paar arbeitet man eine Rolle um die mittleren Paare bis zum Uebergang in das nächste Teilstück. Das Paar anhäkeln, die Rolle am oberen Ende in Position legen für die nächste Reihe der Nadellöcher. Das eingehäkelte untere Laufpaar wird dazu benutzt, die Rolle auf den fertigen Teil zu heften, d.h. man häkelt in jedes Nadelloch ein, indem ein Faden unter der Rolle und ein Faden über der Rolle geführt wird, einmal knoten. Bevorzugt man eine Rippe, wird diese anstelle der Rolle durchgeführt. Beim Arbeiten der Rippe wird in das fertige Teil eingehäkelt. Abgesehen von dem gewünschten dreidimensionalen Effekt ist es von Vorteil, fortlaufend ohne Heraus- und Wiederaufnehmen von Kloeppeln arbeiten zu koennen. Falls gewuenscht, kann man die Rippe um ein ganzes Stueck herumarbeiten, wie z.B. bei dem mittleren Bluetenblatt der Glockenblume (Muster 25). In diesem Fall sollten Paare hereingenommen und am oberen Teil abgelegt werden, um sie zur Fuellung dieses Teils zu verwenden, nachdem die Rippe fuer das nächste Teil fertiggestellt wurde.

Een technische opmerking

Veel van Elsie Luxtons ontwerpen in dit boek zjin 'raised and rolled' en daardoor bedoeld voor de gevorderde leerling. Omdat leerlingen vaak vragen wat bedoeld wordt met 'raised and rolled', volgt hier een korte beschrijving van der werkwijze.

Eerst wordt de rib, of '10 stick', langs één kant van de omtrek van het gekozen patroondeel geklost en aan de top van dat deel worden kussen en klossen dan gedraaid om dit deel op te vullen mit linnen- of netslag. Daarna worden de speldegaatjes aan één kant op de normale manier gewerkt, maar aan de kant van de rib wordt de loper ofwel aan het bovenlusje ofwel aan het onderlusje van het speldegaatje aangehaakt – niet in het eigenlijke speldegat, aangezien dat een vlakke aanhaking is. Werk aan het eind van het onderdeel de paren rond totdat ze goed liggen om langs het gekloste deel te rollen of te 'ribben' (zie Aanhangsel II). Leg, nadat de twee loopparen aan de onderkant zijn aangehaakt, de middenparen tussen één paar van de aangehaakte loopparen en gebruik dit paar om rond deze middenparen te rollen tot de rol lang genoeg is om het volgende deel te bereiken. Haak het paar zo aan dat de rol aan de top goed ligt voor de volgende reeks speldegaatjes. Het andere aangehaakte paar, dat onderaan is achtergelaten, wordt gebruikt om de rol aan het afgewerkte deel vast te maken: d.w.z. haak in ieder gaatje aan, daarbij één draad onder en één draad boven de rol nemen, en knoop één maal. Waar een gekloste rib de voorkeur heeft, wordt deze geklost in plaats van de rol. In dit geval wordt aan het afgewerkte deel aangehaakt tijdens het klossen van de rib. Behalve het gewenste drie dimensionale effect, is het handig, en veel netter, om een aantal delen na elkaar te kunnen klossen zonder de klossen af te knippen en weer aan te hechten zoals in vlak werk moet. De rib kan, indien gewenst, om een volledig onderdeel gebruikt worden, zoals in het middenblad van de klokbloemen (patroon 25). In dit geval, moeten paren worden ingehangen en opzij gelegd aan de top van het onderdeel, en worden gebruikt om dat deel te vullen als de rib zover is gewerkt dat het volgend deel geklost kan worden.

Note technique

Un grand nombre de modèles d'Elsie Luxton dans ce livre comprennent des parties avec des lacets en relief et des rouleaux et sont, pour cette raison, destinés aux dentellières confirmées. Comme les élèves demandent fréquemment quelle est la signification des termes 'lacet en relief' et 'rouleau', voici une description brève.

On commence par le lacet (ou ruban de 10) le long du contour de la partie choisie; arrivé à l'extrémité (en haut de la partie), on tourne la galette avec les fuseaux pour remplir cette partie soit avec un mat, soit avec une grille. Les épingles sont alors travaillées normalement d'un côté, mais, du côté lacet, les meneurs sont crochetés dans les trous des épingles de ce lacet, c'est-à-dire soit dans la boucle du haut, soit dans celle du bas du trou d'épingle – et non pas dans le trou même (ce qui serait un crochetage à plat). A la fin de la partie mettez les paires en position pour former un rouleau ou un lacet le long de la partie terminée (*voir* Appendice II). Après avoir crocheté les deux meneurs en bas, posez les paires centrales entre une paire de meneurs crochetée et utilisez cette paire pour l'enrouler autour de ces fuseaux du milieu jusqu'à obtenir un rouleau de longueur suffisante pour rejoindre la partie suivante à exécuter. Crochetez la paire et faites de sorte que le rouleau sur la partie terminée soit en position pour la prochaine rangée de trous d'épingles. L'autre paire de meneurs crochetée laissée en bas de la partie est utilisée pour assembler le rouleau à la partie terminée, c'est-à-dire crochetez dans chaque trou, en prenant un fil sous le roleau et une fil sur le rouleau, et nouez-les une fois. Si l'on préfère un lacet en relief, on le fait à la place d'un rouleau. Dans ce cas, on crochète dans la partie terminée au fur et à mesure que l'on exécute le lacet à trois dimensions. Mis à part l'effet en relief désiré, celui-ci est bien plus avantageux et plus net pour continuer à faire plusieurs parties sans avoir à enlever les fuseaux et à recommencer, comme cela est nécessaire dans un travail à plat. Si vous le désirez, le lacet peut contourner toute une partie, comme cela est le cas autour du pétale central des Campanules (Patron 25). Dans ce cas, des paires doivent être conservées et placées en haut de la partie pour être utilisées pour remplir cette partie dès que le lacet a été avancé et est prêt pour l'exécution de la partie suivante.

How to use this book

1 All photographs of the finished work are shown from page 16 to 26 so that comparisons can be easily made and the desired design chosen.
2 Every design is shown in a double-page spread and is illustrated by a photograph of the right side, a photograph of the wrong side, a diagram showing the direction of working, the number of pairs required, and a pricking.
3 Each design has the same numbering for all the illustrations, e.g.
– the right side photograph 1-a,
– the wrong side photograph 1-b,
– the working order 1-c,
– the number of pairs 1-d,
– and the pricking 1-e.
4 The photograph of the wrong side of the lace is shown so that the lacemaker has a direct comparison with his/her work and the author's work during the making of the lace.
5 The patterns have been worked in 180/2 cotton thread and so the number of threads in the diagram refers to 180 thread.
When a coarse thread was required No. 50 sewing cotton was used.
6 In the diagram the direction of working is shown by the arrows and the number of pairs of bobbins required for each part is indicated by the number i.e. 5 = 5 pairs or 10 bobbins.
The coarse pair is shown as C, e.g. 6 + C means 6 pairs of bobbins and a coarse pair.
The rib is shown as R, e.g. R5 means 5 pairs rib.
7 All prickings in this book are shown in the actual size.

Wie man dieses Buch benutzt

1 Zur Veranschaulichung und leichteren Wahl des zu klöppelnden Motivs sind die Fotos der fertigen Spitzen auf den Seiten 16 bis 26 abgebildet.
2 Jeder Entwurf wird auf einer Doppelseite gezeigt, illustriert durch ein Foto von Vorder- und Rückseite der Spitze, einer technischen Zeichnung mit Angabe der erforderlichen Klöppelpaare, des Arbeitsverlaufs sowie dem Klöppelbrief.
3 Zu jedem Entwurf erhalten die dazugehörigen Abbildungen durchweg die gleiche Numerierung, z.B. Foto Vorderseite der Spitze 1-a, Rückseite 1-b, Arbeitsanleitung 1-c, Anzahl der Klöppelpaare 1-d, Musterbrief 1-e.
4 Im Foto wird die Rückseite (linke Seite) der Spitze gezeigt, damit während des Klöppelns ein direkter Vergleich möglich ist.
5 Die Muster wurden mit Baumwollgarn 180/2 geklöppelt, die Anzahl der Fäden im Muster beziehen sich daher stets auf Garnstärke 180. Als Konturfaden wurde Nähgarn Nr. 50 benutzt.
6 In der Arbeitszeichnung wird der Arbeitsverlauf durch Pfeile angegeben, die Anzahl der für die einzelnen Teile erforderlichen Klöppelpaare wird durch entsprechende Zahlen angegeben, z.B. 5 = 5 Paare (10 Klöppel).
Der Konturfaden wird mit 'C' bezeichnet, so bedeutet 6 + C = 6 Klöppelpaare sowie 1 Paar Konturfaden.
Die Rippe wird mit 'R' bezeichnet, R5 bedeutet 5 Paare für die Rippe.
7 Alle Briefe sind in Originalgröße abgebildet.

Hoe dit boek te gebruiken

1 Alle uitgewerte stukken zijn afgebeeld op blz. 16 tot 26 om het vergelijken en het kiezen van een ontwerp te vergemakkelijken.
2 Elk ontwerp is afgebeeld op een dubbele pagina en wordt toegelicht met foto's van voor- en achterkant, diagrammen voor de werkrichting en het aantal paren, en de prikking.
3 Elk ontwerp heeft voor alle illustraties hetzelfde nummer, bijv.
– de foto van der voorkant 1-a,
– de foto van de achterkant 1-b,
– de werkvolgorde 1-c,
– het aantal paren 1-d,
– en de prikking 1-e.
4 De foto van de achterkant is gegeven opdat de kantwerkster al tijdens het klossen haar werk kan vergelijken met dat van de auteur.
5 De patronen zijn gewerkt in katoen nr 180/2, dus de aantallen paren in de diagrammen verwijzen naar garen nr 180.
Wanneer een dikke draad nodig was, is naaigaren nr 50 gebruikt.
6 In het diagram is de werkrichting aangegeven door pijlen. Het benodigde aantal paren voor elk deel is aangegeven door nummers, bijv. 5 = 5 paar of 10 klossen.
Het paar met de dikke draad is C, bijv. 6 + C betekent 6 paar plus een paar met dikke draad.
De rib is voorgesteld door R, bijv. R5 betekent rib van 5 paar.
7 Alle prikkingen in het boek zijn op ware grootte gegeven.

Comment utiliser ce livre

1 Toutes les photos des travaux finis se trouvent pages 16 à 26 pour faciliter le choix d'un modèle.
2 Chaque modèle est présenté sur une double page qui donne une photo de l'endroit et une photo de l'envers du travail, un schéma qui donne le nombre de paires de fuseaux et le sens du travail, un carton.
3 Tous les modèles sont présentés dans le même ordre;
1-a: vue de l'endroit
1-b: vue de l'envers
1-c: sens du travail
1-d: nombre de paires de fuseaux
1-e: carton
4 La photo de l'envers permet une comparaison du travail avec le modèle pendant la réalisation de la dentelle.
5 Tous les modèles sont réalisés avec du fil 180/2; quand un fil plus gros est nécessaire du fil à coudre no. 50 est utilisé.
6 Sur les schémas le sens du travail est indiqué par des flèches et le nombre de paires de fuseaux nécessaires pour chaque partie est désigné par un nombre.
Exemple: 5 = 5 paires ou 10 fuseaux.
La paire de fil gros est désignée par C.
Exemple: 6 + C signifie 6 paires du fuseaux plus une paire de fil gros.
Le lacet est désigné par R.
Exemple: R5 signifie côte de 5 paires.
7 Tous les cartons sont grandeur nature.

Finished pieces (actual size)

1
2
3
4
5
6
7
8

9
11
10
12

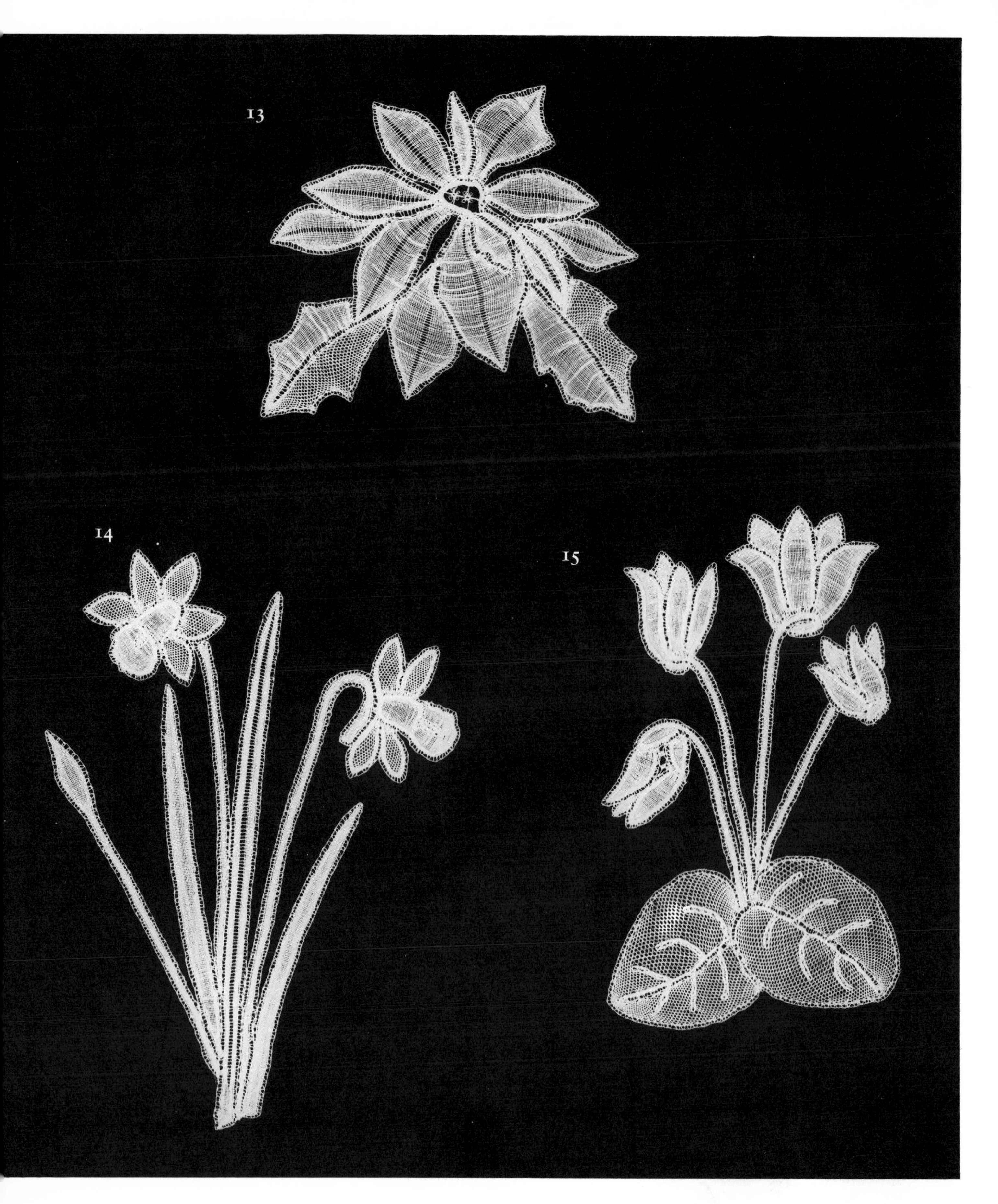
13
14
15

16
17
18

19
20
21

22
23
24

25
26
27

28

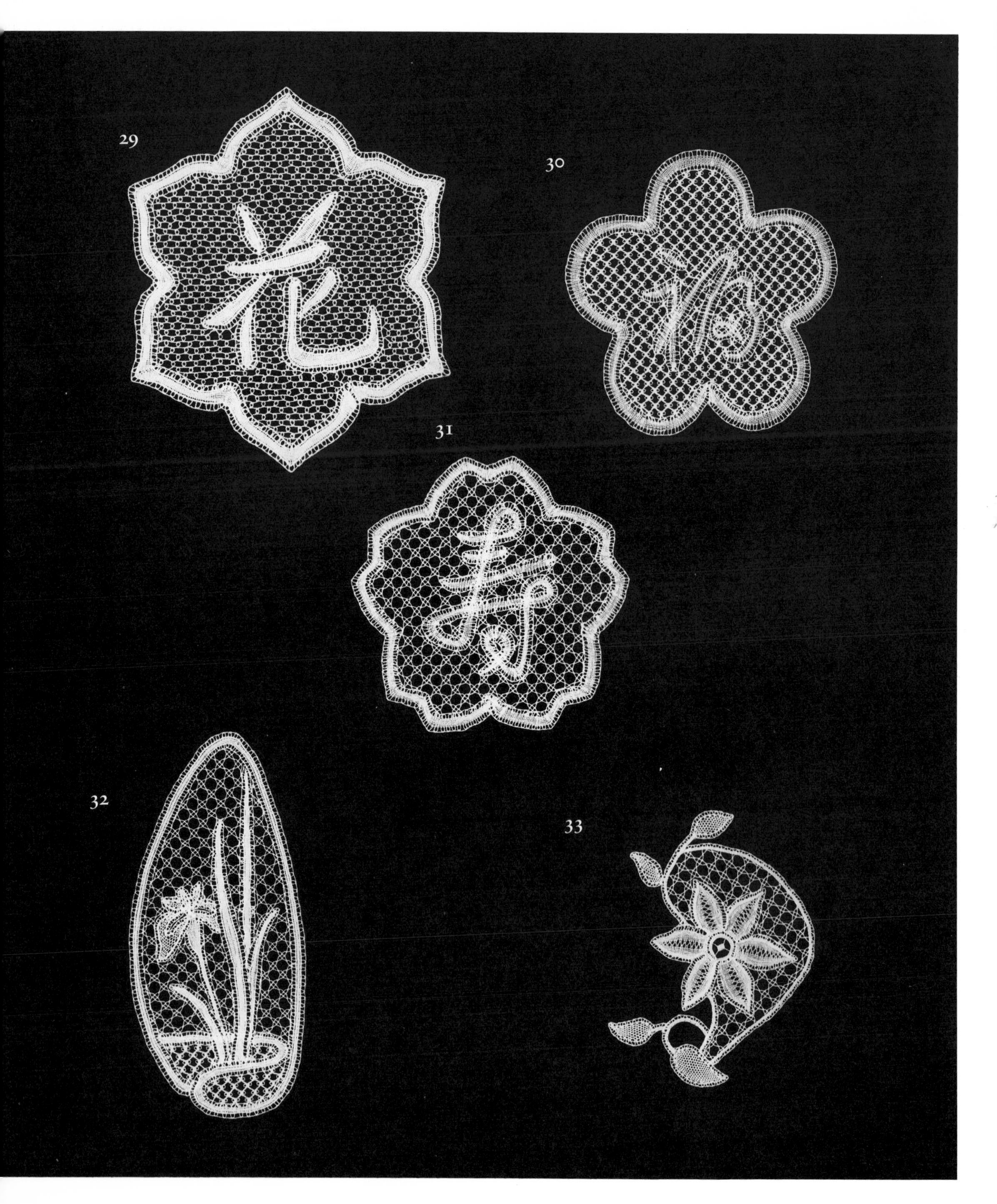
29
30
31
32
33

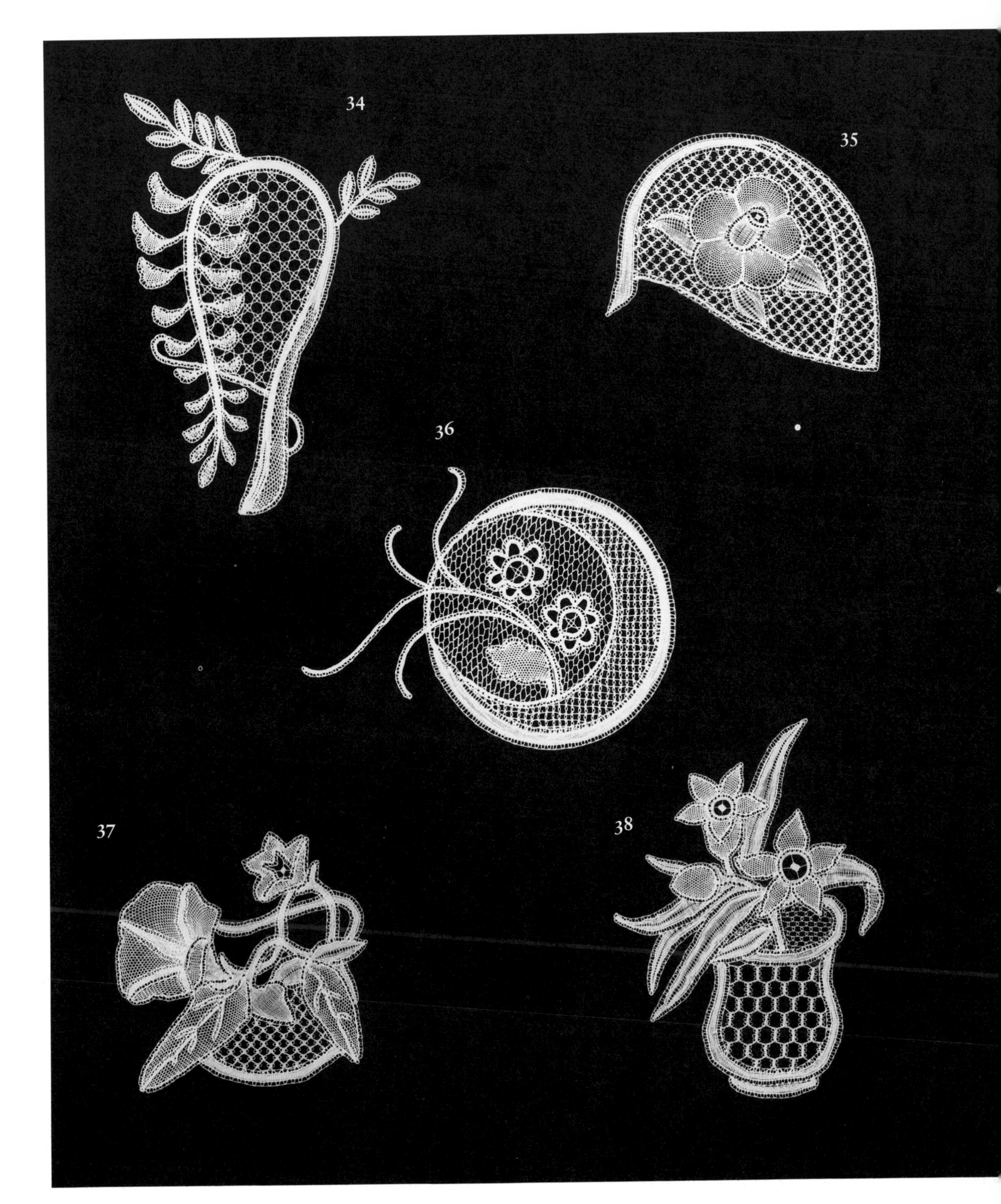
34
35
36
37
38

39
40
41
42
43
44
46
47
45
48

The patterns

1
Daisy (1)

Fig. 1-c working order

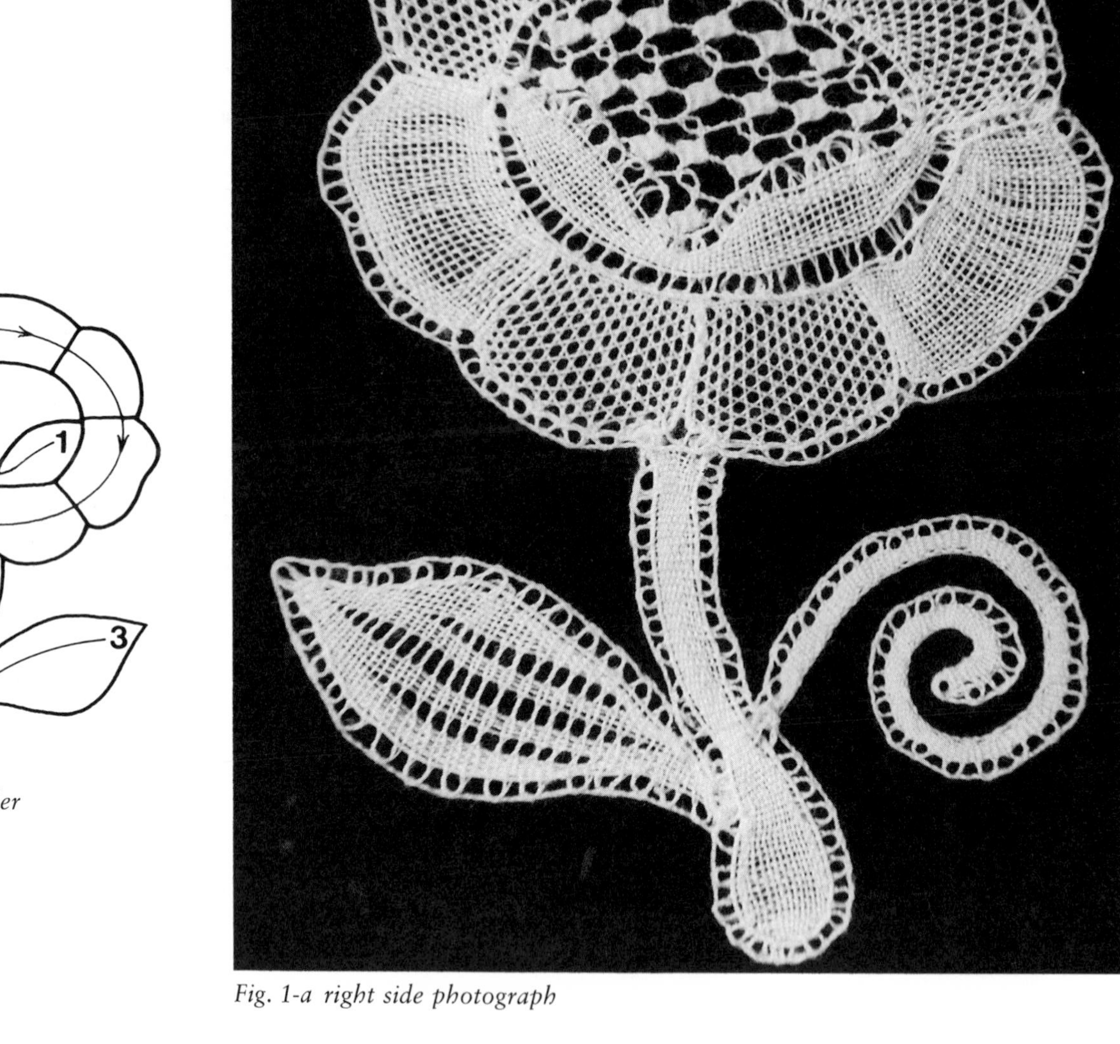

Fig. 1-a right side photograph

Flat work – a pattern recommended for the beginner and suitable to fit into a brooch. The two centre petals are worked first and then the outer petals. The stem is worked from the bottom to the flower, and then the leaf and tendril are sewn into this stem.

Flache Arbeit. Ein Muster für Anfänger, geeignet als Brosche. Die beiden inneren Blütenblätter werden zuerst gearbeitet, dann die äußeren. Der Stiel wird von unten zur Blüte hin gearbeitet, danach Blatt und Ranke an den Stiel anhäkeln.

Vlak werk – een patroon, aanbevolen voor de beginner en geschikt voor een broche. De twee binnenste blaadjes worden eerst geklost en daarna de buitenste. De steel wordt van de basis naar de bloem gewerkt, en daarna worden blad en rank aan deze steel afgehecht.

Travail plat – un dessin recommandé aux débutantes, peut se porter en broche. Travaillez d'abord les deux pétales du centre, ensuite les pétales extérieurs. La tige se travaille du bas vers la fleur, puis la feuille et la vrille sont crochetées dans la tige.

Fig. 1-b wrong side photograph

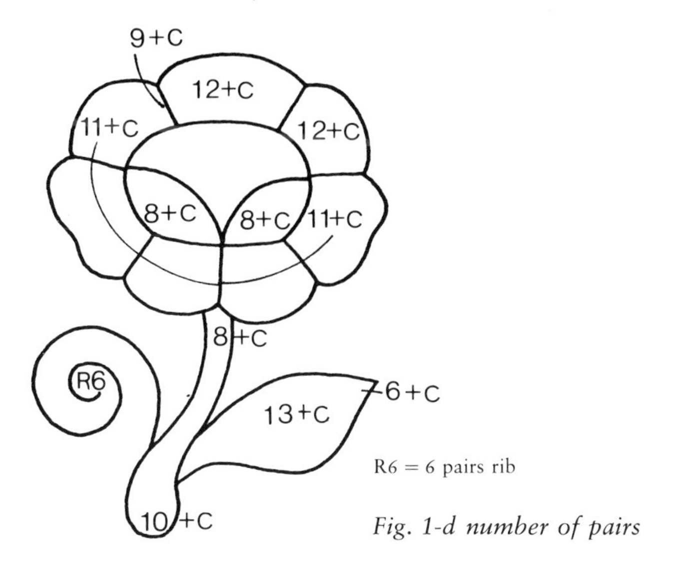

Fig. 1-d number of pairs

Fig. 1-e pricking

2
Wild Rose

Fig. 2-a *right side photograph*

Fig. 2-c working order

Flat work – a pattern for beginners. Divided leaves are worked first – they are a good practice for sewings before starting raised work. Work the flowers. Between each petal weave the coarse thread through all the downrights, around the coarse thread on the other side, and back to its original position.

Flache Arbeit. Ein Muster für Anfänger. Die geteilten Blätter werden zuerst gearbeitet und sind eine gute Übung für das Anhäkeln, ehe man mit der erhabenen Arbeit beginnt. Zwischen jedem Blütenblatt den Konturfaden durch alle Rißpaare weben, um den Konturfaden der anderen Seite herum und zurück zum Ausgangspunkt.

Vlak werk – een patroon voor beginners. De verdeelde blaadjes worden eerst geklost – ze vormen een goede oefening in het aanhaken, voordat met het raised work begonnen wordt. Klos de bloemen. Klos telkens tussen twee blaadjes de dikke draad door alle hangende paren, rond de dikke draad aan de andere kant en weer terug naar zijn oorspronkelijke positie.

Travail plat – un ouvrage pour débutantes. Travaillez d'abord les feuilles lobées – elles sont un bon exercice de crochetage avant d'entreprendre un travail en relief. Entre chaque pétale passez le gros fil de l'autre côté pour revenir à son point de départ.

Fig. 2-b wrong side photograph

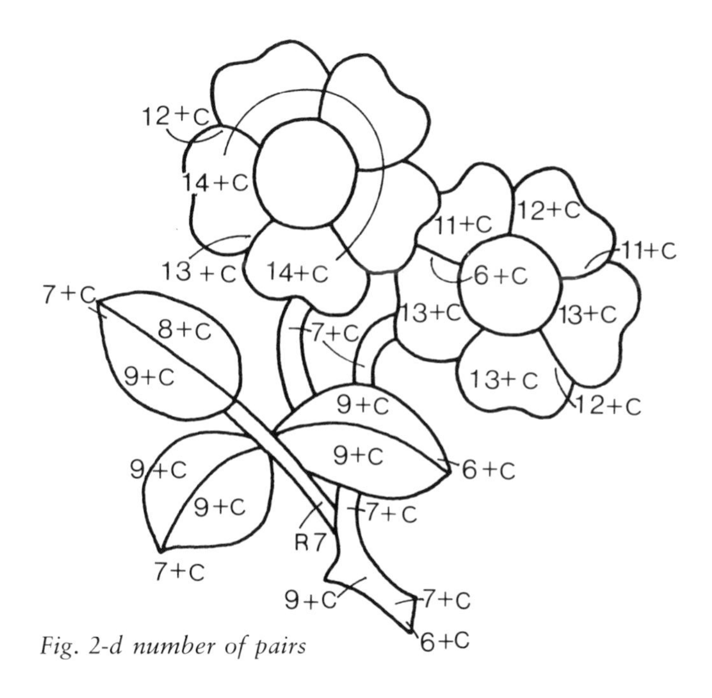

Fig. 2-d number of pairs

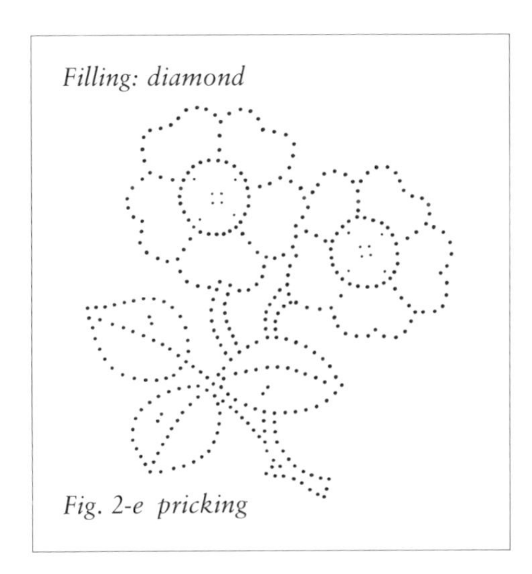

Fig. 2-e pricking

3
Rose (1)

Fig. 3-a right side photograph

Fig. 3-c working order

Fig. 3-b wrong side photograph

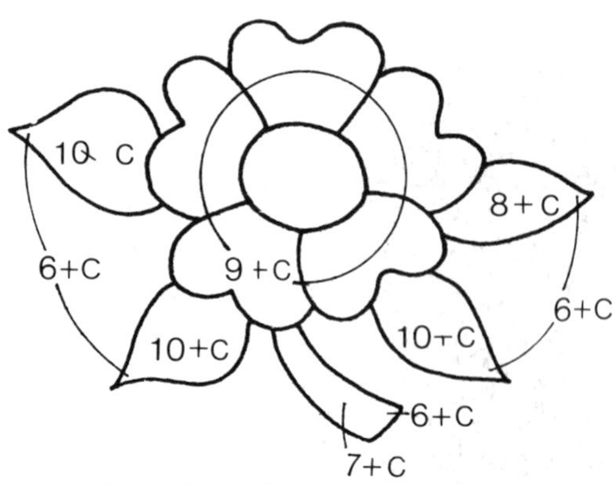

Fig. 3-d number of pairs

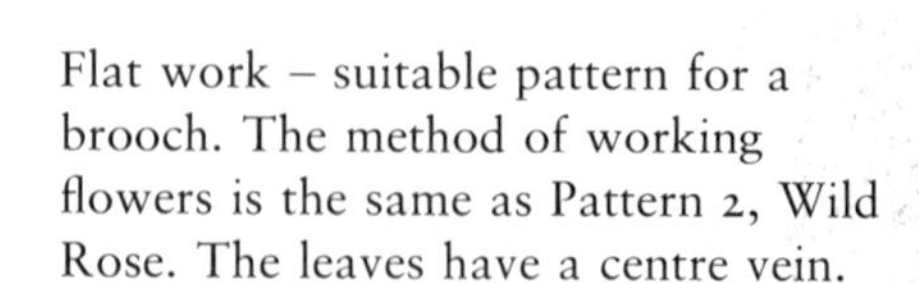

Flat work – suitable pattern for a brooch. The method of working flowers is the same as Pattern 2, Wild Rose. The leaves have a centre vein.

Filling: straight pin

Fig. 3-e pricking

Flache Arbeit. Geeignetes Motiv für eine Brosche. Die Arbeitsweise entspricht Muster 2 – Hundsrose. Die Blätter haben eine Mittelader.

Vlak werk – geschikt patroon voor een broche. De werkmethode is dezelfde als in patroon 2, Wild Rose. De bladeren hebben een middennerf.

Travail plat – peut se porter en broche. La méthode de travail est la même qu'au Patron 2, Wild Rose. Les feuilles ont une nervure centrale.

4
Daisy (2)

Fig. 4-a *right side photograph*

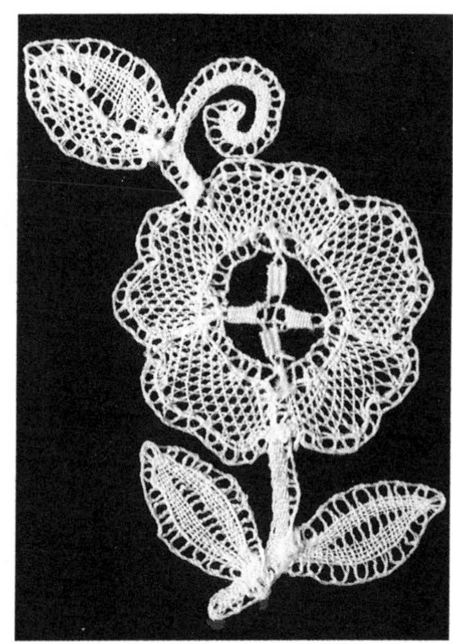

Fig. 4-b *wrong side photograph*

Fig. 4-c *working order*

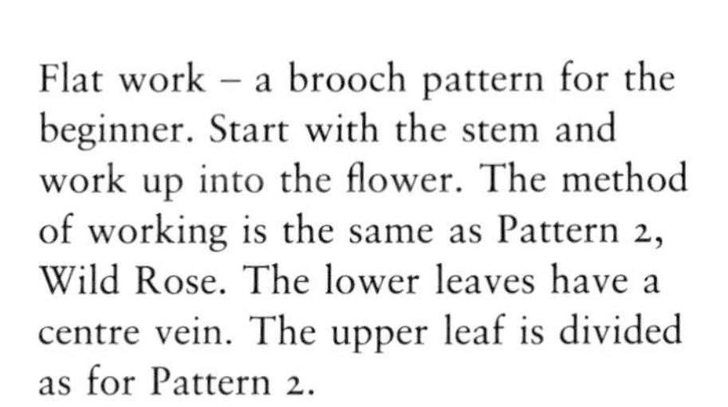

Flat work – a brooch pattern for the beginner. Start with the stem and work up into the flower. The method of working is the same as Pattern 2, Wild Rose. The lower leaves have a centre vein. The upper leaf is divided as for Pattern 2.

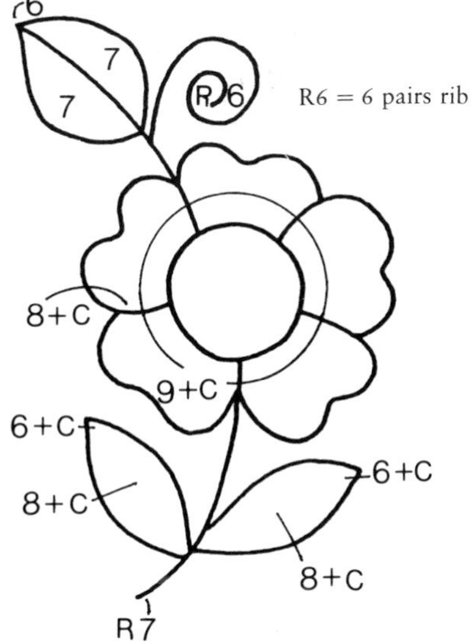

Fig. 4-d *number of pairs*

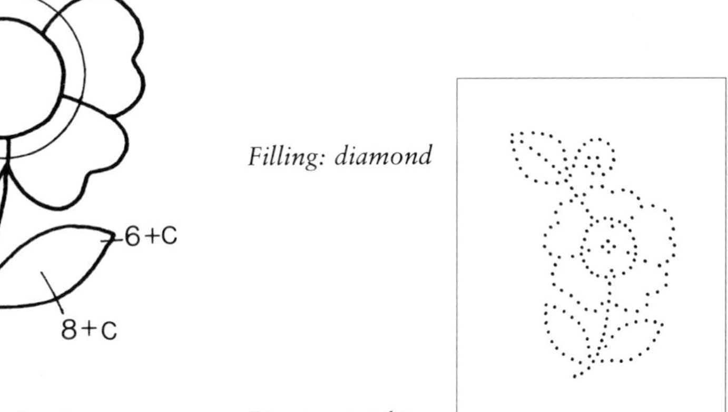

Filling: *diamond*

Fig. 4-e *pricking*

Flache Arbeit. Anfängermuster für eine Brosche. Beim Stiel beginnen und zur Blüte hocharbeiten. Die Arbeitsweise entspricht Muster 2 – Hundsrose. Die unteren Blätter durchläuft eine Ader, das obere Blatt wird unterteilt wie bei Entwurf 2.

Vlak werk – patroon voor beginners, geschikt voor een broche. Begin met de steel en werk omhoog tot in de bloem. De werkmethode is gelijk aan die in patroon 2, Wild Rose. De bladeren hebben een middennerf. Het bovenste blad is verdeeld als in patroon 2.

Travail plat – un dessin pour une broche, destiné aux débutantes. Commencez par la tige et travaillez en montant vers la fleur. La méthode de travail est la mâme qu'au Patron 2, Wild Rose. Les feuilles d'en bas ont une nervure centrale. La feuille d'en haut est divisée comme dans le Patron 2.

5
Primrose

Fig. 5-c working order

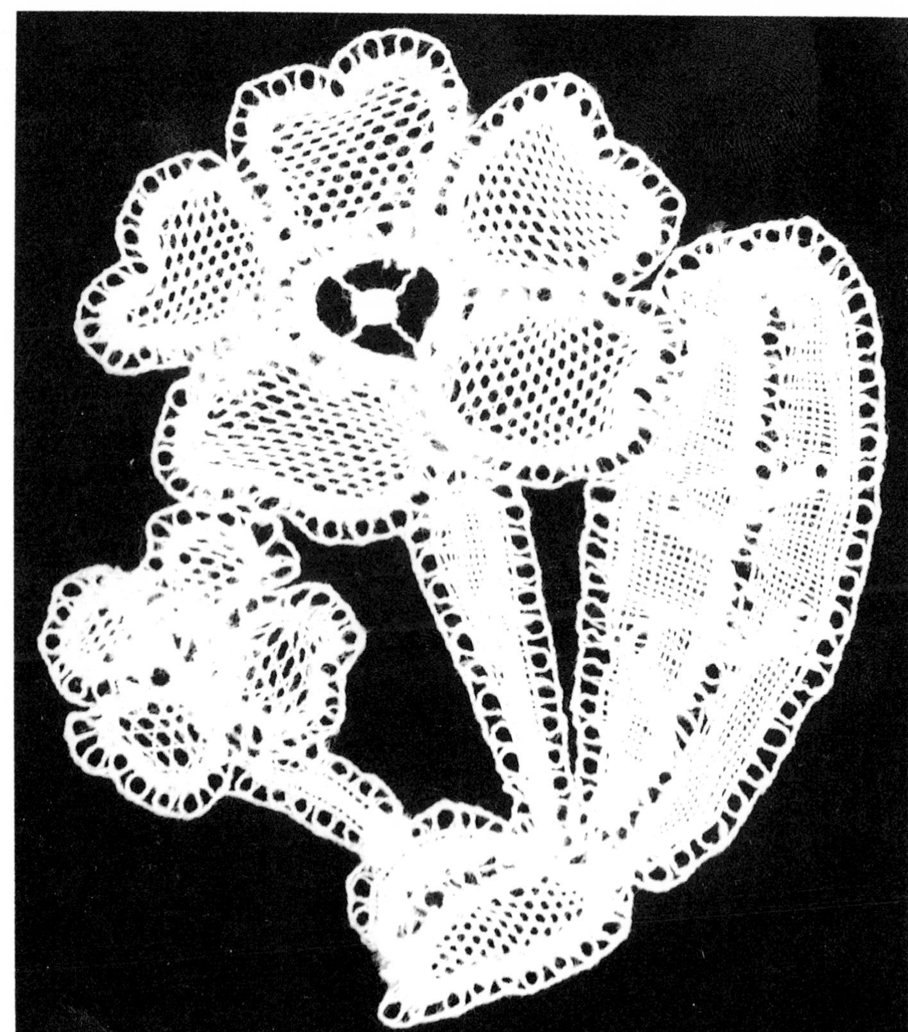

Fig. 5-a right side photograph

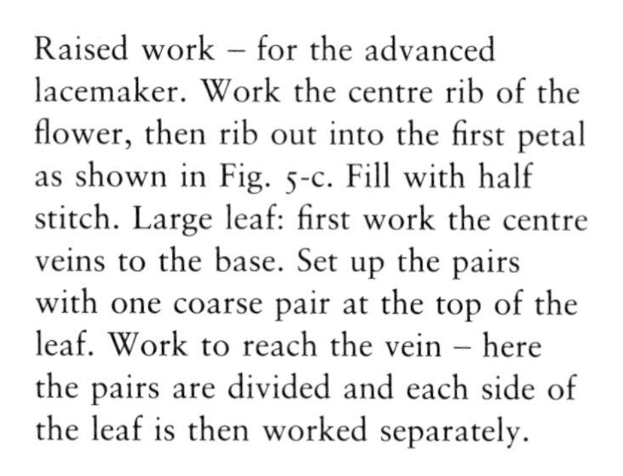

Raised work – for the advanced lacemaker. Work the centre rib of the flower, then rib out into the first petal as shown in Fig. 5-c. Fill with half stitch. Large leaf: first work the centre veins to the base. Set up the pairs with one coarse pair at the top of the leaf. Work to reach the vein – here the pairs are divided and each side of the leaf is then worked separately.

Erhabene Arbeit. Für Fortgeschrittene. Beginn mit innerer Mitte der Blume, Übergang zum ersten Blütenblatt gemäß Abbildung 5-c. Füllung in Halbschlag. Großes Blatt: Zuerst werden die Adern des Blattes zum Stiel hin gearbeitet. Dann die Klöppelpaare und 1 Paar Konturfaden an der Blattspitze aufstecken. Bis zu den Adern klöppeln, die Paare teilen und die Blatthälften separat klöppeln.

Raised work – voor de gevorderde kantkloster. Werk de rib in het hart van de bloem, vervolg de rib in het eerste bloemblaadje zoals aangegeven in fig. 5. Vul met netslag. Groot blad: werk eerst de middennerf tot onderaan. Begin met de paren plus een dik paar aan de top van het blad. Werk tot aan de nerf – hier worden de paren verdeeld en beide zijden van het blad apart verder geklost.

Travail en relief – pour dentellières confirmées. Travaillez le lacet au centre de la fleur, puis utilisez-le pour le premier pétale, comme montré sur la figure 5. Remplissez avec une grille. Feuille: Travaillez les nervures centrales en direction de la base. Placez les paires avec une paire de gros fil à la pointe de la feuille. Continuez vers la nervure où les paires seront divisées pour terminer séparément chaque côté de la feuille.

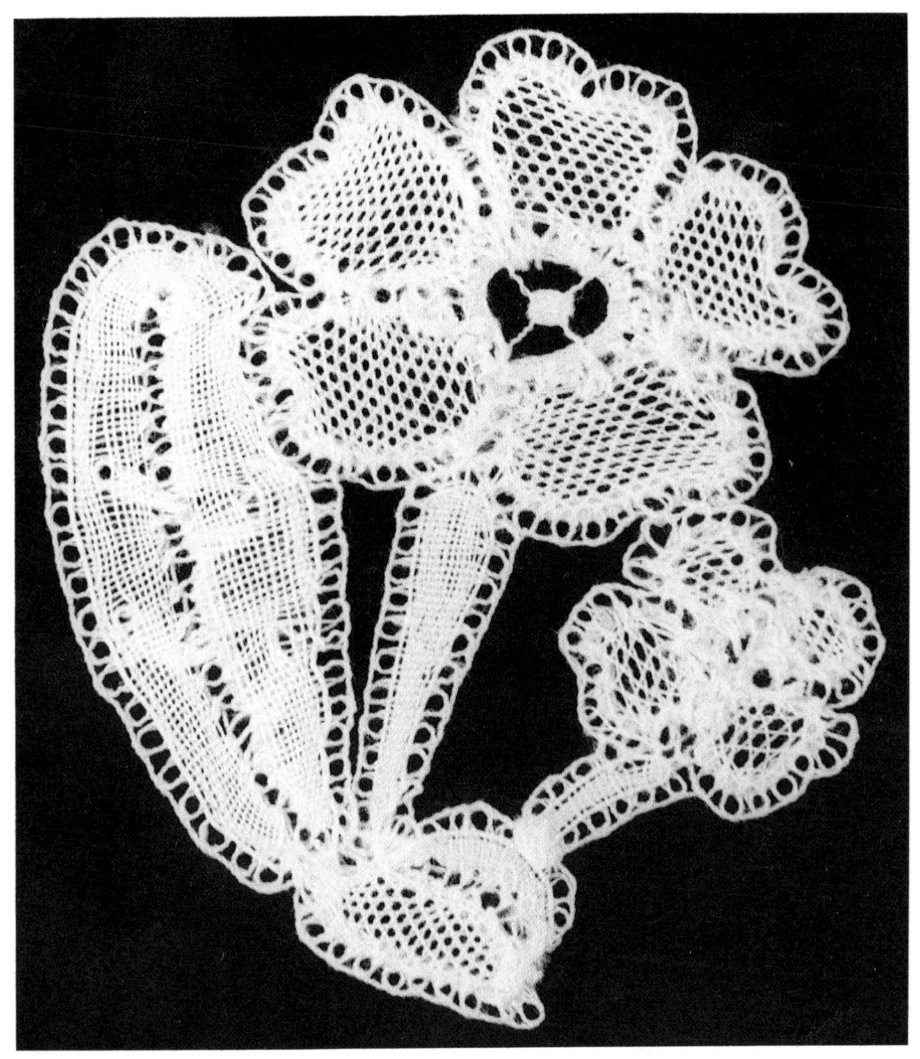

Fig. 5-b wrong side photograph

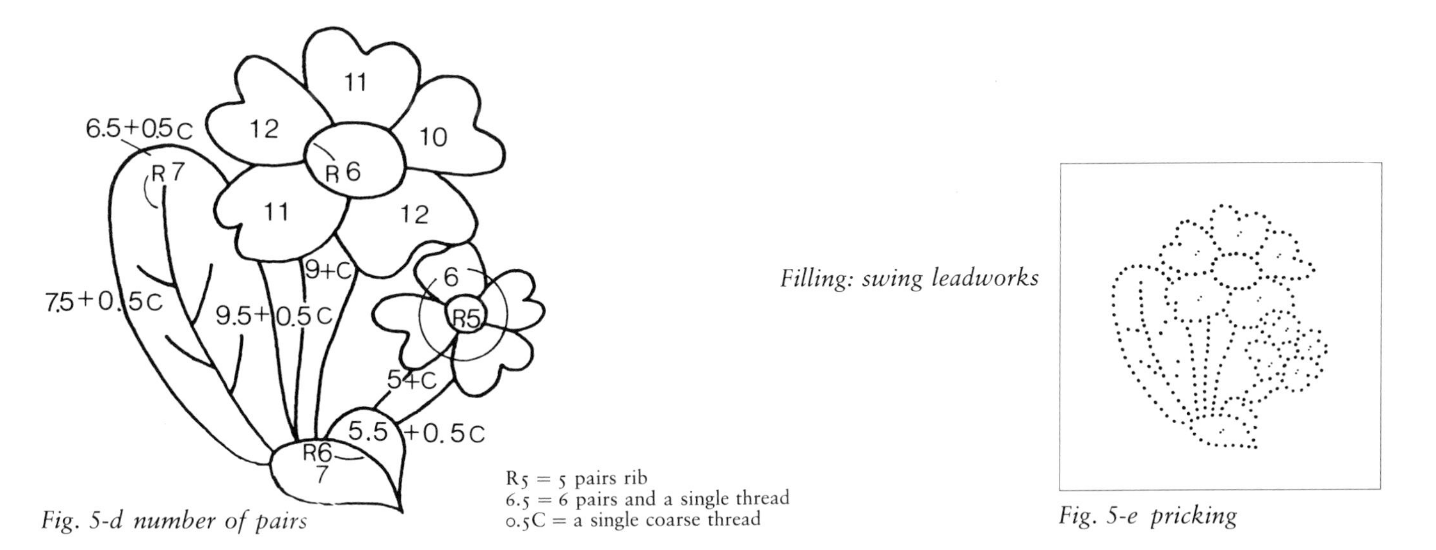

Fig. 5-d number of pairs

R5 = 5 pairs rib
6.5 = 6 pairs and a single thread
0.5C = a single coarse thread

Filling: swing leadworks

Fig. 5-e pricking

6
Pansy

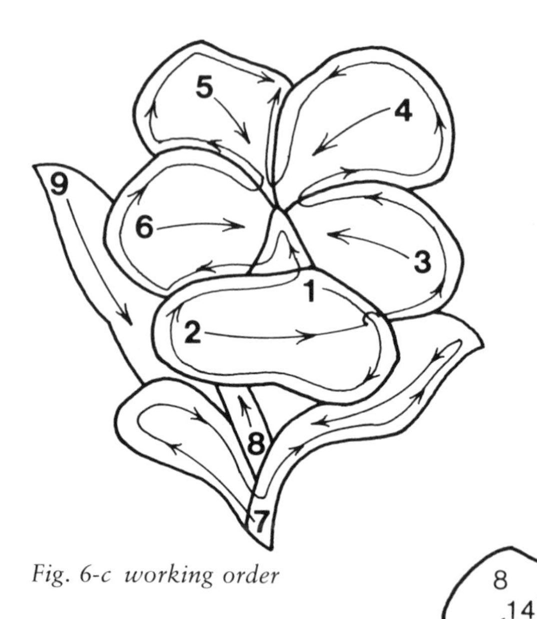

Fig. 6-c working order

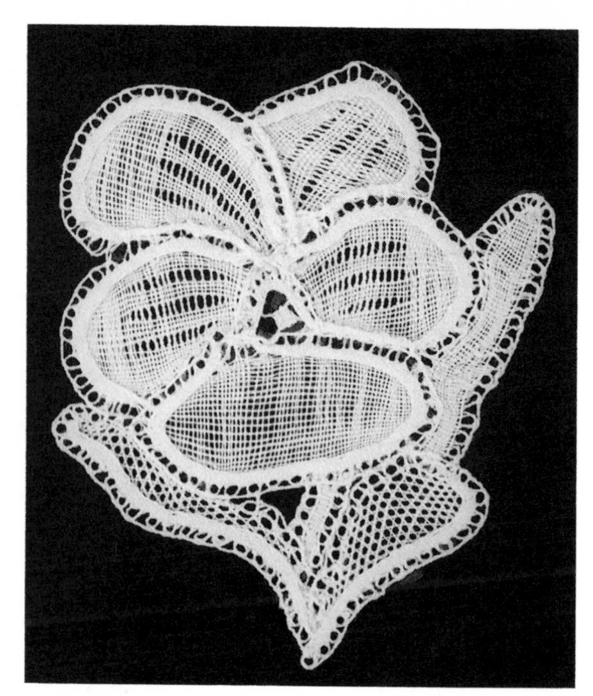

Fig. 6-a right side photograph

R5 = 5 pairs rib

Fig. 6-d number of pairs

Filling: swing leadworks

Fig. 6-e pricking

For the advanced lacemaker. Rib around the lower centre petal, then around the centre of the flower. Fill the lower petal and work the remaining petals in a similar way to Pattern 5, Primrose.

Fig. 6-b wrong side photograph

Für Fortgeschrittene. Rippe um das untere mittlere Blütenblatt arbeiten, anschließend den Innenkreis der Blume. Füllung für ein unteres Blütenblatt, die restlichen Blütenblätter gemäß Muster 5 – Primel, arbeiten.

Voor de gevorderde kantkloster. Werk eerst een rib rond het blad midden onder, dan rond het midden van de bloem. Vul het onderste blad en werk de overige blaadjes als in patroon 5, Primrose.

Pour dentellières confirmées. Exécutez le lacet autour du pétale du centre en bas, puis autour du centre de la fleur. Remplissez le pétale inférieur et travaillez les pétales restants de la même manière que le Patron 5, Primrose.

7
Iris

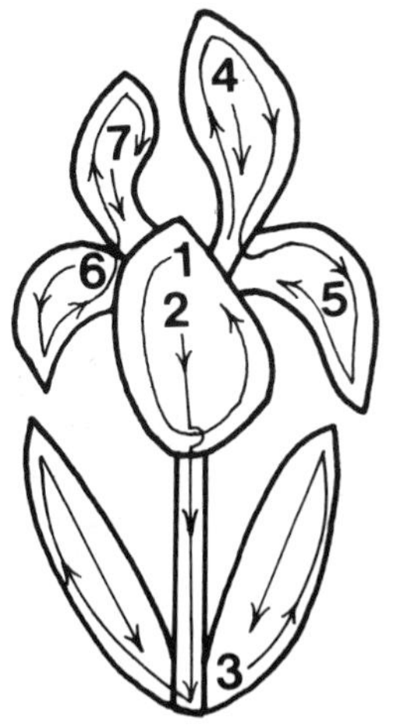

Fig. 7-c working order

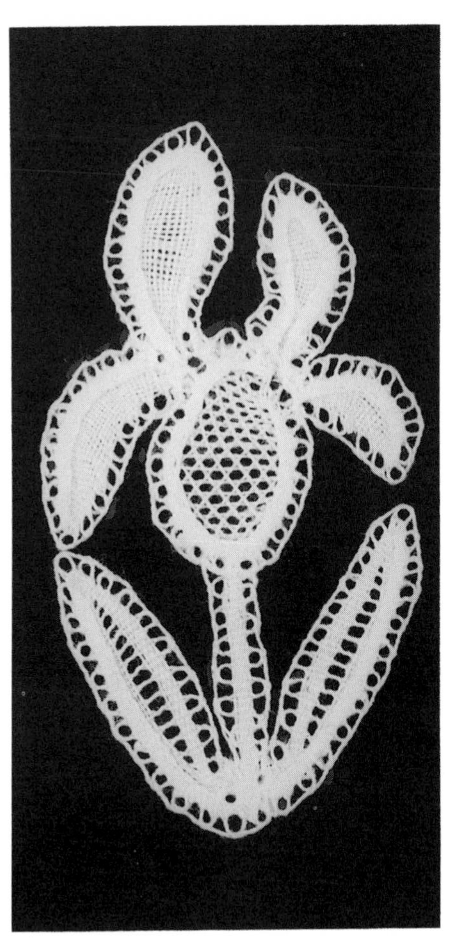

Fig. 7-a right side photograph

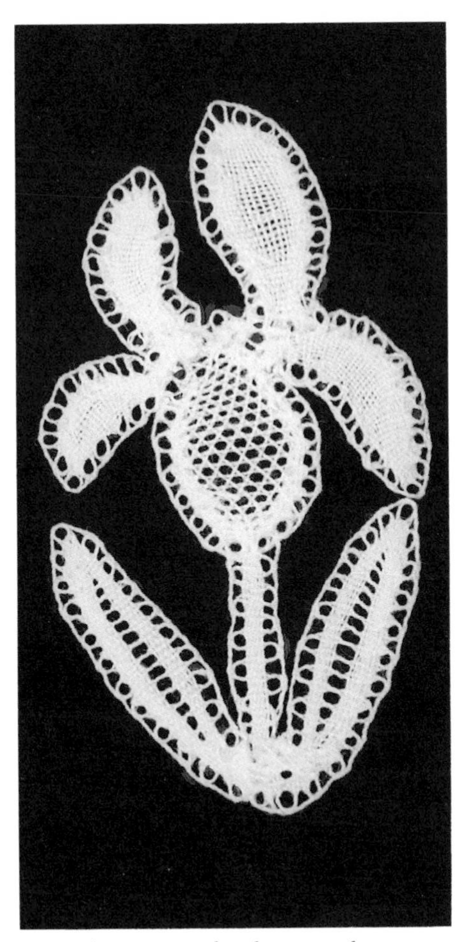

Fig. 7-b wrong side photograph

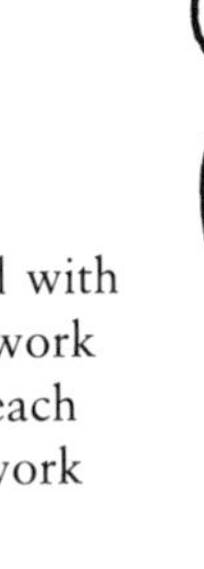

R7 = 7 pairs rib

Fig. 7-d number of pairs

Fig. 7-e pricking

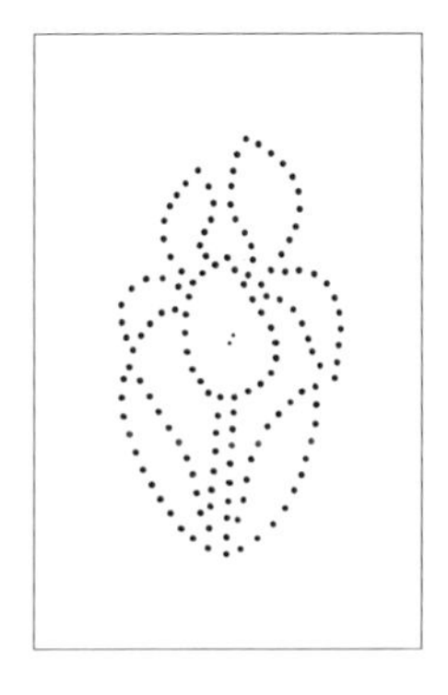

Work the flower calyx first – fill with half stitch and use the pairs to work the stem. Continue on to raise each leaf in turn and sew off. Now work the raised petals of the flower.

Zuerst den Blütenkelch arbeiten, mit Halbschlag füllen und mit diesen Paaren den Stiel klöppeln. Die Blätter im Wechsel erhaben arbeiten und abknoten. Anschließend die erhabenen Blütenblätter der Blume arbeiten.

Klos eerst de kelk – vul met netslag en gebruik dezelfde paren voor de steel. Klos nu de blaadjes in raised work en hecht af. Klos nu de raised bloemblaadjes.

Faites d'abord le calice de la fleur – remplissez-le avec une grille et utilisez les paires pour exécuter la tige.

8
Clarkia

Fig. 8-c working order

Fig. 8-a right side photograph

A variety of different techniques are used in this pattern.

In diesem Muster werden verschiedene Techniken angewandt.

In dit patroon worden verschillende technieken gebruikt.

Un choix de différentes techniques est utilisé pour ce patron.

Fig. 8-b wrong side photograph

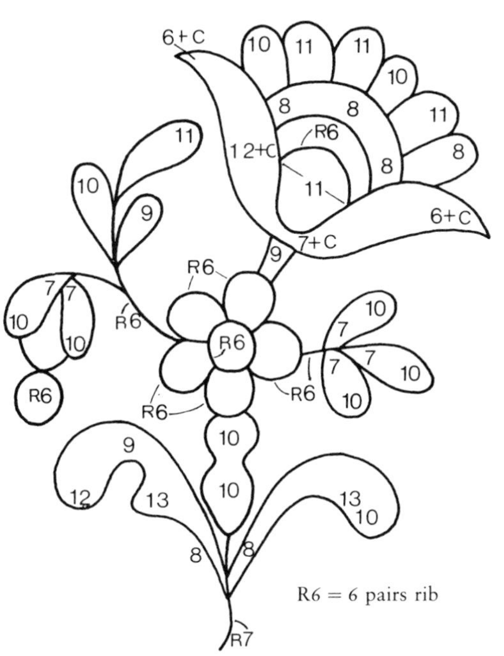

Fig. 8-d number of pairs

Fillings: leadwork bars, swing leadworks

Fig. 8-e pricking

9
Daisy (3)

Fig. 9-a right side photograph

Fig. 9-b wrong side photograph

Fig. 9-c working order

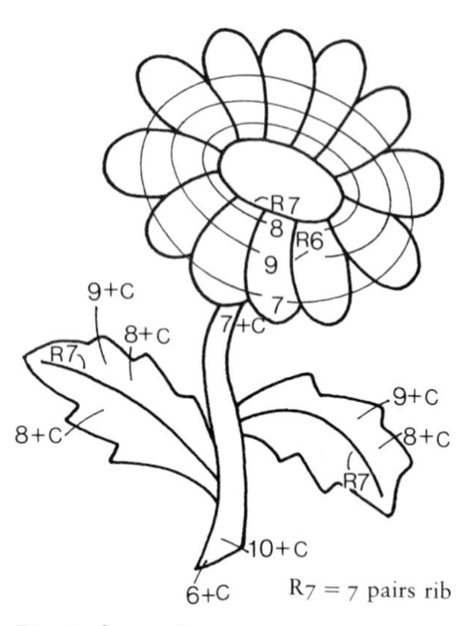

Fig. 9-d number of pairs

Fig. 9-e pricking

Work rib to form the centre of the flower. Continue into first petal. Rib to form the outline of the petals and fill with whole stitch. The leaves have a centre rib.

Rippe für das Innere der Blume arbeiten, Übergang zum ersten Blütenblatt. Rippe als Umrandung der Blütenblätter arbeiten und mit Ganzschlag füllen. Die Blätter werden durch eine Ader unterteilt.

Klos de rib die het hart van de bloem vormt. Vervolg de rib in het eerste bloemblaadje. Klos dan een rib voor de omtrek van de bloemblaadjes en vul deze met linnenslag. De bladeren hebben een middennerf.

Faites le lacet qui forme le milieu de la fleur. Continuez pour travailler le premier pétale. Exécutez le lacet qui servira de contour de pétales, puis remplissez avec du mat. Les feuilles ont une nervure centrale.

10
Dahlia (1)

Fig. 10-a *right side photograph*

Fig. 10-b *wrong side photograph*

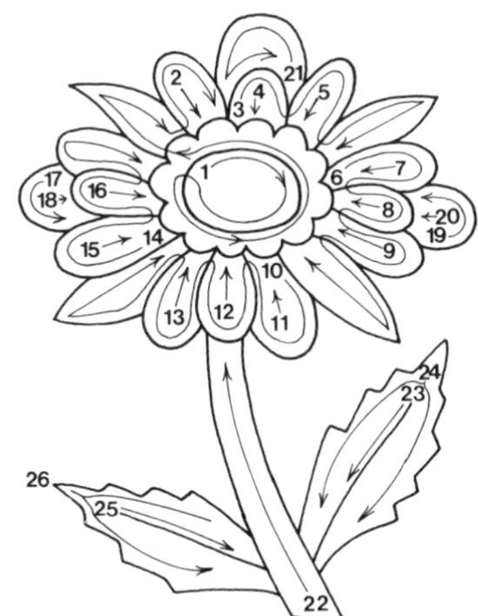

Fig. 10-c *working order*

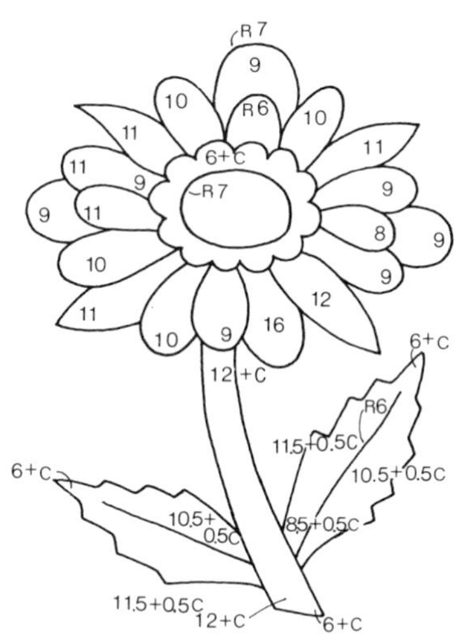

Fig. 10-d *number of pairs*

R6 = 6 pairs rib
11.5 = 11 pairs and a single thread
0.5C = a single coarse thread

Fig. 10-e *pricking*

Rib the centre oval first, then work half stitch petals around the circle. The outer petals are raised and filled with whole or half stitch. Work the centre rib, and start each leaf from the top.

Zuerst die Rippe für das innere Oval und dann die Blütenblätter in Halbschlag arbeiten. Die äußeren Blütenblätter sind erhaben und werden mit Halb- oder Ganzschlag gefüllt. Nach dem Arbeiten der Ader werden die Blätter jeweils an der Spitze beginnend geklöppelt.

Maak eerst de rib om het ovale hart, klos dan de netslagblaadjes om dit hart. De buitenste bloemblaadjes zijn raised en gevuld met linnen- of netslag. Klos de midden rib, en begin elk blad aan de top.

Faites d'abord le lacet pour l'ovale du centre, puis les pétales en grille tout autour. Les pétales extérieurs sont en relief et remplis d'une grille et d'un mat. Exécutez la nervure du centre et commencez chaque feuille en haut.

11
Petunia

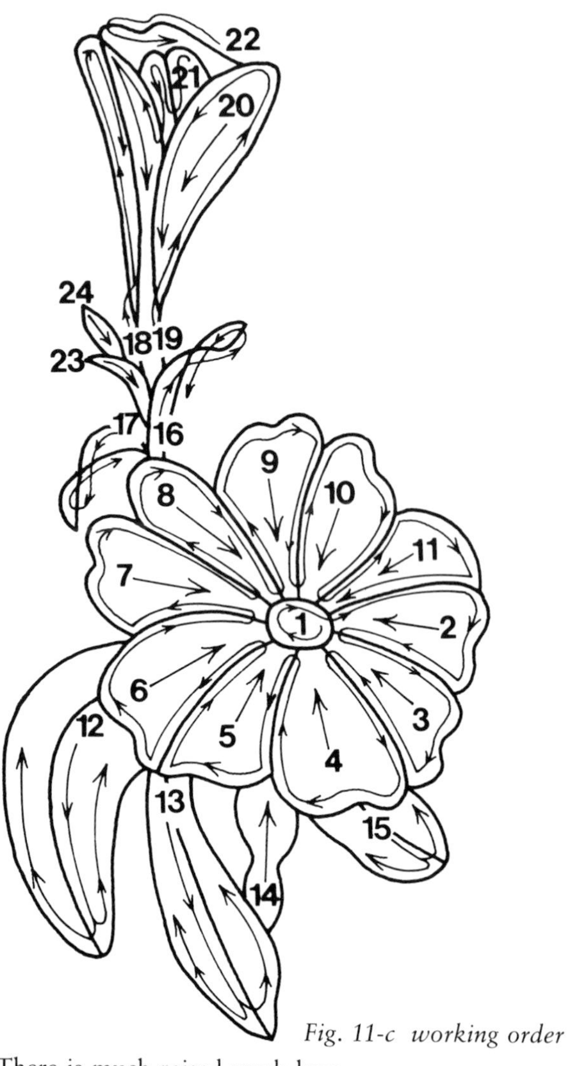

Fig. 11-c working order

There is much raised work here, sometimes with a rib made instead of a roll. Having ribbed around the first petal, it is sometimes an advantage to rib around each petal instead of making a roll. This gives a much neater finish. The leaves have a centre rib.

Fig. 11-a right side photograph

Der Entwurf enthält viel erhabene Arbeit, mitunter wird eine Rippe einer Rolle vorgezogen. Hat man einmal eine Rippe um das erste Blütenblatt gearbeitet, ist es vorteilhaft, diese für alle Blütenblätter anzuwenden anstatt eine Rolle durchzuführen, da es einen glatteren Abschluß ergibt. Die Blätter werden durch eine Ader geteilt.

Hier is veel raised work, soms gewerkt met een rib in plaats van een rol. Na de rib rond het eerste bloemblad is het soms handiger om een rib rond ieder bloemblad te maken dan een rol. Dit geeft een nettere afwerking. De bladeren hebben een middennerf.

Beaucoup de travail en relief, parfois avec un lacet à la place d'un rouleau. Après finition du lacet autour du premier pétale, il peut être judicieux de faire un lacet autour de chaque pétale au lieu d'un rouleau. Ceci donne une finition plus nette. Les feuilles ont une nervure au centre.

Fig. 11-b wrong side photograph

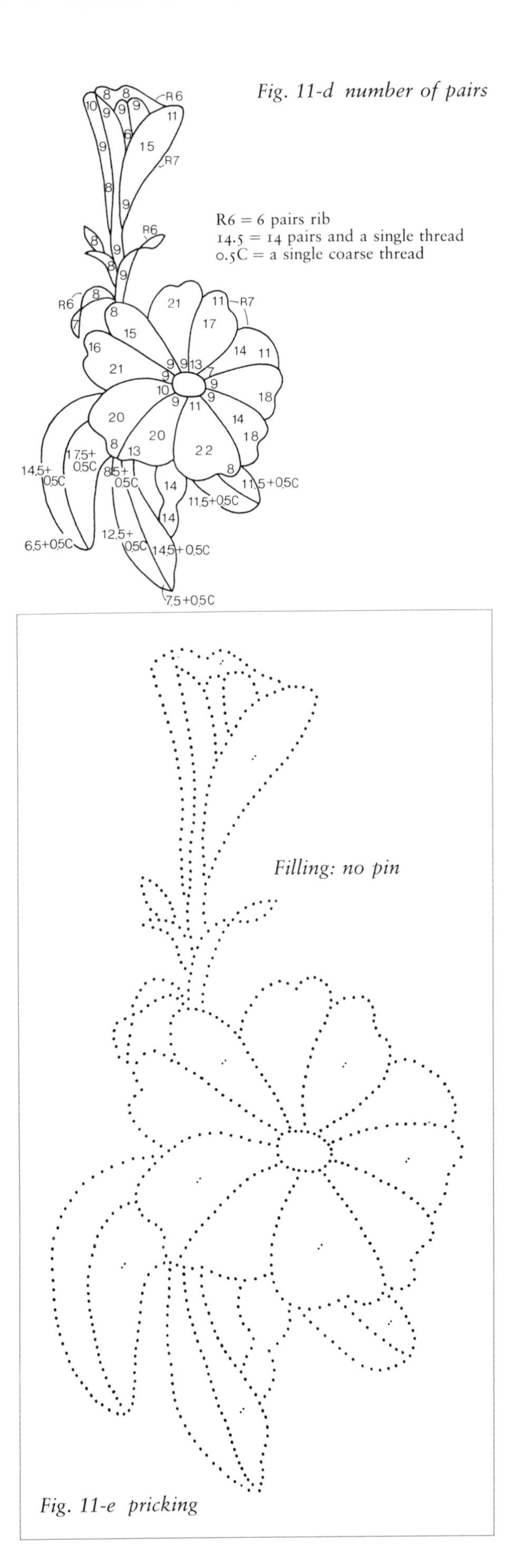

Fig. 11-d number of pairs

Fig. 11-e pricking

12 Periwinkle

Fig. 12-a right side photograph

Fig. 12-c working order

This is a good flowing design suitable for wedding veils etc. Flowers worked as in Pattern 5, Primrose. The No Pin filling is quite suitable for a small area but more difficult to control in a large filling. Divided leaf: work from the base into one side of the leaf. Reduce pairs at the top to turn, and work down into the second side. Here, take the sewings into the pinholes of the first half. The coarse thread should lie next to the sewings at this point.

Ein fließendes Muster, für einen Schleier u.ä. geeignet. Die Blüten werden gem. Muster 5 – Primel gearbeitet. Die 'No-Pin' (Ohne Nadel) Füllung eignet sich für kleine Flächen, für größere Füllungen ist sie schwierig zu handhaben.

Geteiltes Blatt: Eine Hälfte des Blattes von unten arbeiten, an der Spitze Klöppelpaare herausnehmen, umdrehen und die zweite Hälfte klöppeln. Die Fäden in die Nadelpunkte der ersten Blatthälfte einhäkeln. Der Konturfaden sollte hier anliegen.

Dit is een mooi vloeiend ontwerp, geschikt voor bruidssluiers e.d. De bloemen zijn geklost als in patroon 5 Primrose. De 'No Pin' vulling is heel geschikt voor kleine stukjes, maar moeilijker te beheersen in een grote vulling. Verdeeld blad: werk vanuit de basis naar één kant van het blad. Verminder bij de top het aantal paren om te keren, en werk het tweede bladdeel naar beneden. Haak hier aan in de speldegaatjes van de eerste helft. De dikke draad moet hier tegen de aanhakingen liggen.

Voici un dessin gracieux de fleurs à utiliser sur un voile de mariée, etc. Les fleurs sont exécutées comme pour le patron 5, 'Primevère'. Le fond sans épingle est tout à fait adapté à une petite surface, mais plus difficile à rèussir dans le cas d'un grand remplissage.
Feuille lobée: Travaillez de la base vers un côté de la feuille. Réduisez les paires à la pointe pour tourner et travaillez le deuxième côté vers le bas, en faisant les crochetages dans les trous d'épingles de la première moitié. A cet endroit, les gros fil doit se trouver à côté des crochetages.

Fig. 12-b wrong side photograph

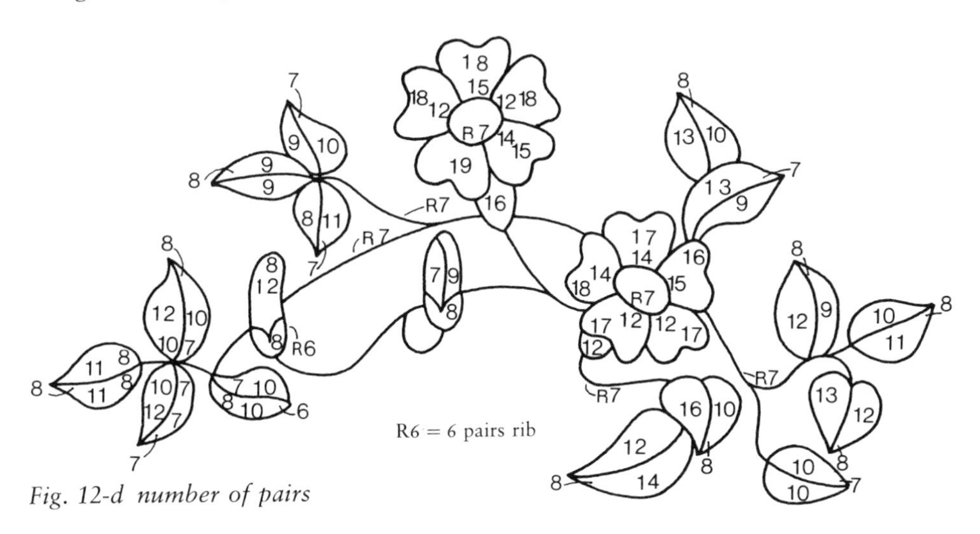

Fig. 12-d number of pairs

Filling: no pin

Fig. 12-e pricking

13 Poinsettia

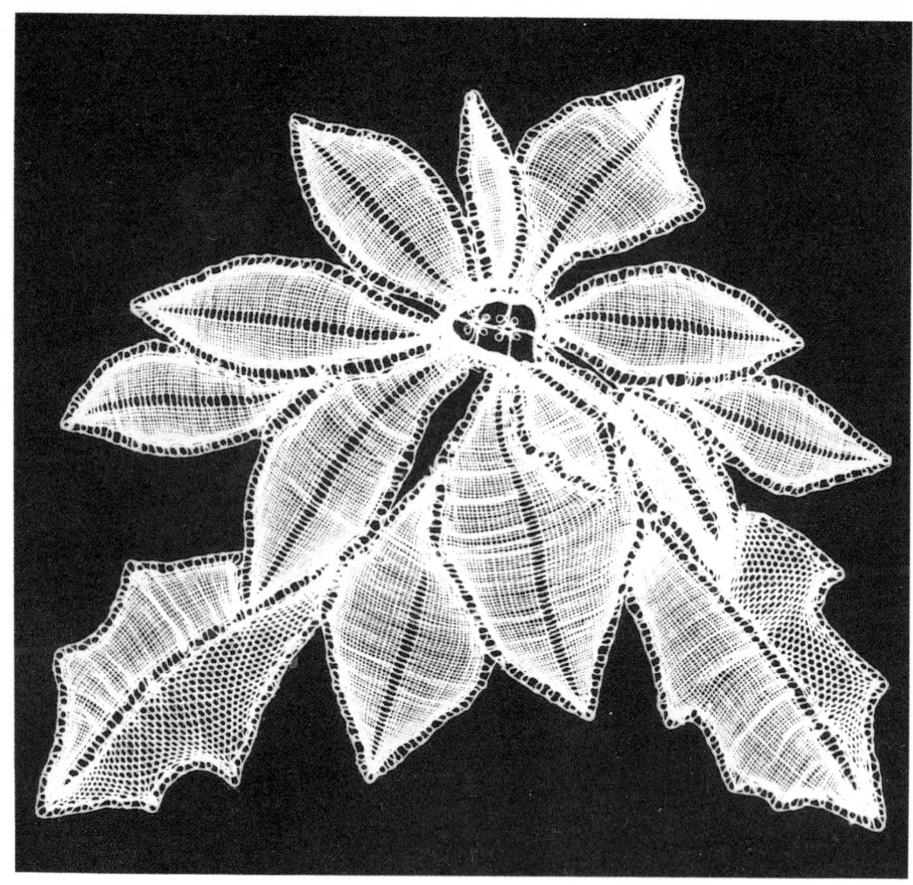

Fig. 13-a right side photograph

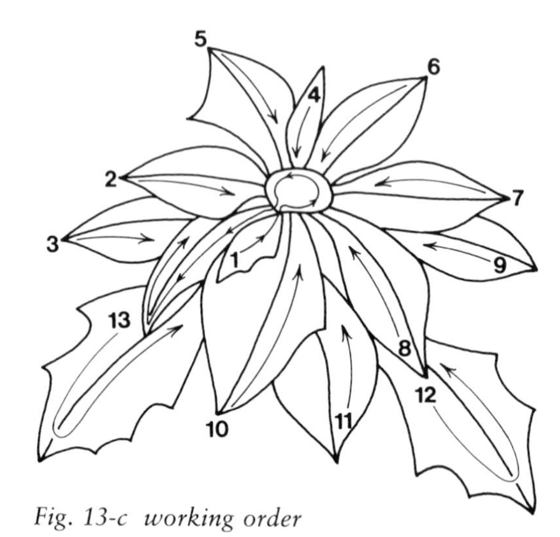

Fig. 13-c working order

Flat work but a very effective design. Ideal for use as a Christmas card. The leaf bracts are plain, and outer leaves are divided.

Flache Arbeit. Sehr attraktiver Entwurf, ideal für Weihnachtskarten. Die Innenblätter sind einfach, die Außenblätter geteilt.

Vlak werk, maar een zeer sprekend ontwerp. Ideaal voor een Kerstkaart. De schutbladeren zijn eenvoudig, en de buitenbladeren zijn verdeeld.

Travail plat avec un effet remarquable. Idéal pour cartes de voeux de Noël. Les bractées des feuilles sont simples, les feuilles extérieures sont lobées.

Fig. 13-b wrong side photograph

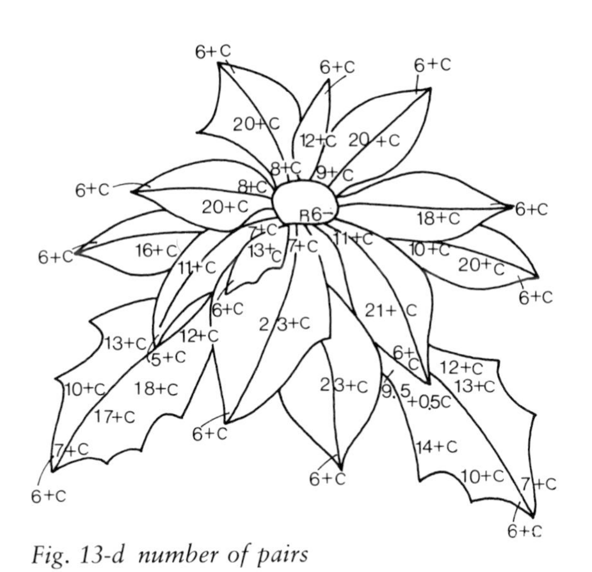

Fig. 13-d number of pairs

R6 = 6 pairs rib
9.5 = 9 pairs and a single thread
0.5C = a single coarse thread

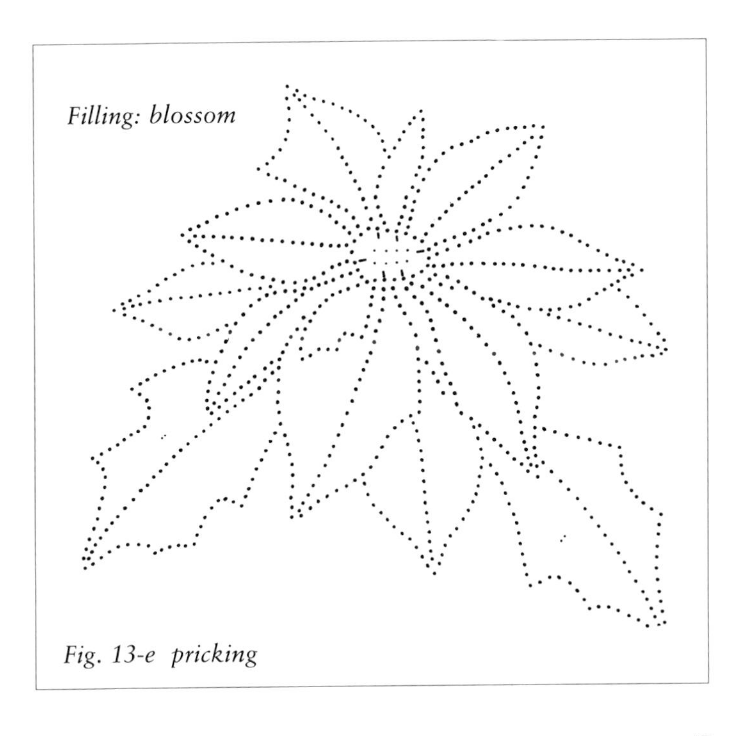

Fig. 13-e pricking

14
Daffodil

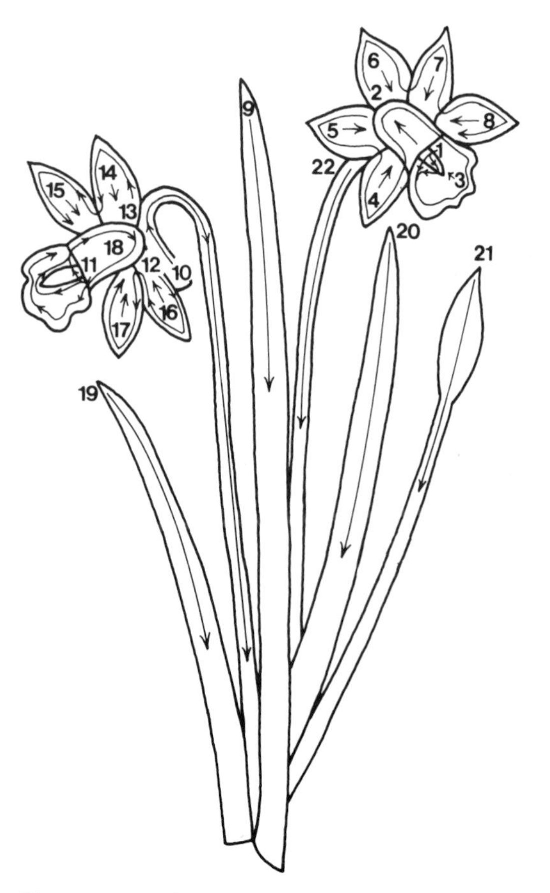

Fig. 14-c working order

Fig. 14-a right side photograph

A Spring flower design that works well for Honiton lacemaking. The flowers are raised but the leaves are flat. The centre leaf has a twisted vein.

Eine für Honiton gut geeignete Frühlingsblume. Die Blüten werden erhaben gearbeitet, die Blätter flach. Für die Ader des mittleren Blattes werden die Fäden gedreht.

Een ontwerp met voorjaarsbloemen, dat heel goed in Honiton gemaakt kan worden. De bloemen zijn raised gewerkt, maar de bladeren zijn vlak. Het middenblad heeft een gedraaide nerf.

Un dessin de fleurs de printemps qui se travaille bien en dentelle Honiton. Les fleurs sont en relief, mais les feuilles sont plates. La feuille centrale a une nervure torsadée.

Fig. 14-b wrong side photograph

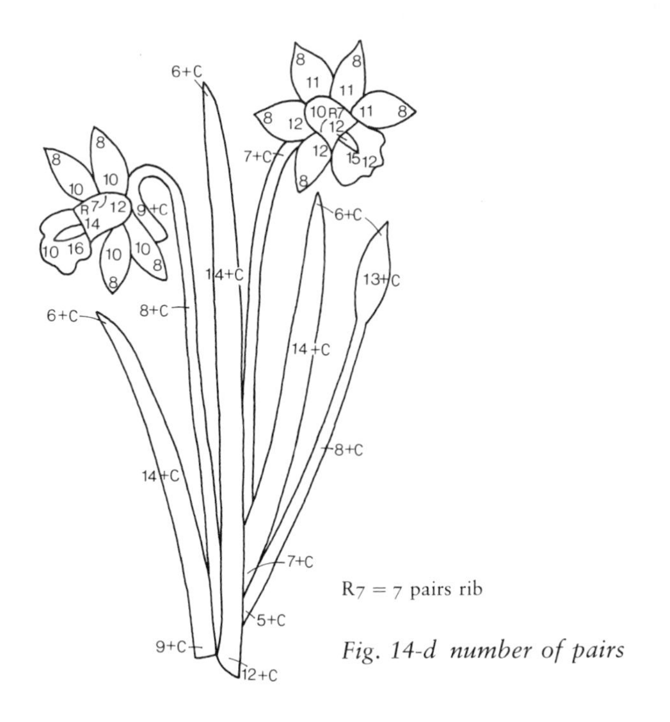

R7 = 7 pairs rib

Fig. 14-d number of pairs

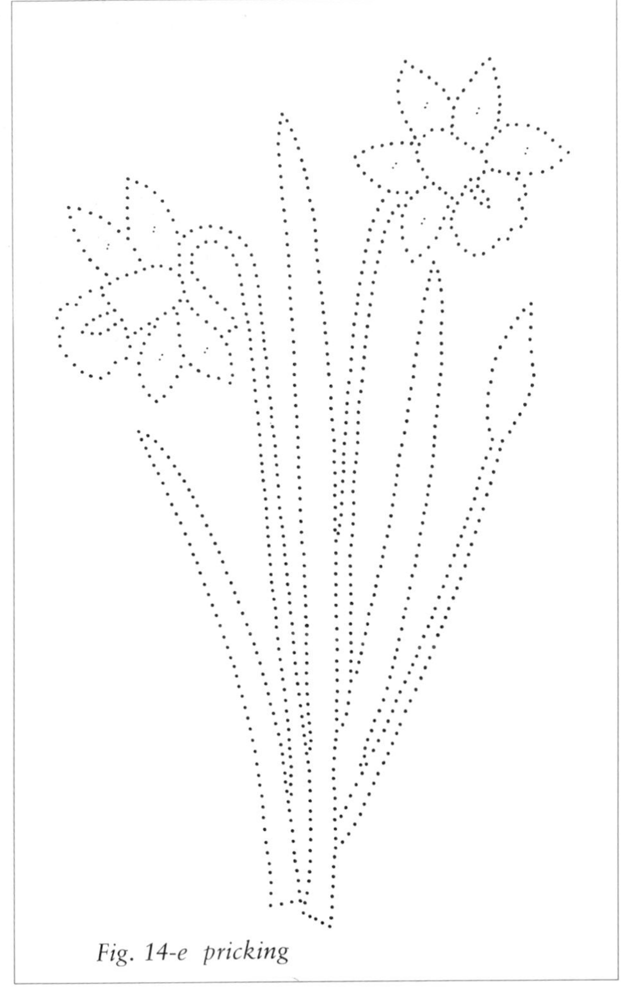

Fig. 14-e pricking

15 Cyclamen

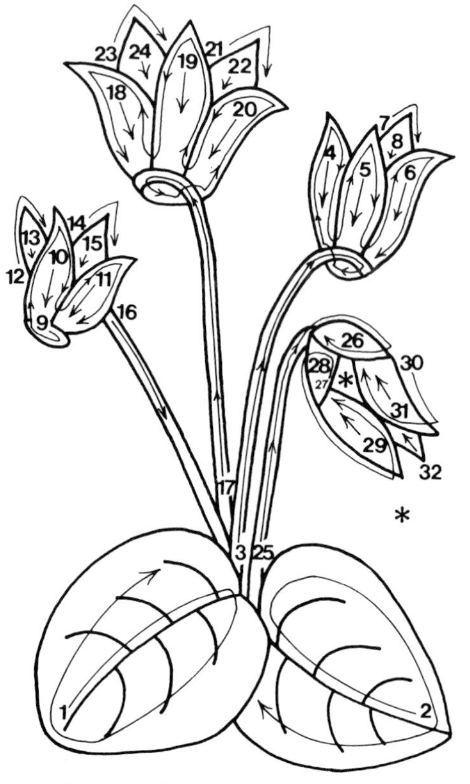

Fig. 15-c working order

Fig. 15-a right side photograph

This pattern is an adaptation of an original, and more suitable for the advanced lacemaker. The leaves should be worked first as in Pattern 5, Primrose.

Das Muster ist die Variation eines Originals. Für Fortgeschrittene. Beginn mit den Blättern gem. Beschreibung in Primrose, Muster 5.

Dit patroon is een variatie op een origineel, en geschikt voor de gevorderde kantkloster. De bladeren moeten eerst gewerkt worden als in patroon 5, Primrose.

Ce patron est une adaptation d'un original et destiné plutôt à la dentellière confirmée. Les feuilles devraient être faites en premier selon le Patron 5, Primrose.

Fig. 15-b wrong side photograph

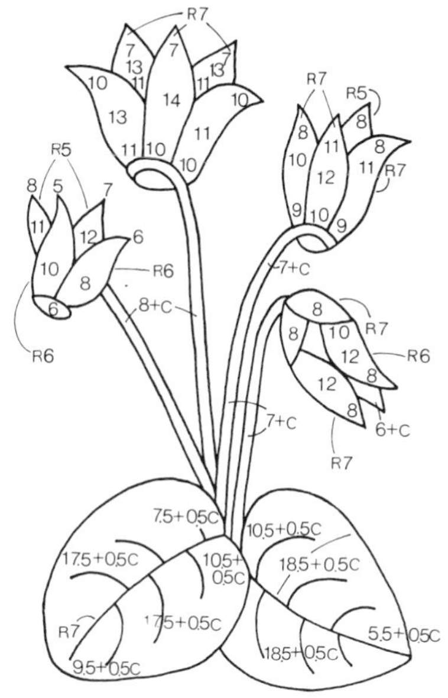

Fig. 15-d number of pairs

R7 = 7 pairs rib
9.5 = 9 pairs and a single thread
0.5C = a single coarse thread

Filling: swing leadworks

Fig. 15-e pricking

16 Christmas Rose

Fig. 16-a right side photograph

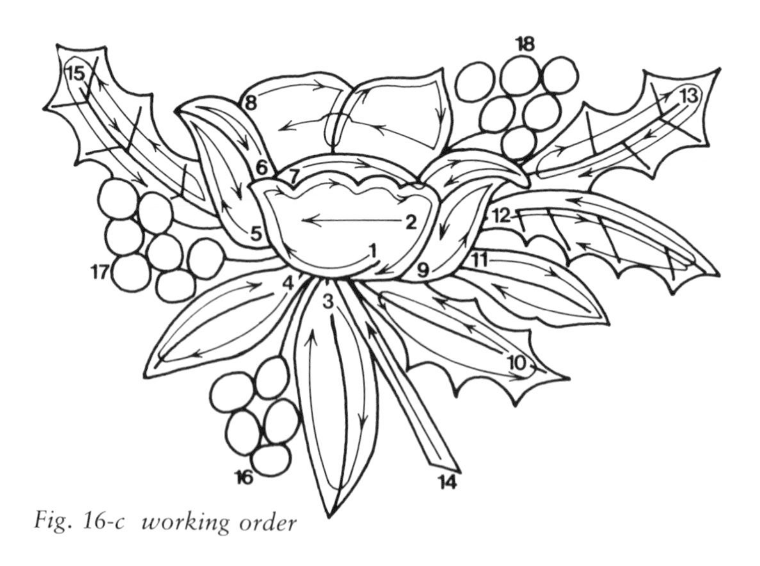

Fig. 16-c working order

A pattern for Christmas. The rose has much raised work. The holly leaves have a centre vein, windows and pearls. The berries are worked with rib, then filled with cloth stitch.

Ein Weihnachtsmotiv. Die Rose besteht vorwiegend aus erhabener Arbeit. Die Blätter der Stechpalme haben in der Mitte eine Ader mit 'Windows & Pearls' (Fenster und Perlen). Für die Beeren eine Rippe arbeiten und mit Leinenschlag füllen.

Een patroon voor Kerstmis. In de roos is veel raised work. De hulstbladeren hebben een middennerf, 'windows' en picots. De bessen worden als rib gewerkt en dan gevuld met linnenslag.

Un dessin pour Noël. La rose a beaucoup de parties en relief. Les feuilles de houx ont une nervure centrale, des fenêtres et des perles. Les baies sont exécutées avec des lacets, puis remplies de mat.

Fig. 16-b wrong side photograph

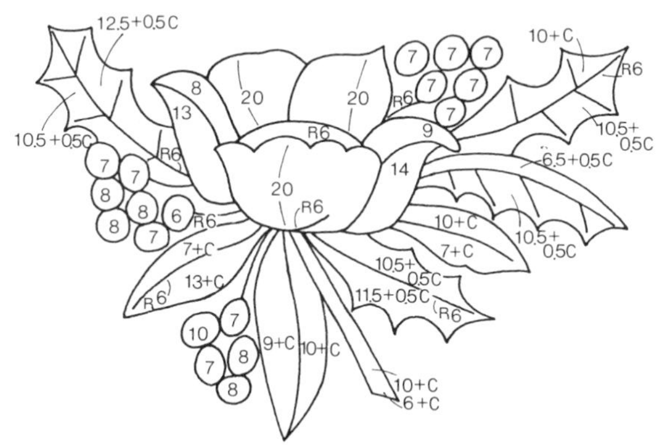

Fig. 16-d number of pairs

R6 = 6 pairs rib
12.5 = 12 pairs and a single thread
0.5C = a single coarse thread

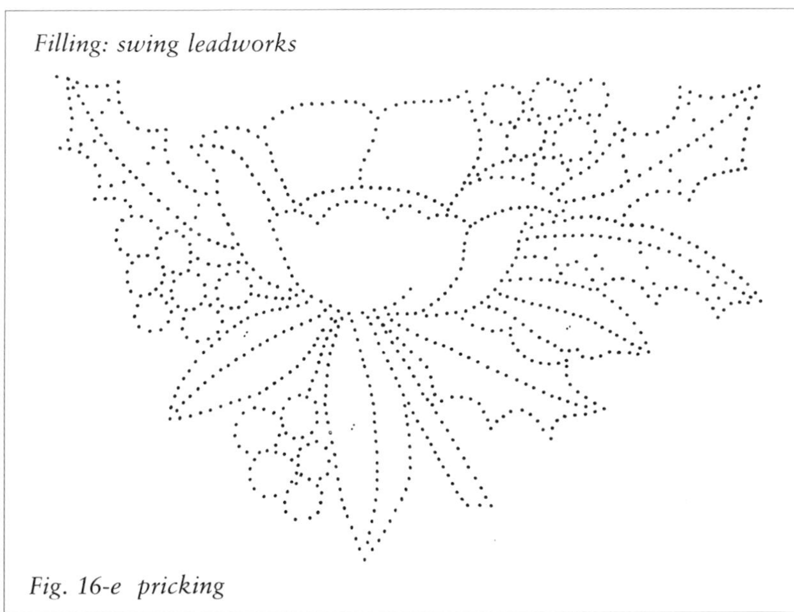

Fig. 16-e pricking

17
Lily

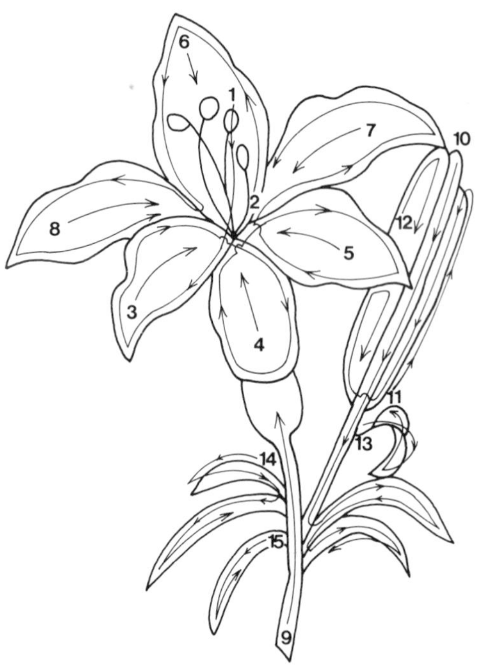

Fig. 17-c working order

Fig. 17-a right side photograph

The stamens should be worked first, then use the pairs to work into the nearest flower petal and fill. Work the other petals in a similar way. The top of each leaf has a rib.

Mit den Staubgefäßen beginnen und mit diesen Paaren das nächstliegende Blütenblatt klöppeln und füllen. Die restlichen Blütenblätter genauso arbeiten. Der obere Rand der Blätter hat eine Rippe.

De meeldraden moeten eerst geklost worden. Gebruik daarna de paren voor het dichtstbijzijnde bloemblad en vul dit. Klos de andere bloemblaadjes op dezelfde manier. Elk blad heeft aan de bovenkant een rib.

Faites les étamines d'abord, puis utilisez les paires pour le pétale le plus proche et remplissez. Exécutez les autres pétales d'une manière similaire. Le haut de chaque feuille a un lacet.

Fig. 17-b wrong side photograph

Fig. 17-e pricking

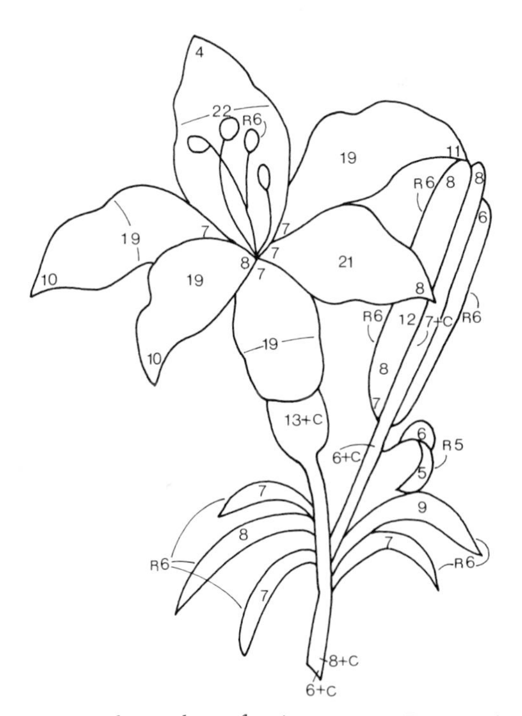

Fig. 17-d number of pairs R6 = 6 pairs rib

18
Campanula

Fig. 18-c working order

Fig. 18-a right side photograph

One side petal of the flower is raised and filled. Work into the calyx and then the other side petal is worked. One leaf has a turned tip; at the top, the rib is changed from one side to the other at the turn (at **X**).

Ein seitliches Blütenblatt wird erhaben gearbeitet und gefüllt; zum Blütenkelch hin arbeiten, danach das andere seitliche Blütenblatt arbeiten. Die Spitze eines Blattes ist geknickt. Oben wechselt die Rippe beim Drehen von der einen zur anderen Seite.

Een buitenblaadje van de bloem is raised en wordt dan gevuld. Ga over naar de kelk en maak daarna het andere buitenblaadje van de bloem. Eén blad heeft een omgeslagen punt; de rib aan de bovenkant gaat bij x naar de andere kant van het blad.

Un pétale latéral de la fleur est en relief et rempli. Continuez avec le calice, puis faites l'autre pétale latéral. Une feuille a un coin tordu; en haut, le lacet passe d'un côtée à l'autre, au changement de direction (à X).

Fig. 18-b wrong side photograph

Fig. 18-e pricking

R5 = 5 pairs rib

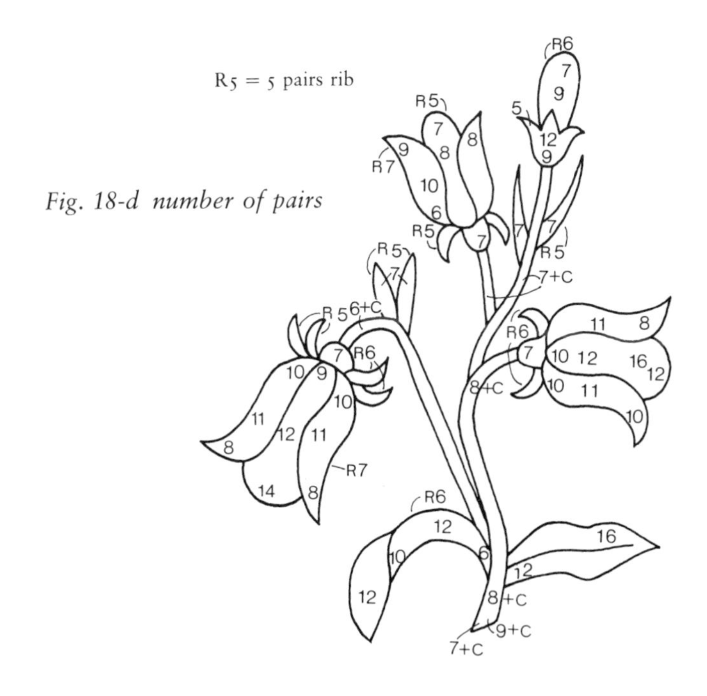

Fig. 18-d number of pairs

19
Helleborus

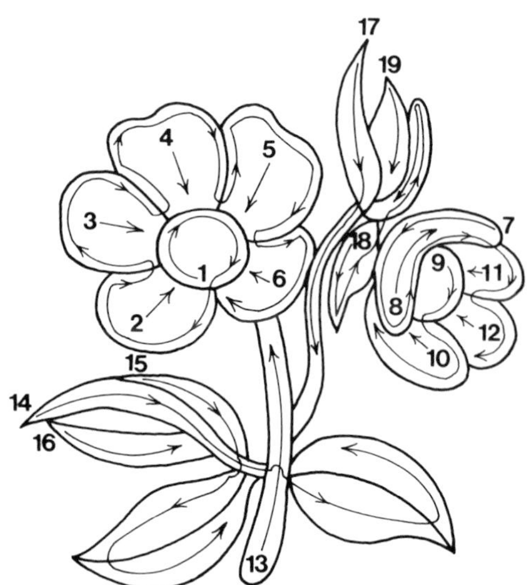

Fig. 19-c working order

Fig. 19-a right side photograph

This is mostly raised work. Work the centre circle of the larger flower first and bring rib to form outline of first petal. Fill with half stitch. Work remaining petals. For the smaller flower, work the upper petal first. Continue to work each petal as the larger flower.

Vorwiegend erhabene Arbeit. Mit dem inneren Kreis der größeren Blume beginnen, die Rippe bildet die Umrandung des ersten Blütenblattes. Füllung in Halbschlag. Restliche Blütenblätter klöppeln. Bei der kleineren Blume wird mit dem oberen Blütenblatt begonnen, die restlichen Blütenblätter wie bei der größeren Blume arbeiten.

Dit is voornamelijk raised work. Klos het hart van de grote bloem eerst en ga met de rib over naar de omtrek van het eerste bloemblad. Vul dit met netslag. Klos nu de overige bloemblaadjes. Klos bij de kleine bloem eerst het lage voorblad. Werk de overige bloemblaadjes als de grote bloem.

Ici il y a beaucoup de relief. Travaillez d'abord le cercle central de la plus grande fleur et faites le contour du premier pétale avec le lacet. Remplissez en grille. Exécutez les autres pétales. Pour la petite fleur, faites d'abord le pétale inférieur de devant. Continuez par les autres pétales comme pour la grande fleur.

Fig. 19-b wrong side photograph

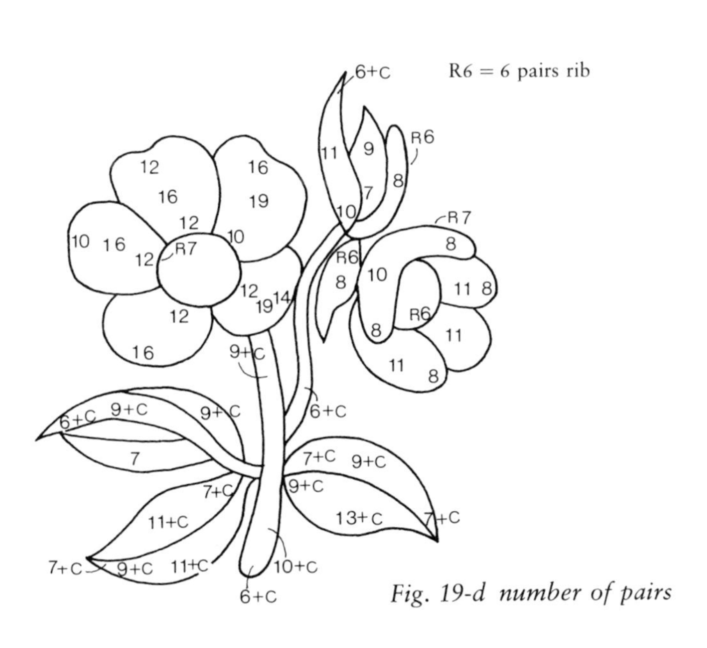

Fig. 19-d number of pairs

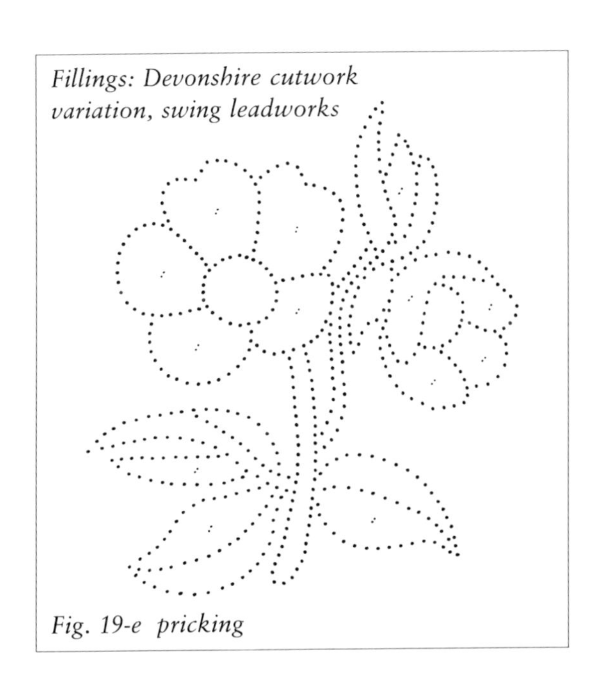

Fillings: Devonshire cutwork variation, swing leadworks

Fig. 19-e pricking

20
Autumn Crocus

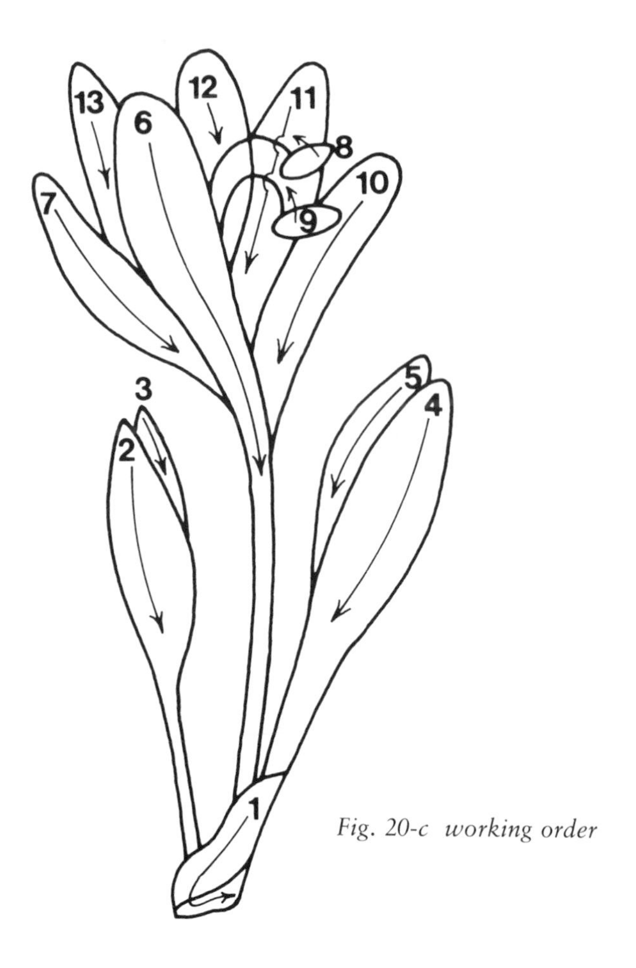

Fig. 20-c working order

Fig. 20-a right side photograph

Flat work. Work the base first, followed by the buds. Then work the first petal and down the main stem. The stamens should now be worked before the remaining petals, as these work over them. The buds are flat work.

Flache Arbeit. Zuerst den unteren Teil und die Knospen arbeiten. Danach das erste Blütenblatt und den Hauptstiel hinab. Die Staubgefäße vor den restlichen Blütenblättern arbeiten, da sie diese überlappen. Die Knospen bestehen aus flacher Arbeit.

Vlak werk. Klos eerst de basis, gevolgd door de knoppen, dan het eerste bloemblad en de hoofdstengel naar beneden. Nu moeten de meeldraden geklost worden vóór de andere bloemblaadjes omdat die daar overheen geklost moeten worden. De knoppen zijn in vlak werk.

Travail à plat. Faites d'abord la base, puis les boutons. Exécutez ensuite le premier pétale et descendez la tige principale. Les étamines seront à faire ensuite, avant les autres pétales, parce qu'elles seront travaillées par-dessus. Les boutons sont plats.

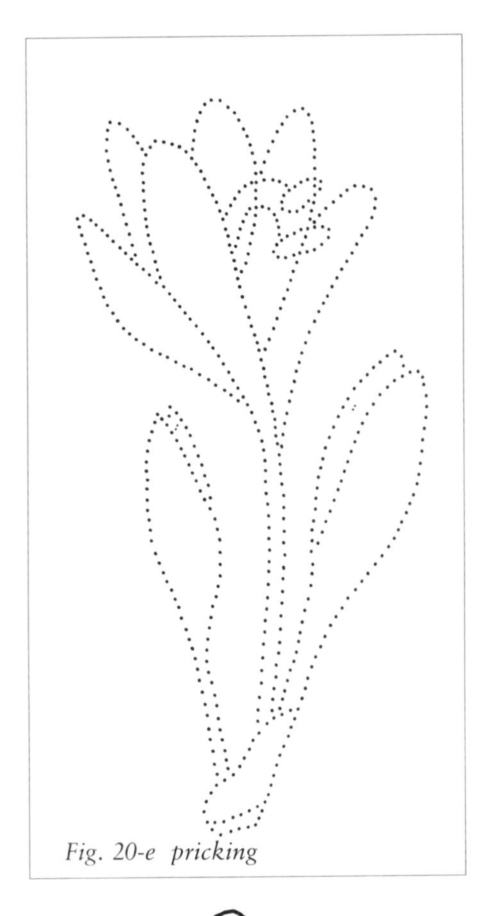

Fig. 20-e *pricking*

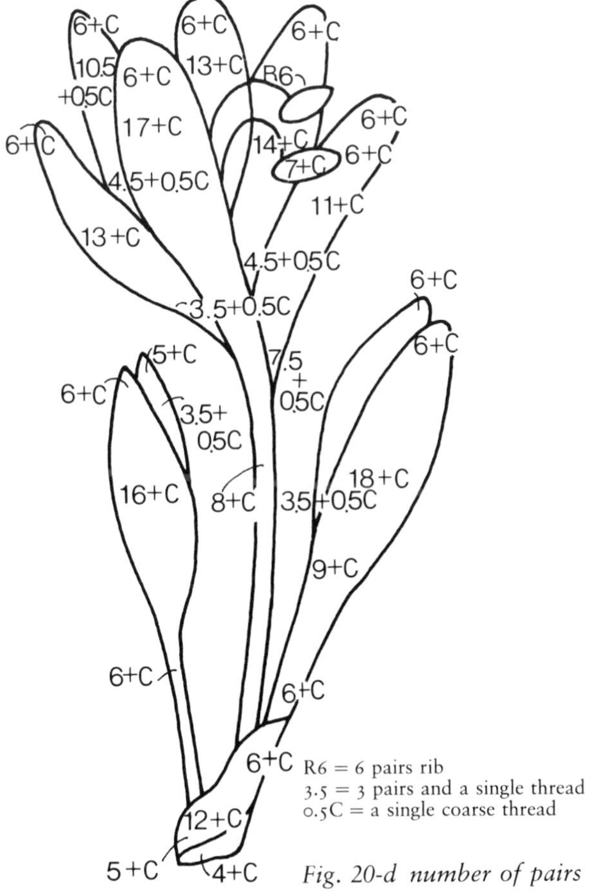

Fig. 20-d *number of pairs*

Fig. 20-b *wrong side photograph*

21
Azalea

Fig. 21-a right side photograph

Fig. 21-c working order

Work the centre rib of the flower first. Use these pairs to rib, and form the outline of petals, in turn, and fill. Some leaves can have a rib at the top and some can be plain.

Zuerst die innere Rippe der Blume arbeiten. Mit den gleichen Paaren im Wechsel die Umrandung der Blütenblätter bilden und füllen. Die Blätter können eine Rippe haben oder sind einfach.

Werk eerst de rib in het hart van de bloem. Gebruik deze paren voor de rib, die de omtrek van alle bloemblaadjes vormt en vul ze. Sommige bladeren kunnen een rib aan de bovenkant hebben en andere kunnen gewoon vlak zijn.

Travaillez d'abord le lacet au milieu de la fleur. Utilisez la même paire pour le lacet et le contour des pétales que vous ferez les uns après les autres; remplissez. Certaines feuilles peuvent avoir un lacet un haut, d'autres peuvent se présenter à plat.

Fig. 21-d *number of pairs*

Fig. 21-b *wrong side photograph*

Fig. 21-e *pricking*

22
Prickly Poppy

Fig. 22-c working order

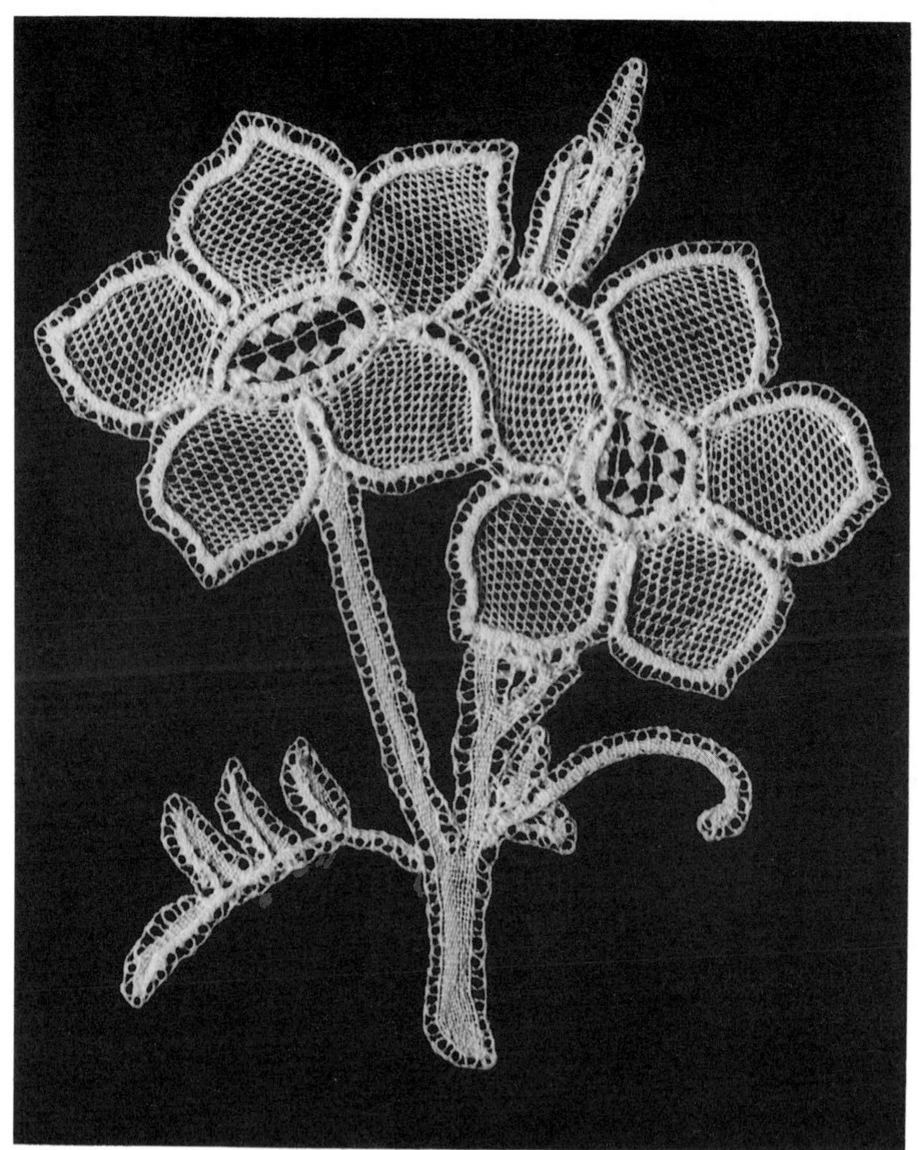

Fig. 22-a right side photograph

The flowers are similar to work as in Pattern 19, Helleborus.

Die Blume wird gemäß Muster 19 gearbeitet.

De bloemen kunnen op dezelfde manier gewerkt worden als in patroon 19, Helleborus.

Les fleurs se travaillent d'une manière similaire à celles du Patron 19, Helleborus.

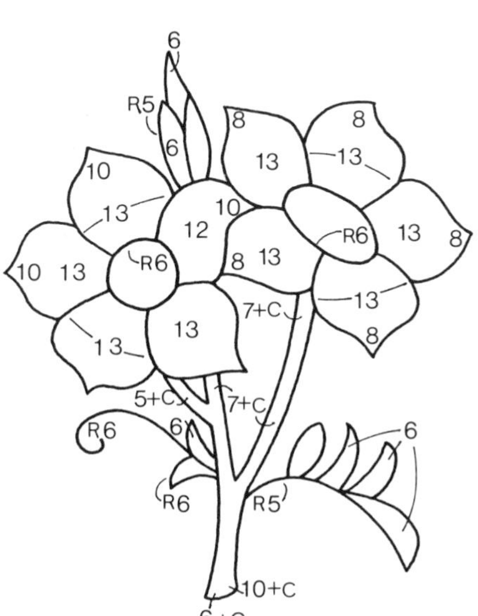

Fig. 22-d number of pairs

R5 = 5 pairs rib

Fig. 22-b wrong side photograph

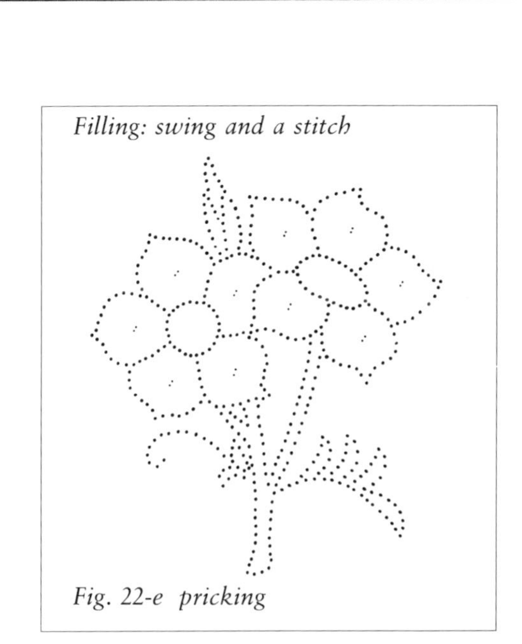

Fig. 22-e pricking

23
Magnolia

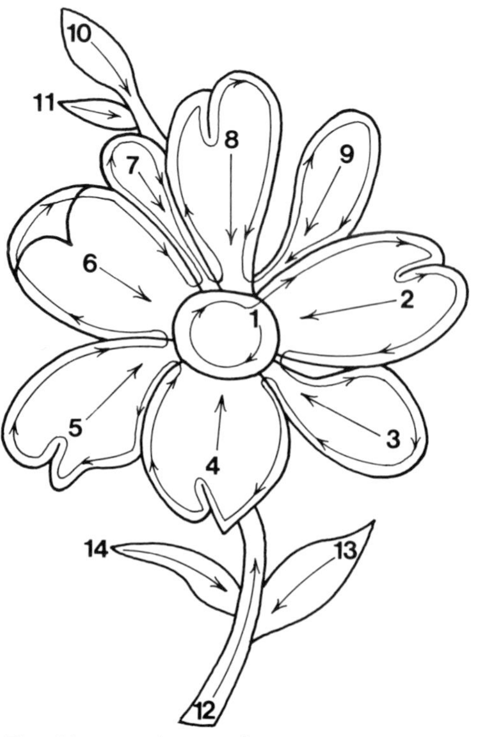

Fig. 23-c working order

Fig. 23-a right side photograph

As with most other flowers, the centre rib is worked first. Continue out into the first petal, and fill each in turn. The filling used here is Blossom, page 112.

Wie bei nahezu allen anderen Blumen wird die innere Rippe zuerst gearbeitet. Übergang zum ersten Blütenblatt, anschließend alle nacheinander füllen. Die angewandte Füllung wird auf Seite 112 beschrieben.

Net als bij de meeste andere bloemen wordt de rib in het hart eerst geklost. Ga dan over naar het eerste en de volgende bloembladeren en vul ze één voor één. Hier is als vulling 'Blossom', pagina 112 gebruikt.

Comme pour la plupart des autre fleurs, travaillez le lacet du milieu d'abord. Continuez par le premier pétale, puis remplissez chacun à son tour. Le fond utilisé ici est celui de la Blossom page 112.

Fig. 23-b wrong side photograph

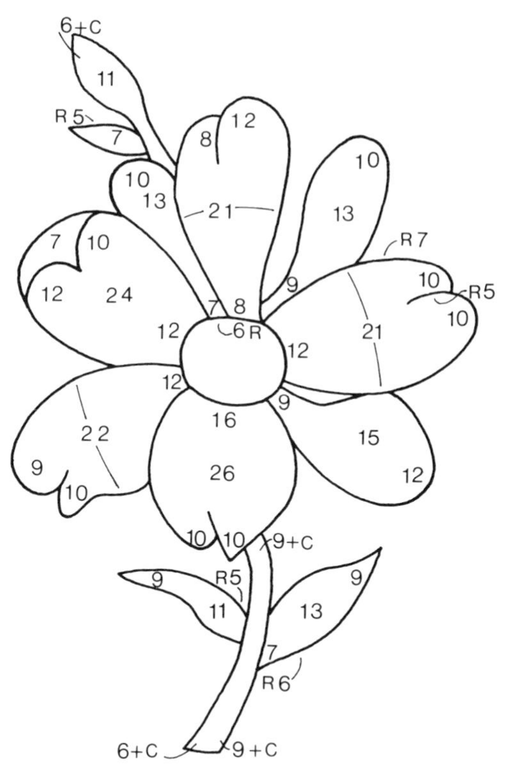

Fig. 23-d number of pairs R5 = 5 pairs rib

Filling: whole stitch block variation

Fig. 23-e pricking

24
Cowslip

Fig. 24-c working order

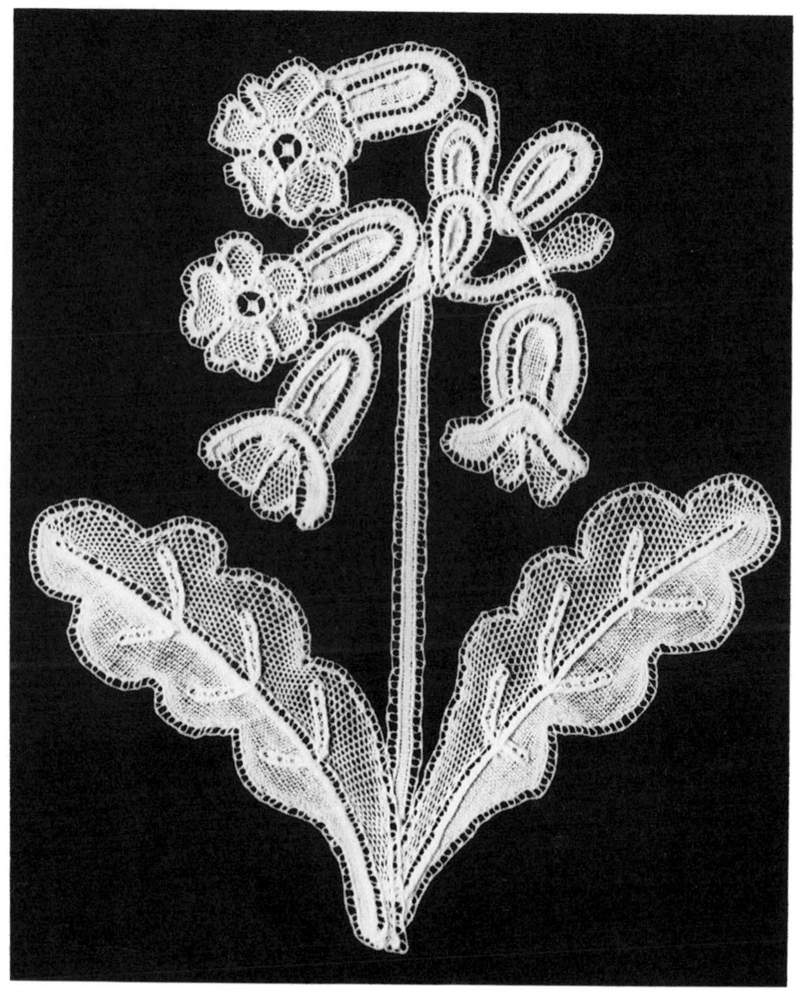

Fig. 24-a right side photograph

This is a very old, traditional pattern. It has been adapted here using less flowers. The leaves are made similarly to a Primrose leaf, Pattern 5.

Dies ist in altes traditionelles Muster und wird hier mit weniger Blüten vorgestellt. Die Blätter werden ähnlich dem Primelblatt von Muster 5 geklöppelt.

Dit is een zeer oud klassiek patroon. Het is hier zo veranderd dat er minder bloemen zijn. De bladeren zijn gemaakt als een Primroseblad, patroon 5.

Voici un dessin traditionnel très ancien. Il a été adapté en mettant moins de fleurs. Les feuilles sont faites de manière similaire à une feuille du Patron 5, Primeuère.

Fig. 24-b wrong side photograph

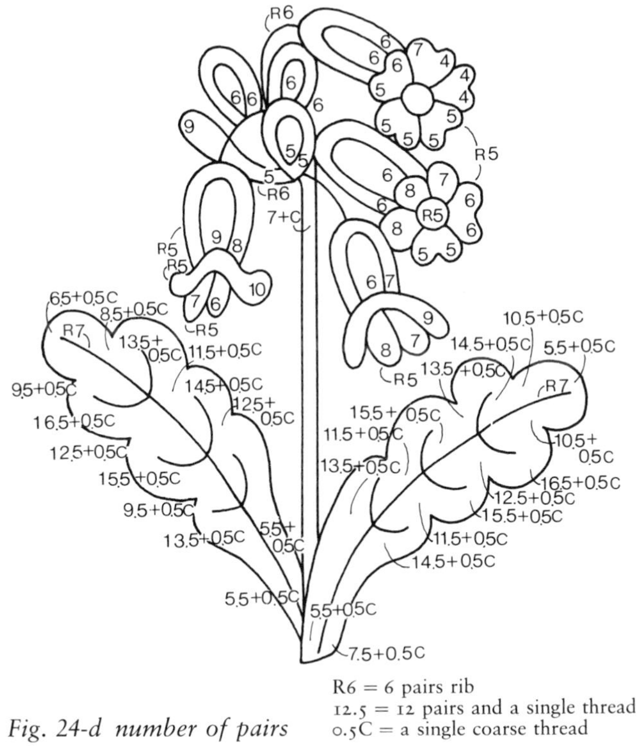

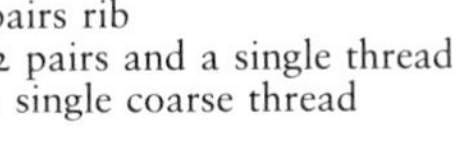

R6 = 6 pairs rib
12.5 = 12 pairs and a single thread
0.5C = a single coarse thread

Fig. 24-d number of pairs

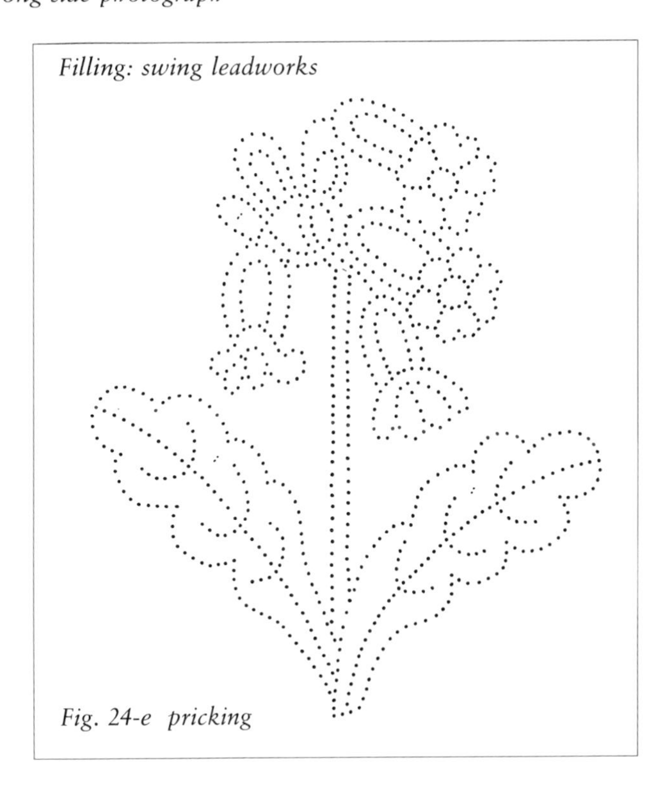

Filling: swing leadworks

Fig. 24-e pricking

25
Gloxinia

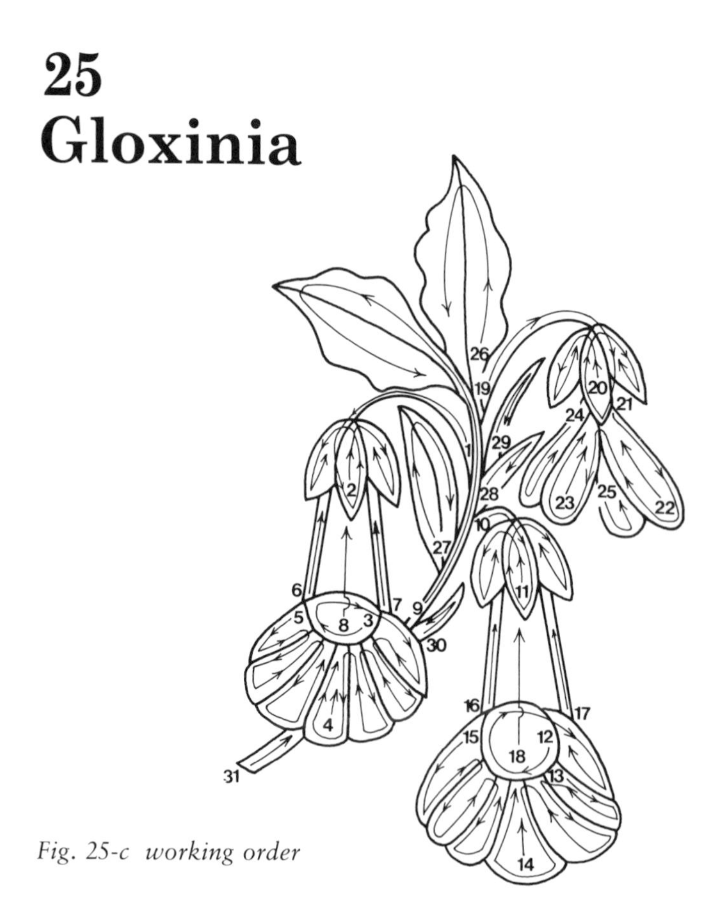

Fig. 25-c working order

Fig. 25-b right side photograph

This has attractive, bell flowers. Work the top section of the flower first. Rib the centre of the base and work out into the first three petals. These will be ribbed and rolled. The centre petal has a rib all around it. The remaining three petals start from the opposite side and are ribbed and rolled so that each side matches. The larger leaves are divided leaves – the small ones have a top rib.

Attraktive Glocken. Mit dem oberen Teil der Blume beginnen. Eine Rippe für die Mitte der Blüte bilden, anschließend die drei ersten Blütenblätter klöppeln. Das mittlere Blütenblatt hat rundum eine Rippe. Die restlichen drei Blütenblätter werden von der entgegengesetzten Seite gearbeitet, so daß beide Teile identisch sind. Die größeren Blätter werden geteilt, die kleineren haben an der Spitze eine Rippe.

Dit patroon heeft fraaie klokvormige bloemen. Werk het bovendeel van de bloem eerst. Rib rond het hart van de bloem en ga over naar de eerste drie bloemblaadjes. Deze worden geribd en gerold. Het middelste bloemblad heeft rondom een rib. De overige drie bloemblaadjes worden vanaf de andere kant begonnen, ze worden geribd en gerold, zodat de beide zijden gelijk zijn. De grote bladeren zijn verdeeld – de kleine hebben een rib aan de bovenkant.

Les clochettes sont séduisantes. Faites d'abord la partie supérieure de la fleur. Exécutez le lacet à la base et continuez avec les trois premiers pétales qui auront un lacet et qui seront roulés. Le pétale du milieu est entouré d'un lacet. Commencez les trois feuilles restantes du côté opposé avec un lacet et un rouleau, de sorte que les côtés correspondent. Les feuilles plus grandes sont lobées, les plus petites ont un lacet sur le dessus.

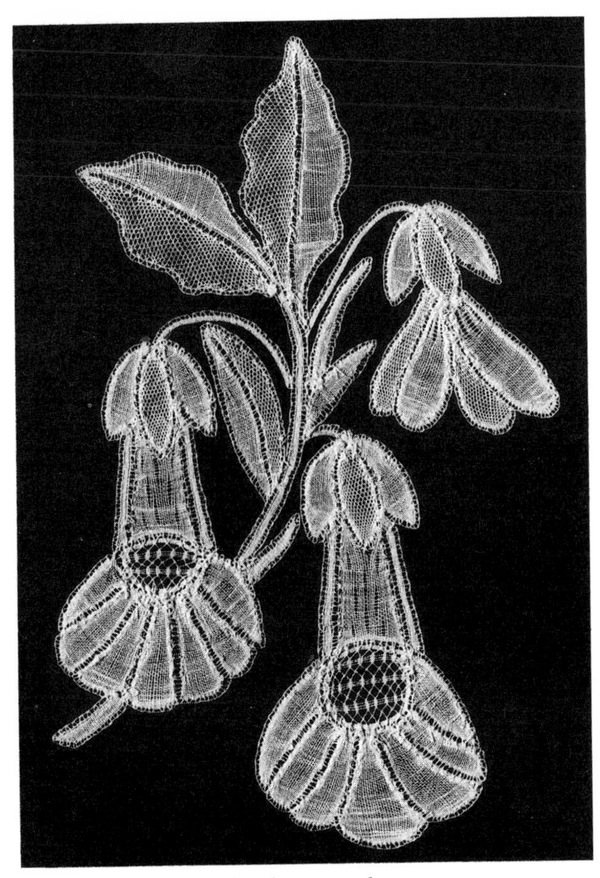

Fig. 25-a wrong side photograph

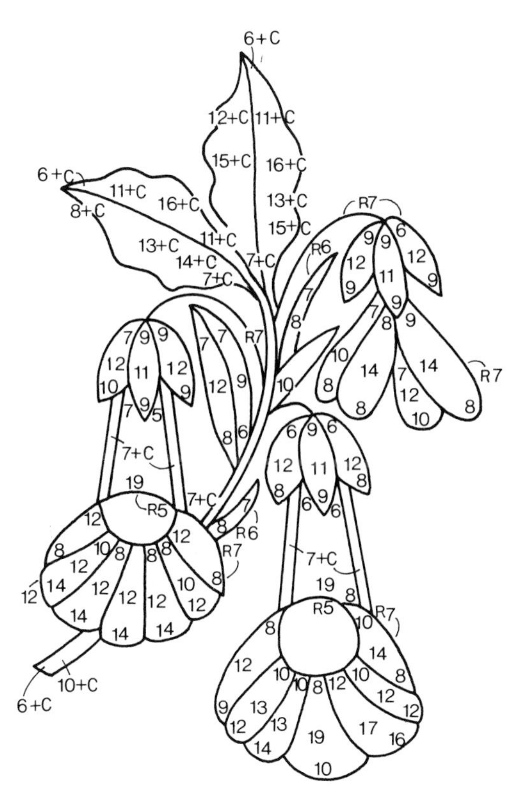

Fig. 25-d number of pairs R6 = 6 pairs rib

Fig. 25-e pricking *Filling: Italian*

26
Violet

Fig. 26-a right side photograph

Fig. 26-b wrong side photograph

Filling: swing leadworks

Fig. 26-e pricking

Fig. 26-c working order

This is an adaptation from a traditional design. The working of the leaves and flowers is similar to Pattern 15, Cyclamen.

R6 = 6 pairs rib

Fig. 26-d number of pairs

Anlehnung an einen traditionellen Entwurf. Ausarbeiten der Blätter und Blüten gem. Muster 15 – Alpenveilchen.

Dit is een variatie op een oud patroon. Het klossen van bladeren en bloemen gaat net als in patroon 15, Cyclamen.

Voici une adaptation d'un dessin traditionnel. Le travail des feuilles et des fleurs est similaire au Patron 15, Cyclamen.

27
Bird of Paradise

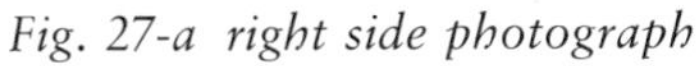

Fig. 27-a *right side photograph*

Fig. 27-b *wrong side photograph*

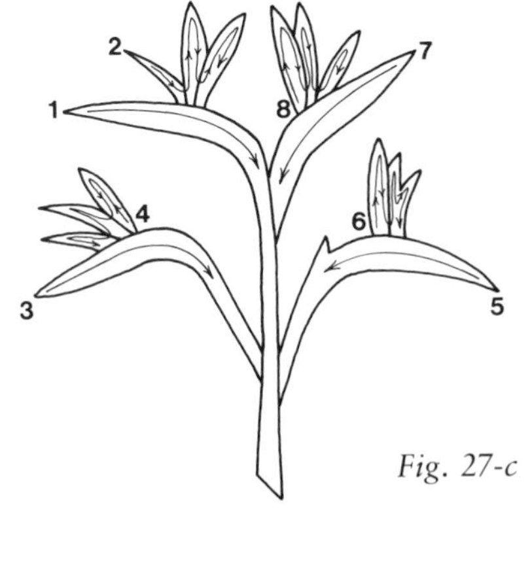

Fig. 27-c *working order*

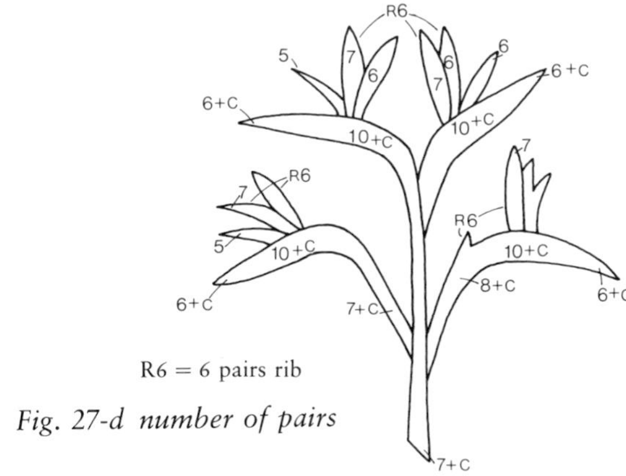

R6 = 6 pairs rib

Fig. 27-d *number of pairs*

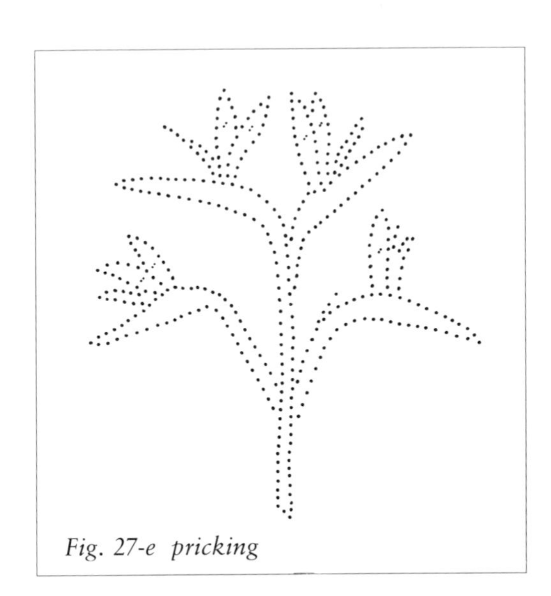

Fig. 27-e *pricking*

The raised sections are easy. This pattern is useful for beginners to practise simple raised sewings.

Die erhabenen Partien sind leicht. Das Muster eignet sich für Anfänger zum Üben einfachen erhabenen Anhäkelns.

De raised delen zijn gemakkelijk. Dit patroon is geschikt voor beginners als oefening in het aanhaken in raised work.

Les parties en relief sont simples à exécuter. Cet ouvrage est utile aux débutantes, car il leur permet de s'exercer aux crochetages simples en relief.

28
Rose (2)

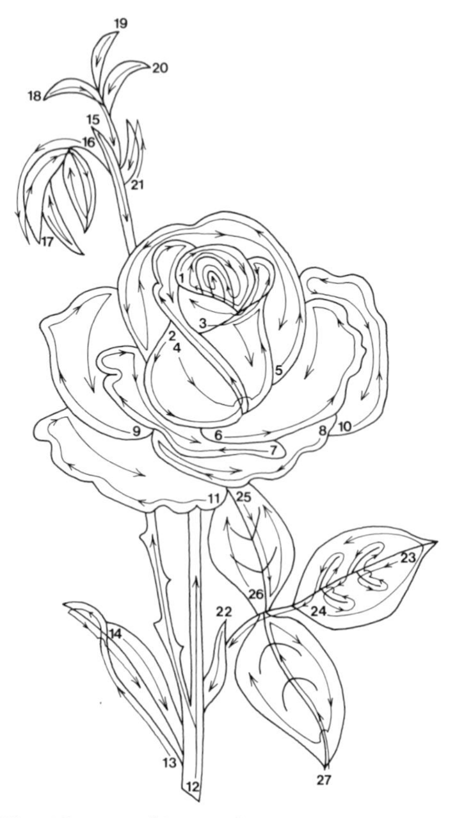

Fig. 28-c working order

Fig. 28-a right side photograph

Roses are popular with all Honiton lacemakers. Each petal has a raised rib outline. Mostly whole stitch is used, filled with a little half stitch in the centre. The leaves are veined and worked as in Pattern 5.

Rosen sind beliebte Honitonmotive. Die einzelnen Blütenblätter haben als Umrandung erhabene Rippen. Füllung vorwiegend in Ganzschlag mit etwas Halbschlag in der Mitte. Die Blätter haben Adern und werden gem. Muster 5 ausgeführt.

Rozen zijn bij alle Honiton-klosters populair. Ieder bloemblad heeft een rib als omtrek. Voornamelijk is linnenslag gebruikt, opgevuld met wat netslag in het hart. De bladeren zijn generfd en geklost als in patroon 5.

Toutes les dentellières de Honiton aiment les roses. Chaque pétale a un contour de lacet en relief. Le plus souvent, c'est le mat qui est utilisé comme fond avec une petite grille au centre. Les feuilles ont des nervures et sont exécutées comme indiqué dans le Patron 5, Primrose.

Fig. 28-b wrong side photograph

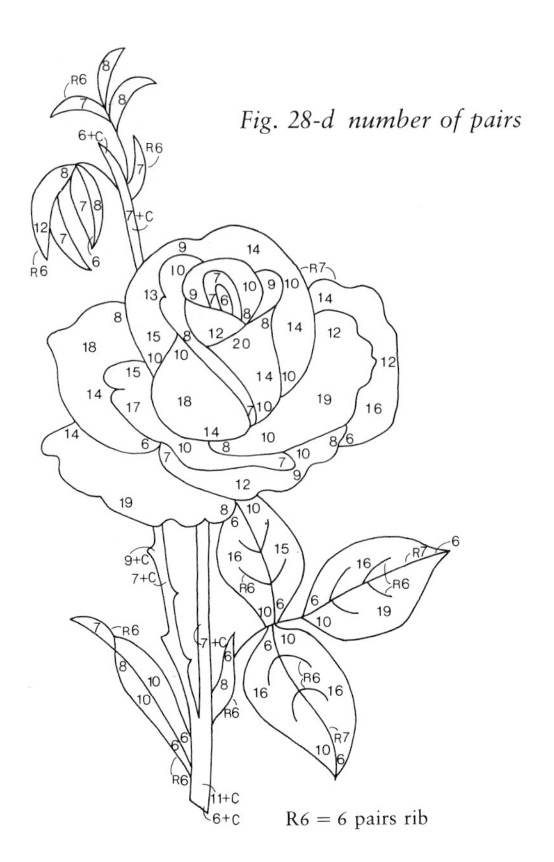

Fig. 28-d number of pairs

R6 = 6 pairs rib

Fig. 28-e pricking

29
Hana

Fig. 29-c working order

Fig. 29-a right side photograph

Flat work – a beginners' pattern suitable for use on a powder compact or set in a paperweight. The Japanese word 'Hana' means flower, and this flower shape is that of the Night Starlily. Work the flower shape first, then the calligraphy.

Flache Arbeit – geeignet als Einsatz für eine Puderdose oder einen Briefbeschwerer. Das japanische Wort 'Hana' bedeutet Blume, dargestellt wird eine Lilie der Nacht. Zuerst die Blume, dann die Schriftzeichen ausführen.

Vlak werk – een patroon voor beginners, geschikt voor op een poederdoos of in een presse-papier. Het Japanse woord 'Hana' betekent bloem, en deze bloemvorm is die van de 'Night Starlily'. Klos eerst de bloemvorm, daarna de kalligrafie.

Travail à plat – un patron pour débutantes, pouvant être utilisé pour le dessus d'un poudrier ou pour un presse-papiers. Le mot japonais 'Hana' signifie 'fleur', et la fleur représentée est un lis étoilé. Faites d'abord la forme de la fleur, puis les lettres calligraphiées.

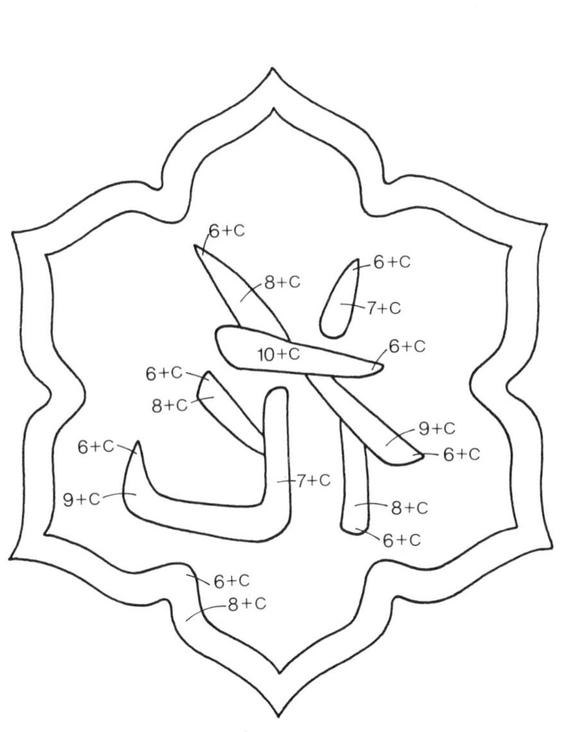

Fig. 29-d number of pairs

Fig. 29-b wrong side photograph

Filling: pin and a stitch

Fig. 29-e prickings

30
Fuku

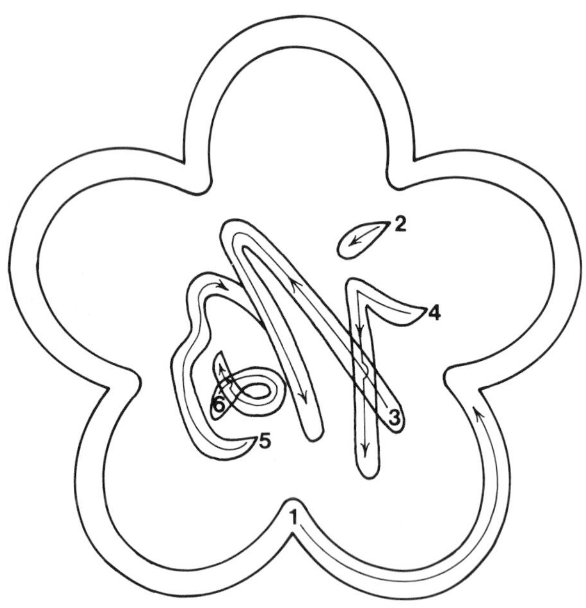

Fig. 30-c working order

Fig. 30-a right side photograph

Flat work – a beginners' pattern suitable for use on a powder compact or set in a paperweight. The Japanese word 'Fuku' means good fortune, and this flower shape is that of the Japanese apricot. Work the flower shape first, then the calligraphy.

Flache Arbeit. Für Anfänger. Geeignet als Einsatz für eine Puderdose oder einen Briefbeschwerer. Das japanische Wort 'Fuku' bedeutet Reichtum, dargestellt wird eine japanische Aprikose. Zuerst die Blume, dann die Schriftzeichen ausführen.

Vlak werk – een patroon voor beginners, geschikt voor poederdoos of presse-papier. Het Japanse woord 'Fuku' betekent geluk, en deze bloemvorm is die van de Japanse abrikoos. Klos eerst de bloemvorm, daarna de kalligrafie.

Travail à plat – un dessin à la portée des débutantes, pouvant être utilisé pour un poudrier ou un presse-papiers. Le mot japonais 'Fuku' signifie 'bonheur' et la fleur est celle d'un abricotier japonais. Faites d'abord la fleur, puis les lettres calligraphiées.

Fig. 30-d number of pairs

Fig. 30-b wrong side photograph

Filling:
whole stitch block variation

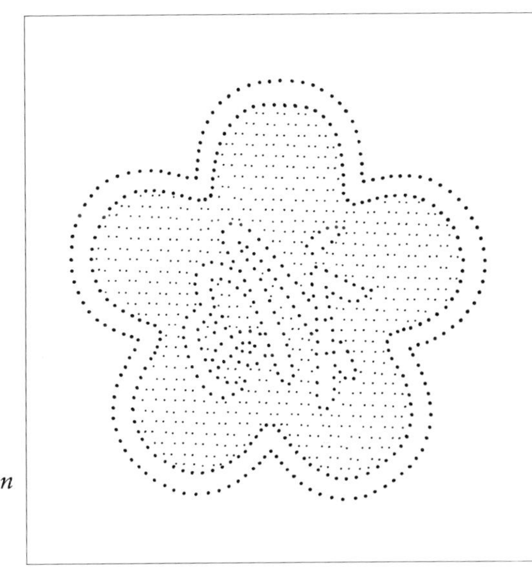

Fig. 30-e prickings

31
Kotobuki

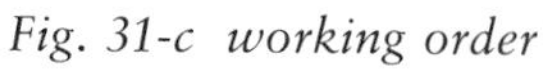
Fig. 31-c working order

Fig. 31-a right side photograph

Flat work – a beginners' pattern suitable for use on a greetings card. The Japanese word 'Kotobuki' means congratulations, and this flower shape is that of cherry blossom. Work the flower shape first, then the calligraphy.

Flache Arbei:. Für Anfänger. Geeignet als Grußkarte. Das japanische Wort 'Kotobuku' bedeutet Glueckwünsche, dargestellt wird eine Kirschblüte.

Vlak werk – een patroon voor beginners, geschikt voor een felicitatiekaart. Het Japanse woord 'Kotobuki' betekent gefeliciteerd, en deze bloemvorm is die van der kersenbloesem. Werk eerst de bloemvorm en daarna de kalligrafie.

Travail à plat – un dessin pour débutantes, pouvant être utilisé sur une carte de voeux. Le mot japonais 'Kotobuki' signifie 'félicitations' et la fleur représente une fleur de cérisier. Faites d'abord la fleur, puis les lettres calligraphiées.

Fig. 31-d number of pairs

Fig. 31-b wrong side photograph

Filling: four pin

Fig. 31-e prickings

32
Ikebana Iris

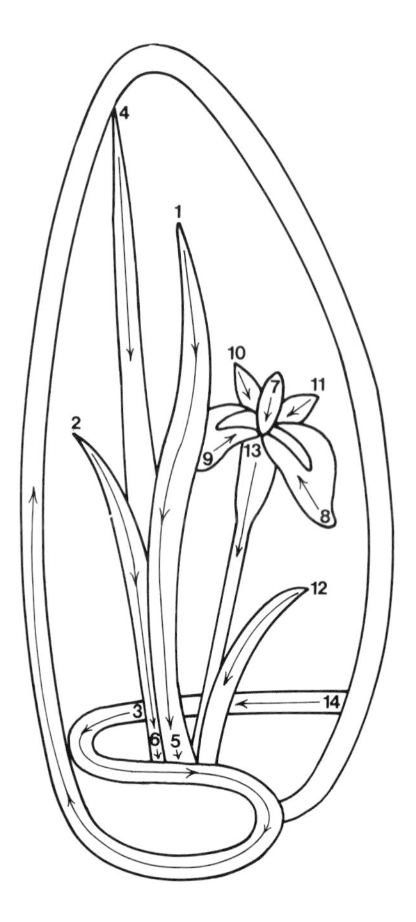

Fig. 32-c working order

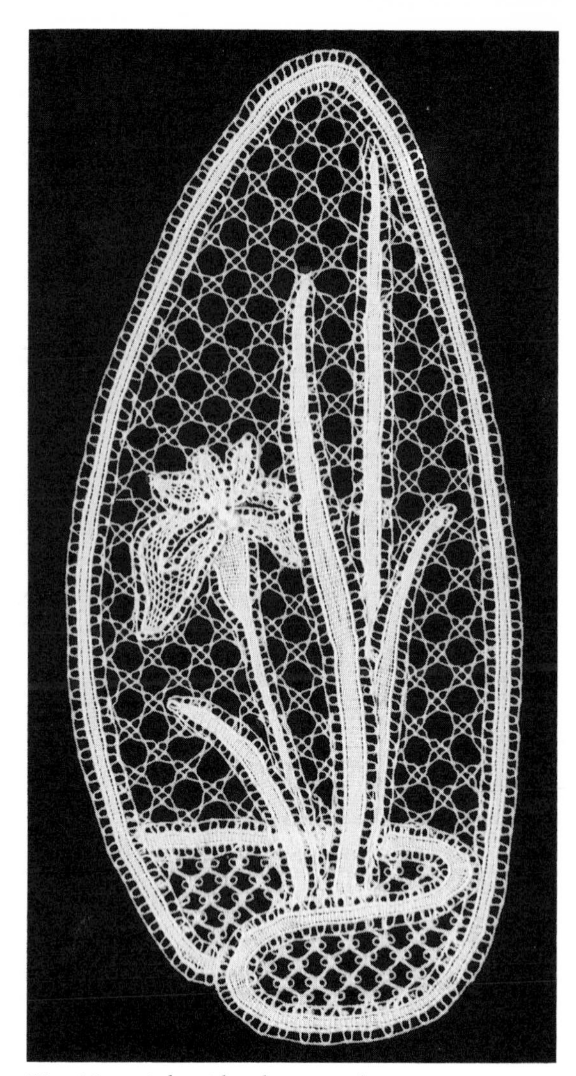

Fig. 32-a right side photograph

Flat work – a design ideal for use on a greetings card. Start with the two leaves and then work the stream to form the outline of the motif. Finally, sew the two leaves on to the stream.

Flache Arbeit. Ideal als Grusskarte. Zuerst die beiden Blätter, dann den Flussbogen klöppeln, mit dem die Umrandung des Motivs gebildet wird. Zum Schluss die beiden Blätter an den Flussbogen häkeln.

Vlak werk – een goed ontwerp voor een felicitatiekaart. Begin met de twee bladeren en klos dan het bandje dat de omtrek van het motief vormt. Hecht tenslotte de twee bladeren af in het bandje.

Travail à plat – un dessin particulièrement adapté à une carte de voeux. Commencez par les deux feuilles, puis faites la partie représentant les contours du motif Crochetez les deux feuilles en dernier.

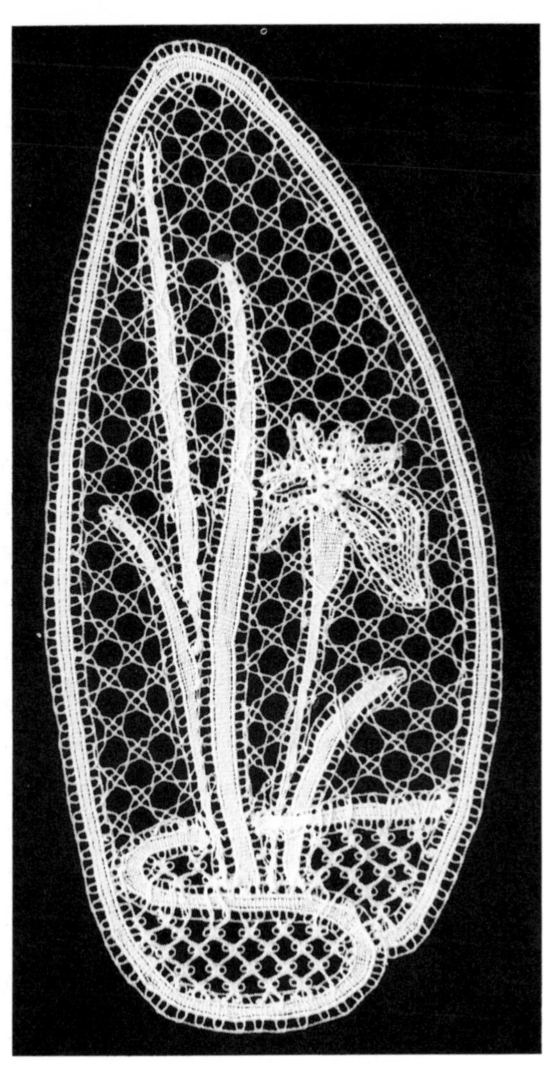

Fig. 32-b wrong side photograph

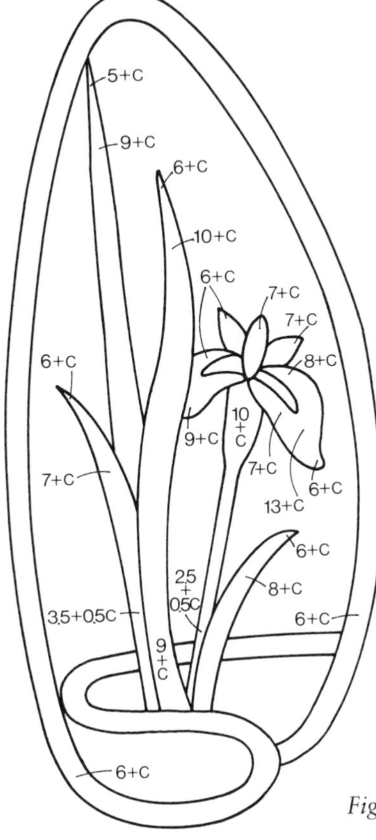

3.5 = 3 pairs and a single thread
0.5C = a single coarse thread

Fig. 32-d number of pairs

Filling: four pin, whole stitch block variation

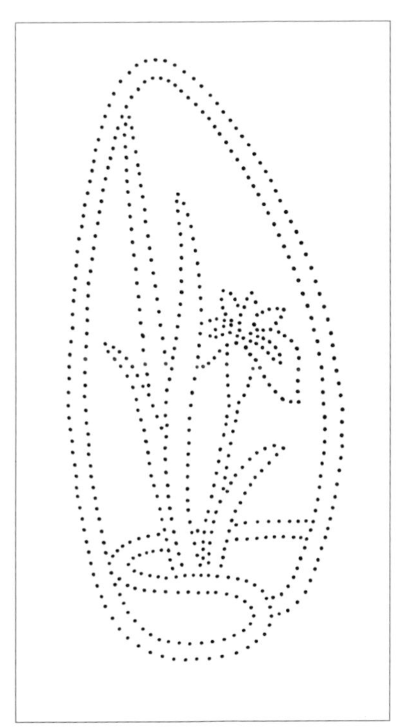

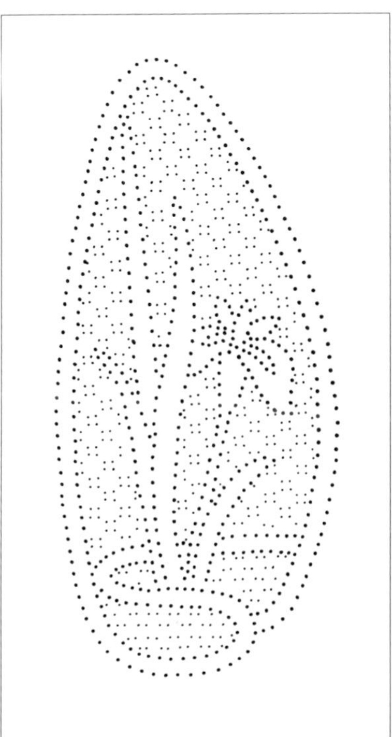

Fig. 32-e prickings

33 Ikebana Clematis

Fig. 33-c working order

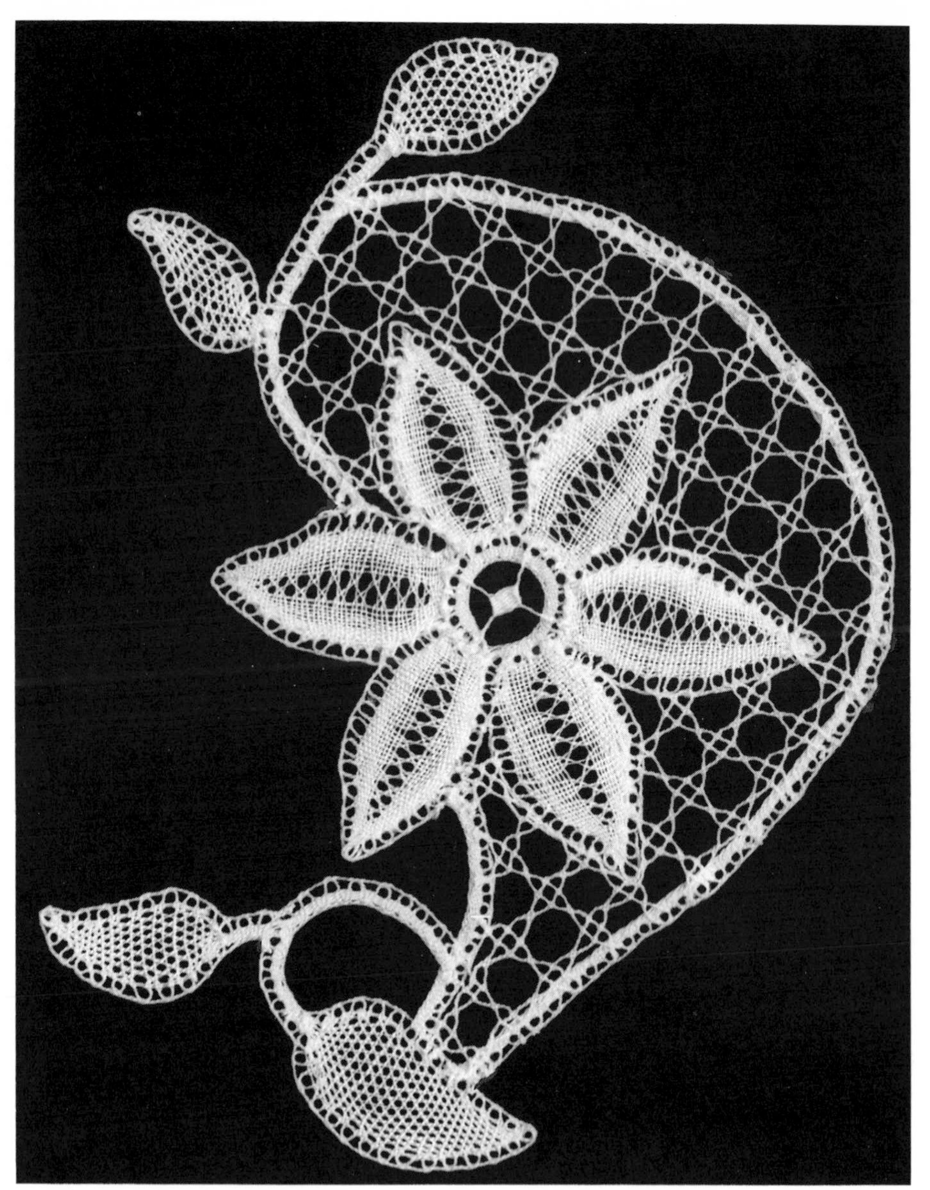

Fig. 33-a right side photograph

This raised work is suitable for use on a powder compact or set in a paperweight. Work the centre rib of the flower, then rib out into the first petal, as shown in Fig. 33-c. Fill the petal with whole stitch and half stitch. Finally, work the leaves, stem, and filling.

Erhabene Arbeit – geeignet als Einsatz für eine Puderdose oder einen Briefbeschwerer. Innere Rippe der Blume ausführen, Uebergang zum ersten Blütenblatt gem. Abbildung 33-c. Füllung in Ganz- und Halbschlag. Anschliessend Blätter, Stiel und Füllung ausführen.

Dit raised work is geschikt voor een poederdoos of een presse-papier. Klos eerst de rib in het hart van de bloem, ga dan met de rib over naar het eerste bloemblad, als in fig. 33-c. Vul het bloemblad met linnenslag en netslag. Klos tenslotte bladeren, steel en vulling.

Ce travail en relief peut être utilisé pour garnir un poudrier ou un presse-papiers. Faites le lacet au milieu de la fleur et continuez-le pour faire le premier pétale (*voir* Fig. 33-c). Remplissez le pétale en mat et en grille. Pour terminer, faites les feuilles, leurs tiges et le fond.

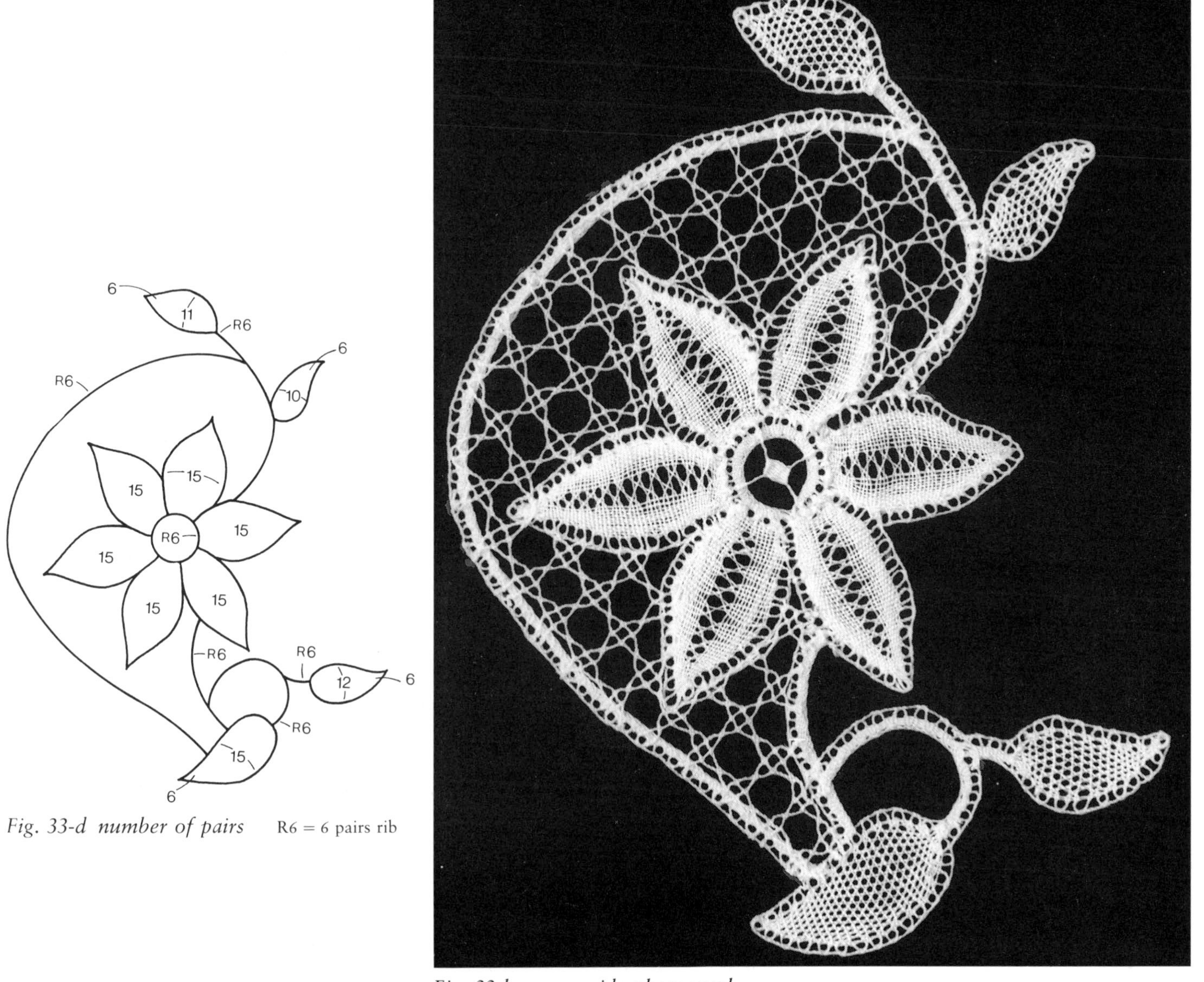

Fig. 33-d number of pairs R6 = 6 pairs rib

Fig. 33-b wrong side photograph

Fillings: four pin, swing leadworks

Fig. 33-e prickings

34
Ikebana Wisteria

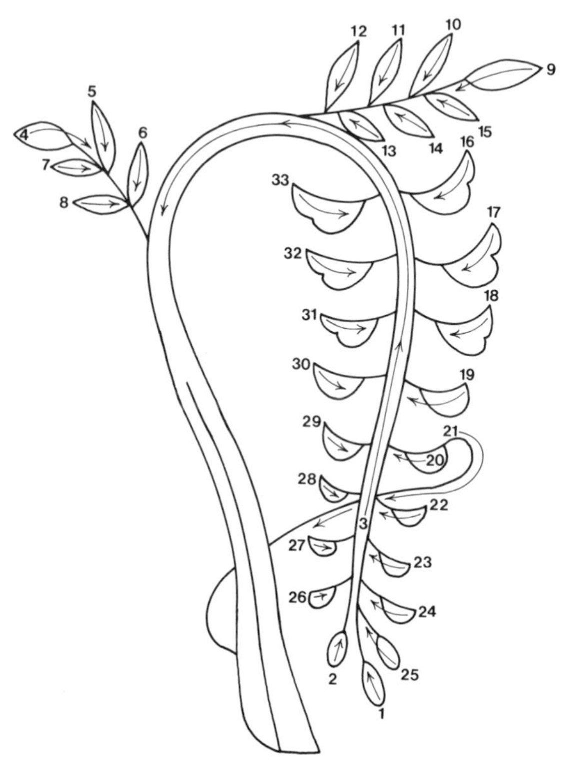

Fig. 34-c working order

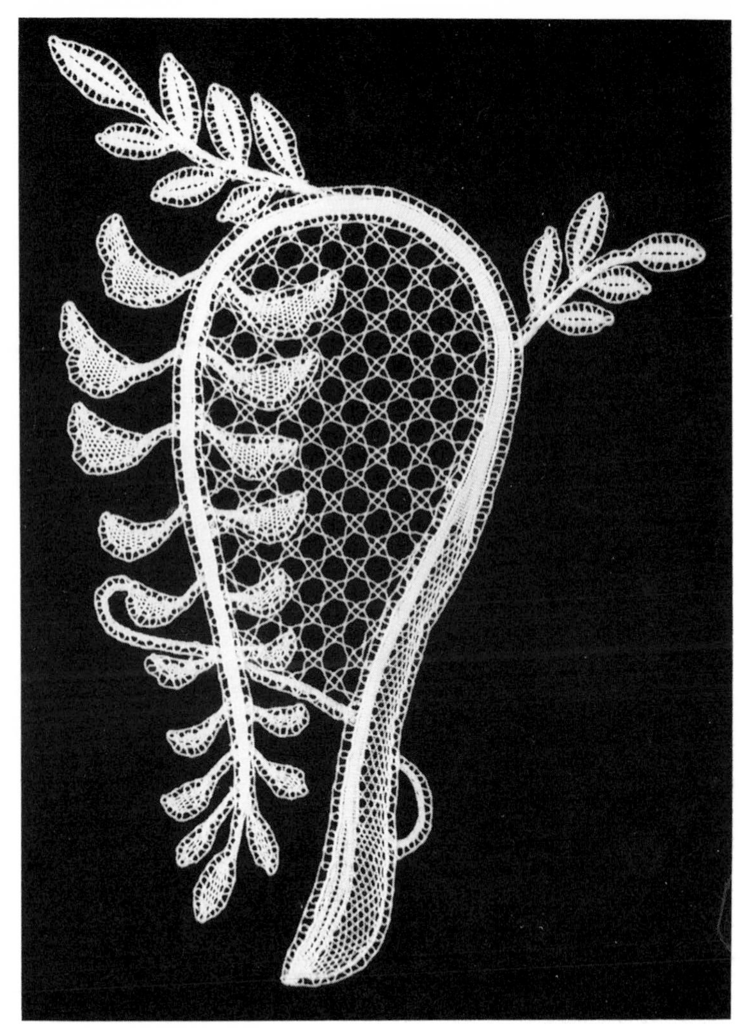

Fig. 34-a right side photograph

Flat work – ideal for use on a greetings card. Work the lowest two buds first and use the pairs to work the main tree stem. Then work the leaves and their stems. The remaining buds and flowers are sewn on to the stem.

Flache Arbeit – ideal für Grusskarten. Die beiden untersten Knospen zürst ausführen und die Kloeppelpaare für den Stiel verwenden. Anschliessend die Blätter und deren Stiel arbeiten. Die restlichen Knospen und Blüten werden an den Stiel gehäkelt.

Vlak werk – mooi voor een wenskaart. Klos de onderste knoppen eerst en en gebruik de paren voor de hoofdtak. Klos daarna de bladeren en hun steeltjes. De overige knoppen en bloemen worden in de steel afgehecht.

Travail à plat – idéal pour l'utilisation sur une carte de voeux. Faites d'abord les deux boutons inférieurs et utilisez les paires pour le tronc d'arbre principal. Exécutez ensuite les feuilles et leurs tiges. Les autres bourgeons et fleurs sont réliés aux branches.

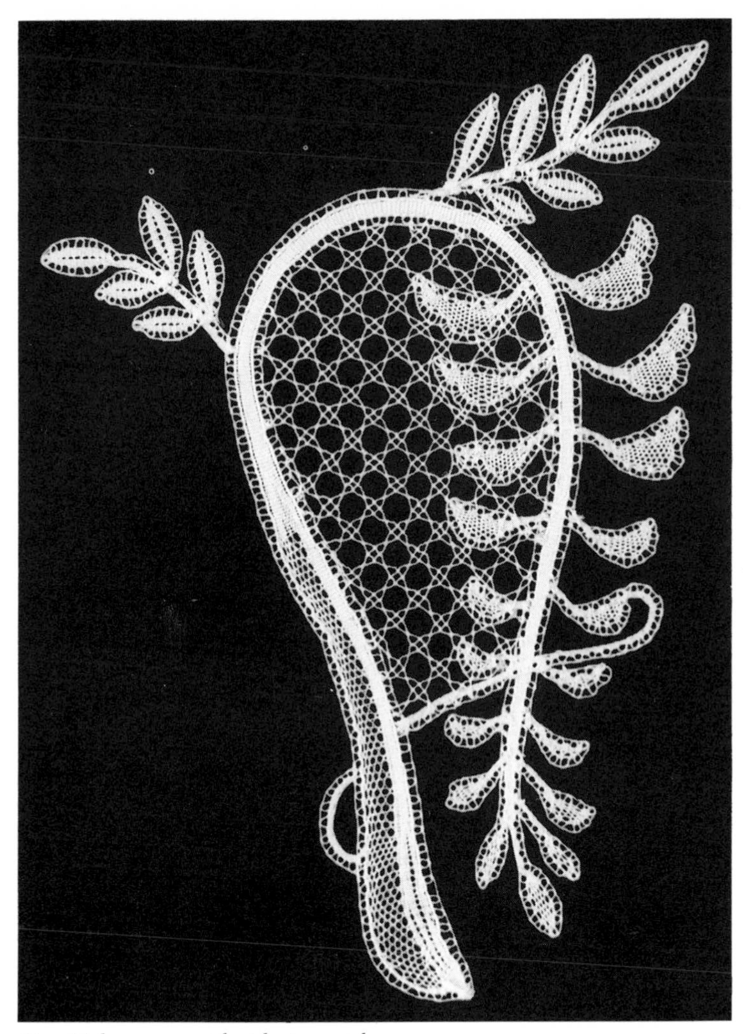

Fig. 34-b wrong side photograph

Fig. 34-e prickings *Filling: four pin*

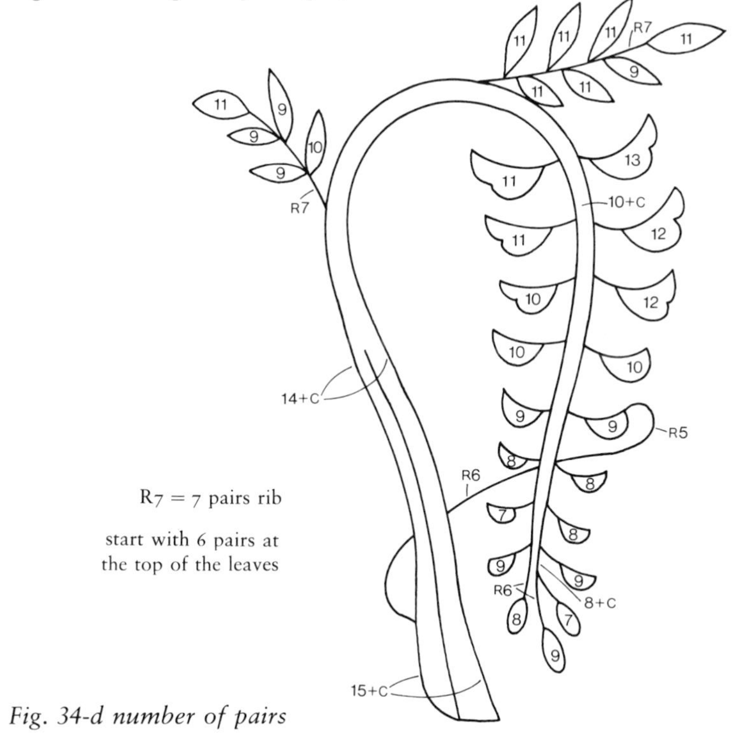

Fig. 34-d number of pairs

35 Ikebana Camellia

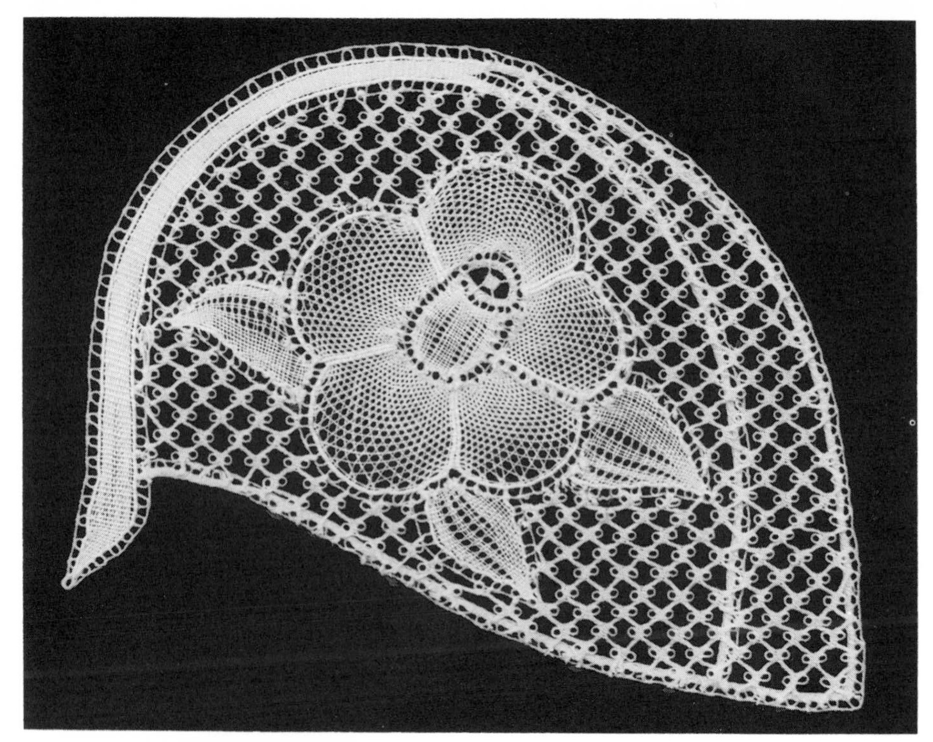

Fig. 35-a right side photograph

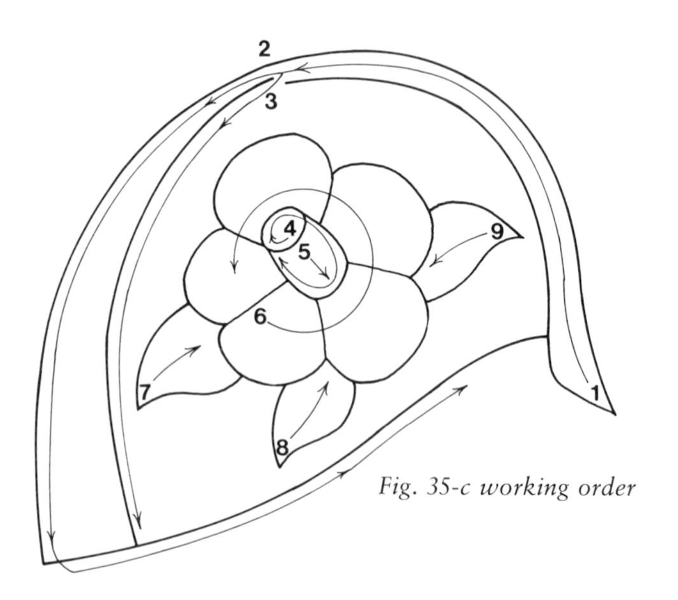

Fig. 35-c working order

This pattern is suitable for a paperweight. Work a branch of the willow tree as the outline of the motif. Then work the centre rib of the flower, and rib out to form the stamen as shown in Fig. 35-c (5). The petals are worked in half stitch, then work the leaves and sew them on to the flower petals.

Muster für einen Briefbeschwerer. Einen Zweig der Trauerweide als Umrandung des Motivs arbeiten. Anschliessend die innere Rippe der Blume arbeiten. Gemäss Abbildung 35-c die Staubgefässe ausführen. Die Blütenblätter in Halbschlag arbeiten, danach die Blätter kloeppeln und an die Blütenblätter häkeln.

Dit patroon is geschikt voor een presse-papier. Klos de wilgetak als de omtrek van het motief. Werk dan de rib in het hart van de bloem en laat die overgaan in de meeldraad als in fig. 35-c. De bloemblaadjes worden in netslag geklost. Klos daarna de bladeren en hecht ze af in de bloemblaadjes.

Ce dessin peut garnir un presse-papiers. Faites une branche de saule comme contour du motif. Travaillez ensuite le lacet de la fleur et continuez-le pour former l'étamine (Fig. 35-c[5]). Les pétales sont exécutés en grille; faites ensuite les feuilles et crochetez-les aux pétales de la fleur.

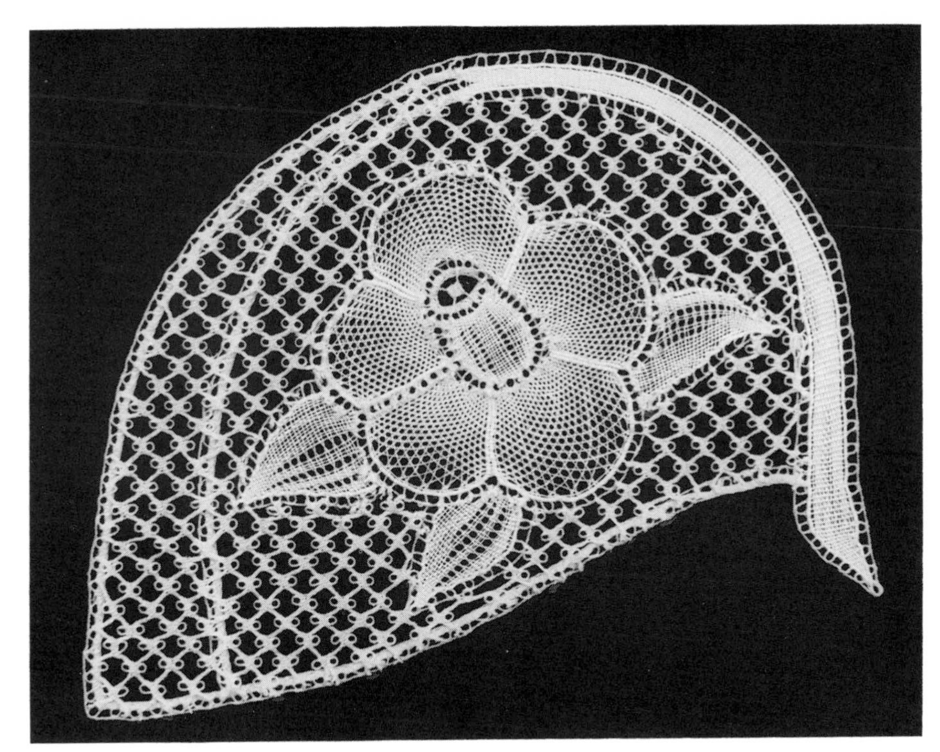

Fig. 35-b wrong side photograph

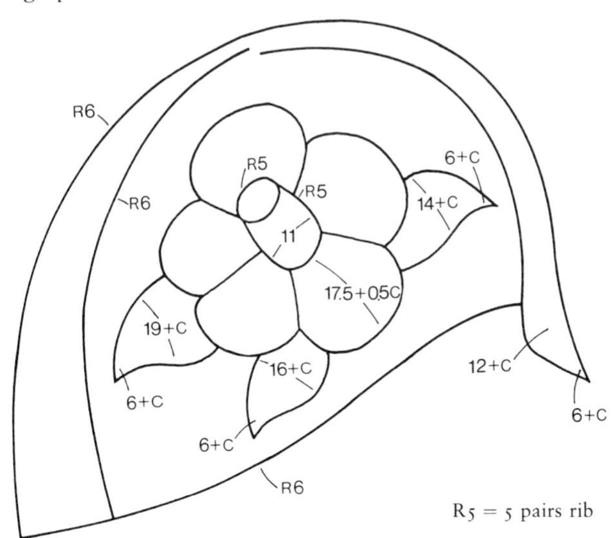

Fig. 35-d number of pairs

R5 = 5 pairs rib

Fillings: whole stitch block variation, swing leadworks

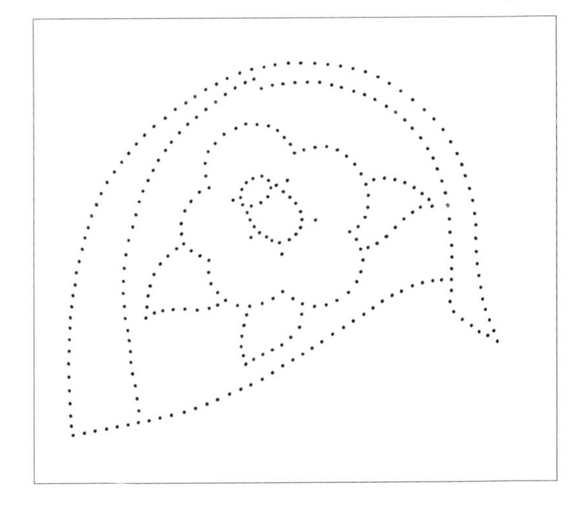

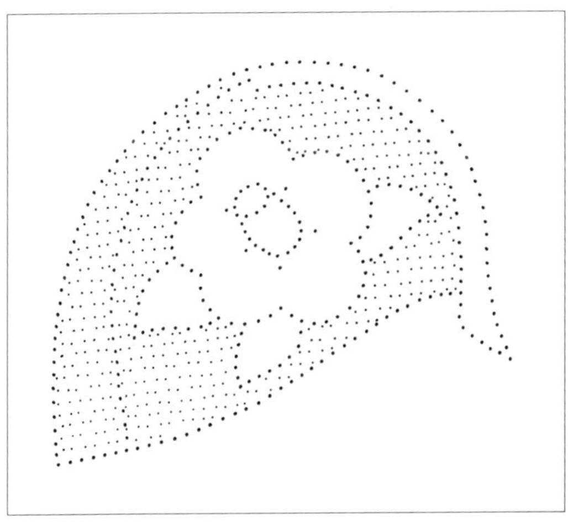

Fig. 35-e prickings

36
Ikebana Chrysanthemum

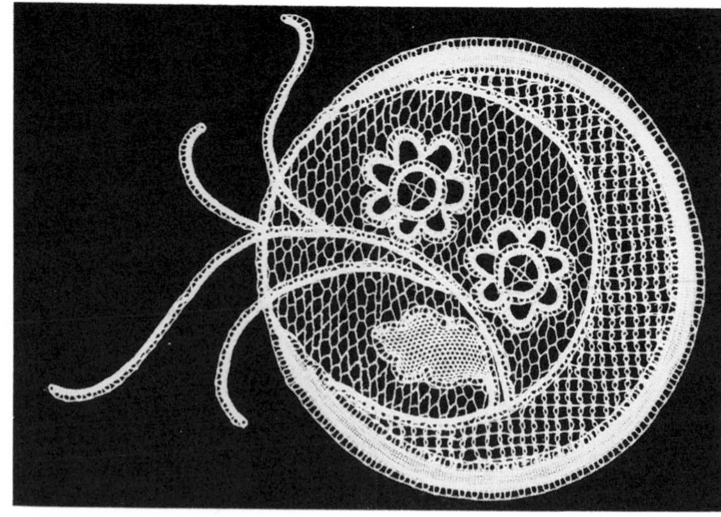

Fig. 36-a right side photograph

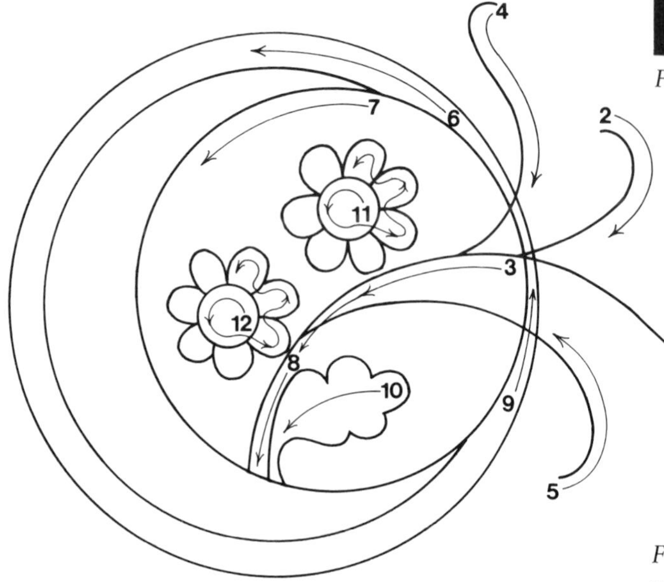

Fig. 36-c working order

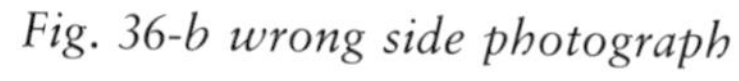

Fig. 36-b wrong side photograph

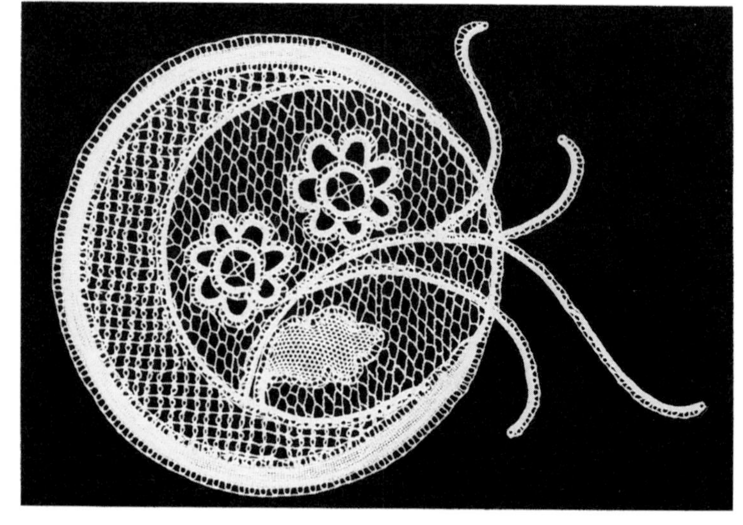

Flat work – ideal for use as a greetings card. Work rib to form a branch, then work the moon shaped vase as shown in Fig. 36c. Work rib to form the centre of the flower and then rib out to the petals.

Flache Arbeit – ideal für Grusskarten. Rippe ausführen, um einen Ast zu gestalten, anschliessend die mondförmige Vase gemäss Abbildung 36-c klöppeln. Rippe für die Mitte der Blume bilden, Übergang zu den Blütenblättern.

Vlak werk – geschikt voor gebruik op een wenskaart. Klos de rib die de tak vormt, werk daarna da maanvormige vaas volgens fig 36-c. Klos de rib in het hart van de bloem en laat die overgaan in de bloemblaadjes.

Travail à plat – idéal pour carte de voeux. Faites le lacet d'abord pour former une branche, et ensuite le vase en forme de lune (*voir* Fig. 36c). Formez le centre de la fleur avec un lacet que vous continuerez pour les pétales.

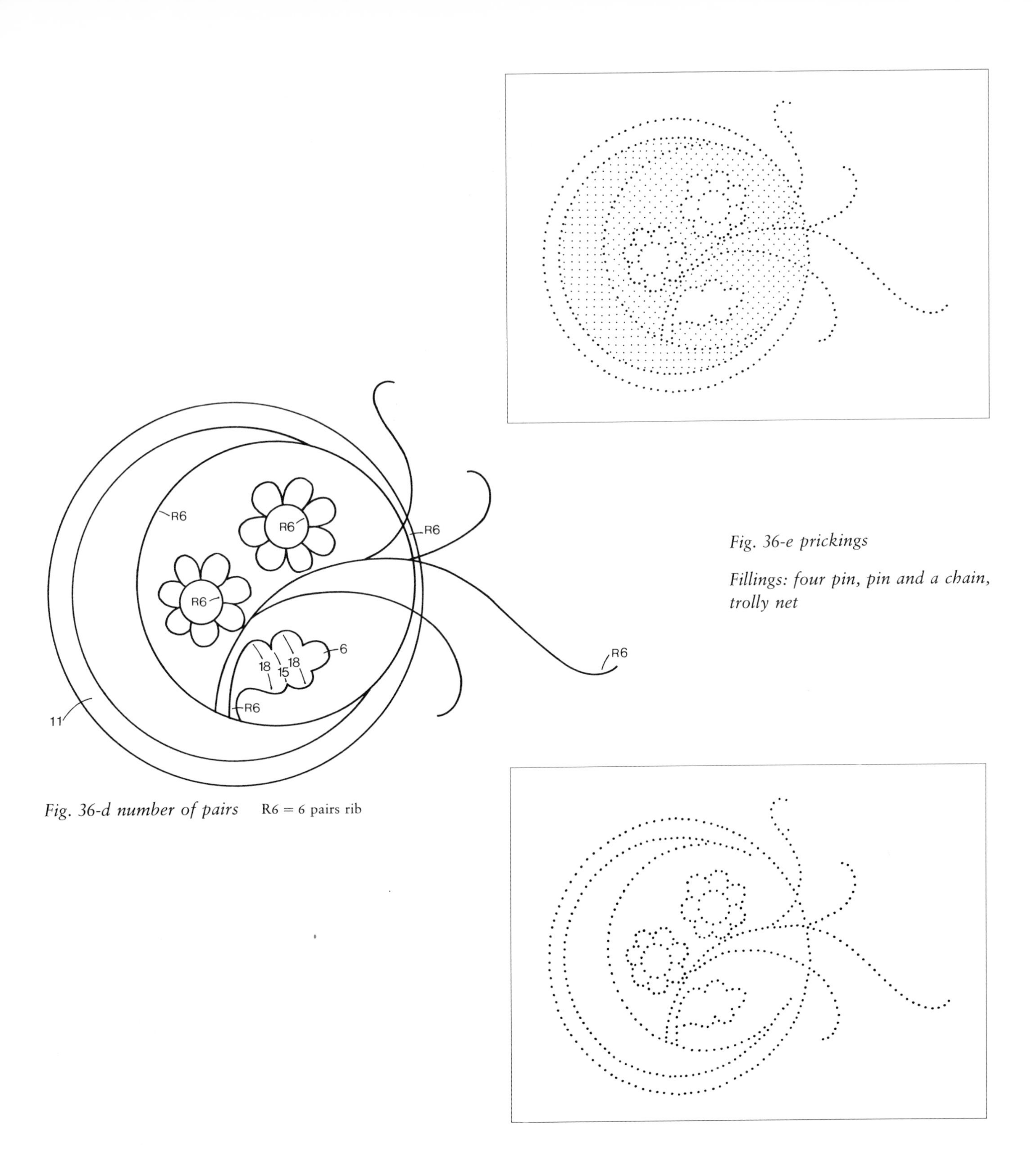

Fig. 36-e prickings

Fillings: four pin, pin and a chain, trolly net

Fig. 36-d number of pairs R6 = 6 pairs rib

37
Ikebana Wild Morning Glory

Fig. 37-a right side photograph

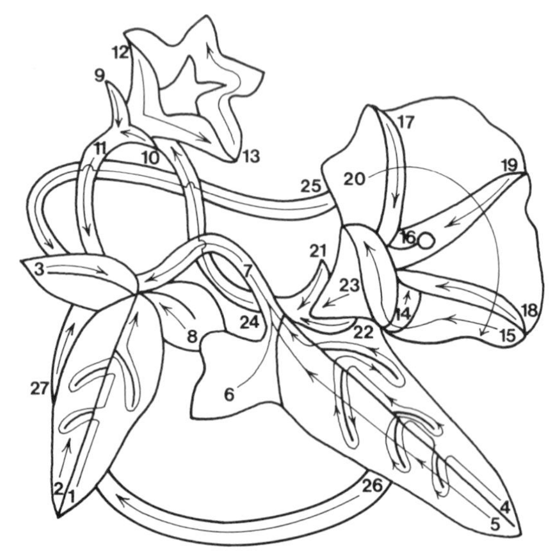

Fig. 37-c working order

A variety of different techniques are used to make this raised work pattern. Work the raised vein first, and then the half stitch leaf.

Anwendung einer Vielzahl verschiedener Techniken zur Gestaltung des erhaben gearbeiteten Musters. Zuerst die Ader ausführen, danach das Blütenblatt in Halbschlag.

Om dit raised patroon te maken zijn verschillende technieken gebruikt. Klos eerst de opliggende nerf en dan het netslagblad.

Ce patron à travail en relief comprend une variétée de différentes techniques. Faites d'abord la nervure en relief, et ensuite la feuille en grille.

Fig. 37-b wrong side photograph

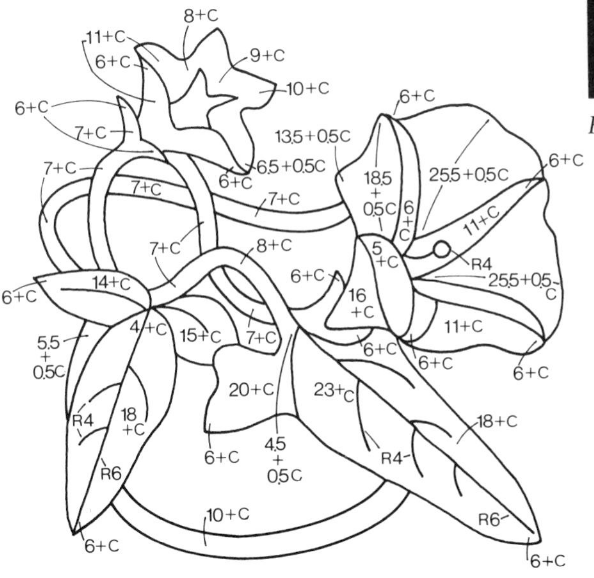

R6 = 6 pairs rib
13.5 = 13 pairs and a single thread
0.5C = a single coarse thread

Fig. 37-d number of pairs

Fillings:
whole stitch block variation,
swing leadworks

Fig. 37-e prickings

38
Ikebana Gentian

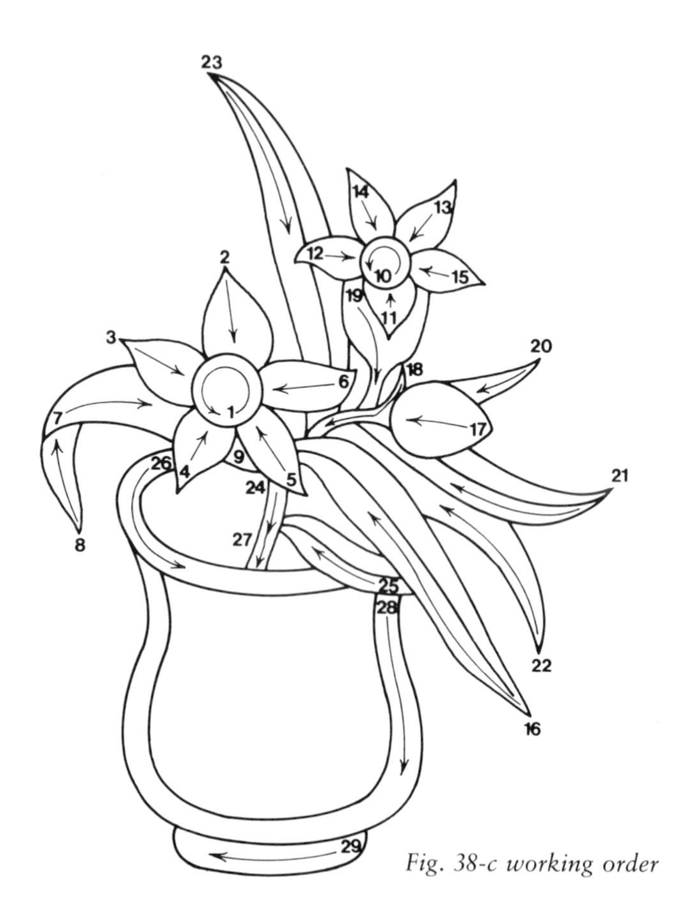

Fig. 38-c working order

Fig. 38-a right side photograph

Work the centre rib of the main flower, then the half stitch petals around the circle.

Die mittlere Rippe der Blume arbeiten, anschliessend die Blütenblätter in Halbschlag ausführen.

Werk de rib in het hart van de grootste bloem, daarna de netslag bloemblaadjes rond het hart.

Exécutez d'abord le lacet au milieu de la fleur principale, puis la grille des pétales autour du cercle.

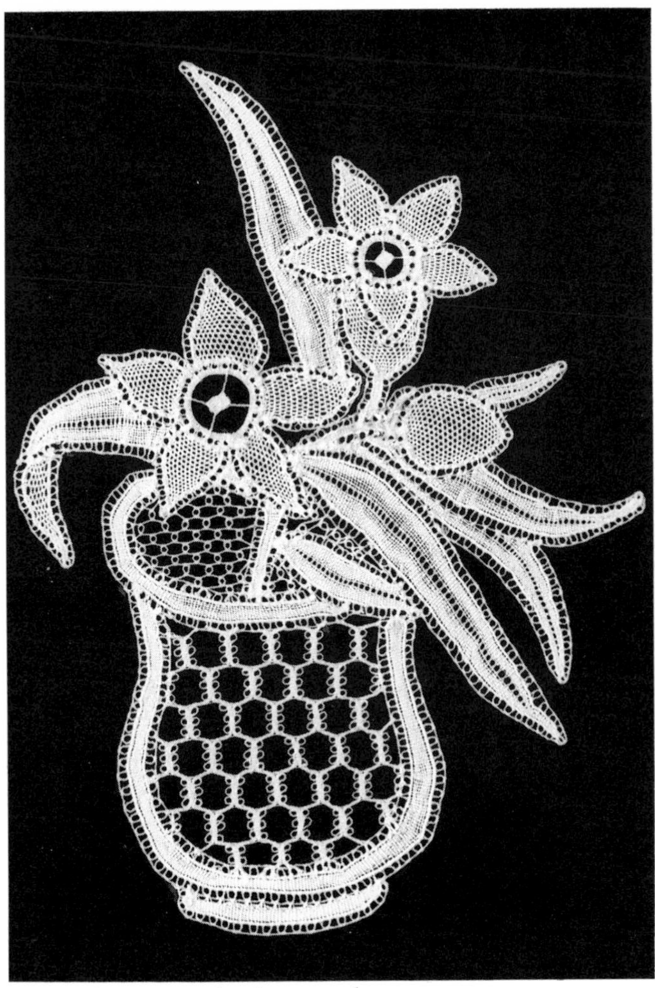

Fig. 38-b wrong side photograph

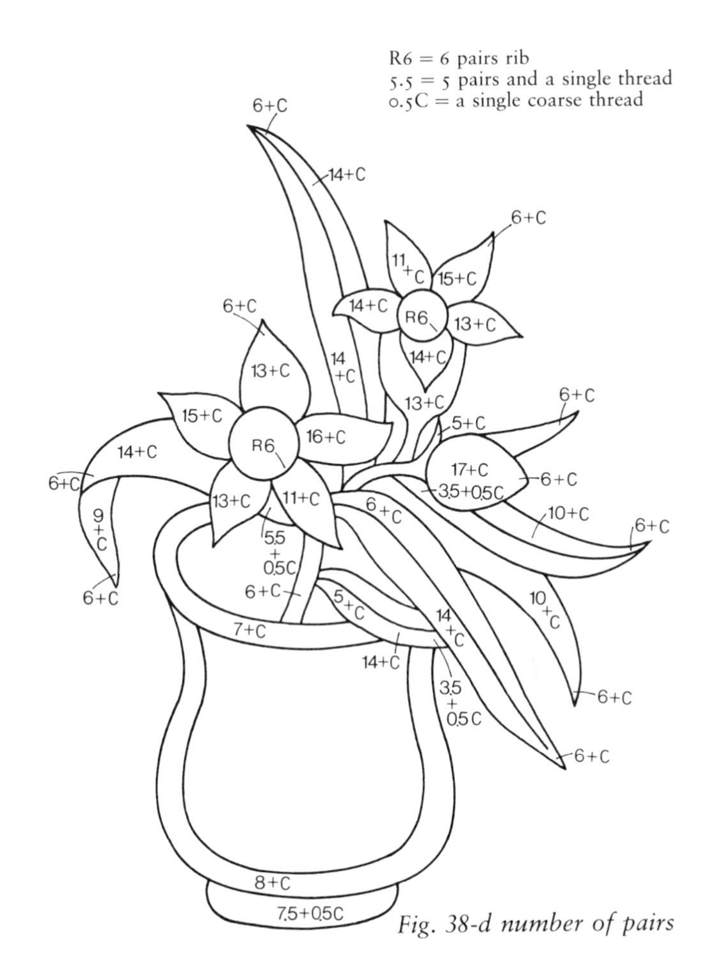

Fig. 38-d number of pairs

Fillings:
pin and a stitch,
whole stitch block,
swing leadworks

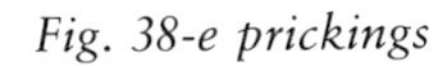

Fig. 38-e prickings

39
Sunflower

Fig. 39-a right side photograph

Fig. 39-b wrong side photograph

Fig. 39-c working order

Fig. 39-d number of pairs

14.5 = 14 pairs and a single thread
0.5C = a single coarse thread

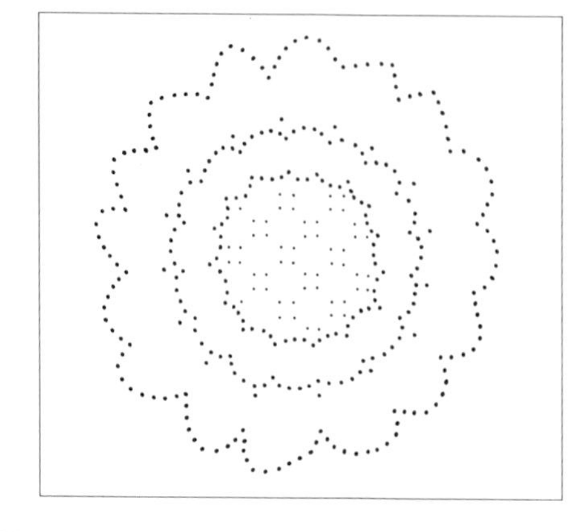

Filling:
four pin and swing leadworks

Fig. 39-e pricking

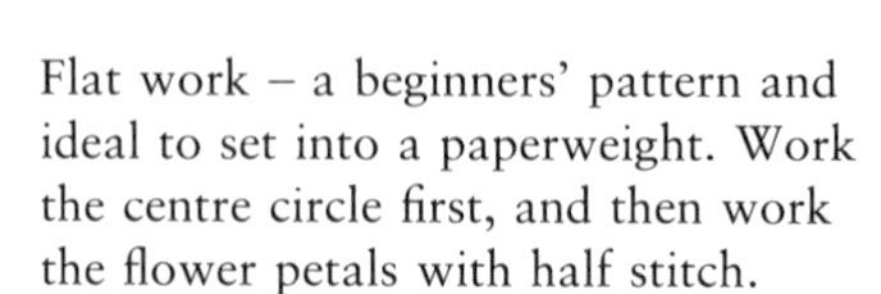

Flat work – a beginners' pattern and ideal to set into a paperweight. Work the centre circle first, and then work the flower petals with half stitch.

Flache Arbeit. Für Anfänger und ideal als Einsatz für einen Briefbeschwerer. Zürst den Innenkreis arbeiten, danach die Blütenblätter in Halbschlag.

Vlak werk – een patroon voor beginners, geschikt voor in een presse-papier. Werk de middencirkel eerst, en daarna de bloemblaadjes in netslag.

Travail à plat – un ouvrage à la portée des débutantes pouvant être utilisé pour un presse-papiers. Faites d'abord le cercle du milieu, puis les pétales en grille.

40
Bamboo Lily

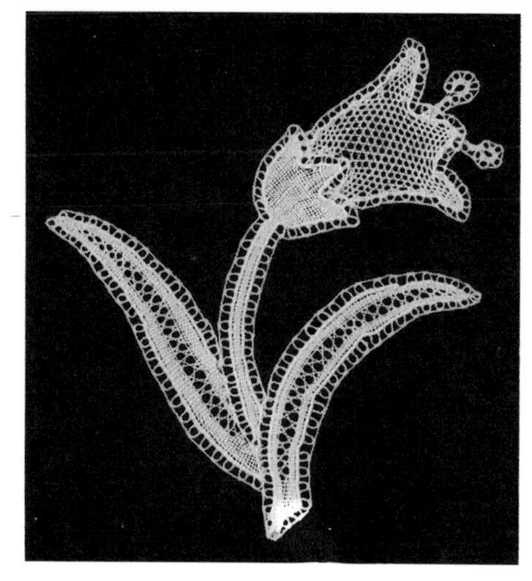

Fig. 40-a right side photograph

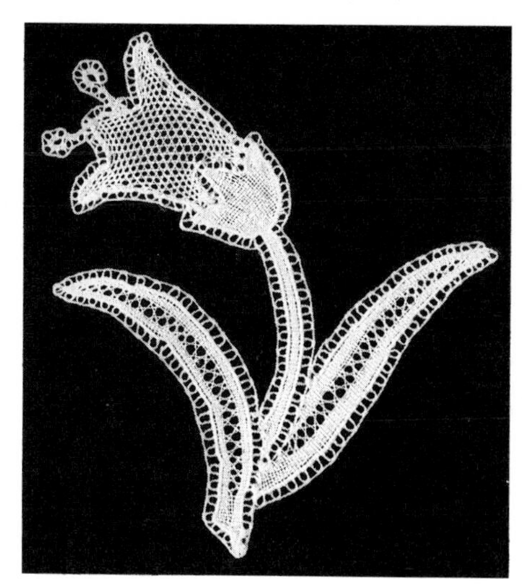

Fig. 40-b wrong side photograph

Fig. 40-c working order

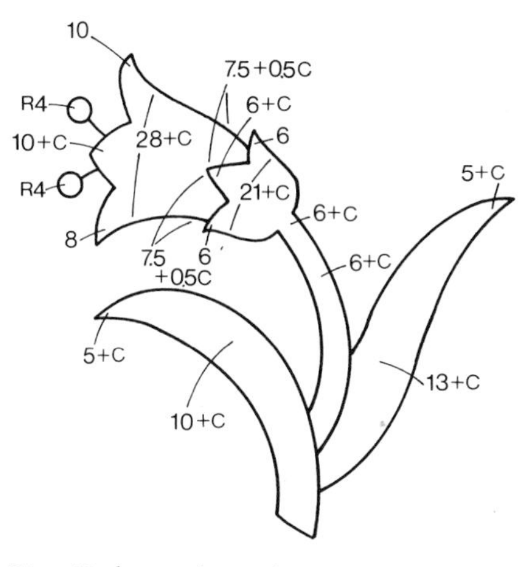

Fig. 40-d number of pairs

R4 = 4 pairs rib
7.5 = 7 pairs and a single thread
0.5C = a single coarse thread

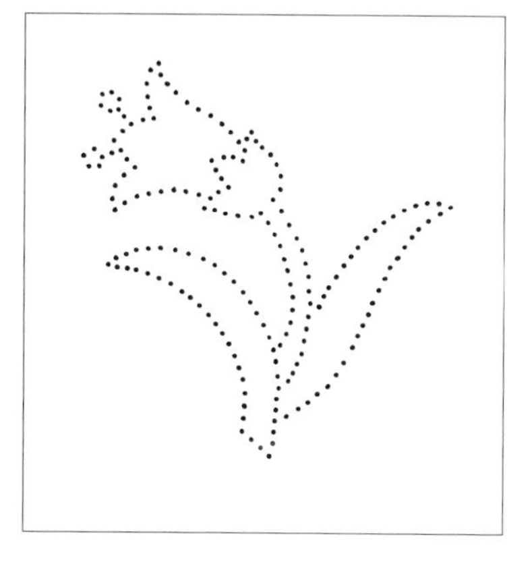

Fig. 40-e pricking

Flat work – a beginners' pattern suitable for setting into a paperweight. Work the leaves with half-stitch veins first. Next, work the flower calyx and decrease the number of pairs to form the stem, which is sewn onto the first leaf.

Flache Arbeit. Für Anfänger. Geeignet als Einsatz für einen Briefbeschwerer. Zürst die Blätter mit Adern in Halbschlag ausführen. Anschliessend den Blütenkelch arbeiten. Die Anzahl der Klöppelpaare verringern, um den Stiel zu bilden, der in das erste Blatt eingehäkelt wird.

Travail à plat – un ouvrage à la portée des débutantes, pouvant être utilisé pour garnir un presse-papiers. Faites d'abord les feuilles à nervures en grille. Ensuite, exécutez le calice de la fleur et diminuez le nombre de paires pour former la tige qui est crochetée dans la première feuille.

Vlak werk – een patroon voor beginners, geschikt voor een presse-papier. Klos de bladeren met de netslag nerf eerst. Klos dan de bloemkelk en verminder het aantal paren om de steel te maken, die aan het eerste blad is aangehaakt.

41 Common Orange Daylily

Fig. 41-a right side photograph

Fig. 41-b wrong side photograph

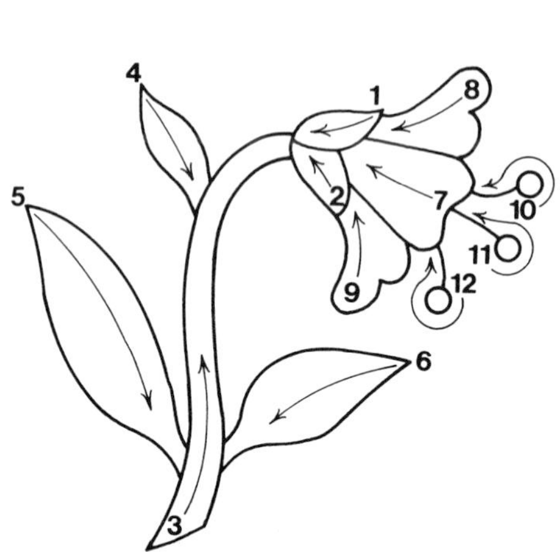

Fig. 41-c working order

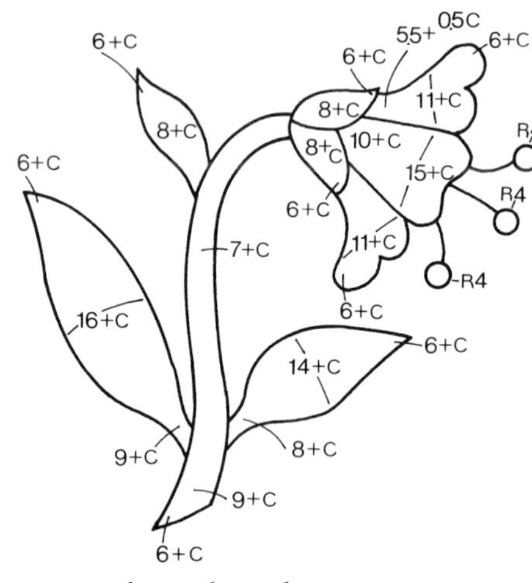

Fig. 41-d number of pairs

R4 = 4 pairs rib
5.5 = 5 pairs and a single thread
0.5C = a single coarse thread

Fig. 41-e pricking

Flat work – a beginners' pattern. Work the flower calyx first, and then work the stem from the bottom up to the calyx. Work the leaves, starting from the tips, and sew into the stem.

Flache Arbeit. Für Anfänger. Zürst den Blütenkelch ausführen, danach den Stiel von unten zum Blütenkelch hocharbeiten. Die Blätter an der Spitze beginnen und in den Stiel einhäkeln.

Vlak werk – een patroon voor beginners. Klos de bloemkelk eerst, en werk dan de steel vanaf de basis omhoog naar de kelk. Klos de bladeren, te beginnen aan de punt, en hecht ze af aan de steel.

Travail à plat – à la portée des débutantes. Exécutez d'abord le calice de la fleur, puis la tige à partir d'en bas jusqu'au calice. Faites les feuilles en commençant par les pointes et crochetez-les à la tige.

42 Oyama Magnolia

Fig. 42-a right side photograph

Fig. 42-b wrong side photograph

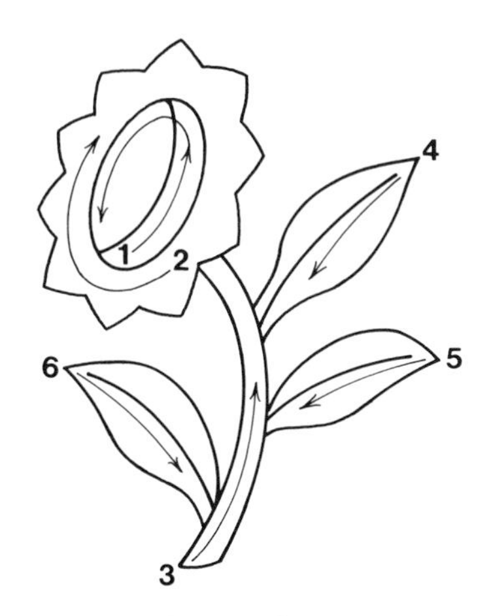

Fig. 42-c working order

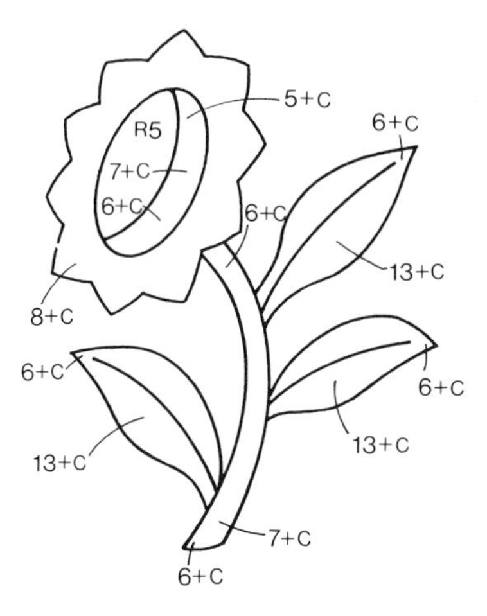

Fig. 42-d number of pairs R5 = 5 pairs rib

Filling: whole stitch block variation

Fig. 42-e pricking

Work the flower centre first and then work the outer petals with half stitch. Work up the stem from the bottom up to the flower. Use whole and half stitch to work the leaves.

Zuerst die Mitte der Blume, dann die aeusseren Blütenblätter in Halbschlag ausführen. Den Stiel unten beginnen und zur Blume hochführen. Die Blätter in Ganz- und Halbschlag klöppeln.

Klos het hart van de bloem eerst en daarna de buitenste bloemblaadjes in netslag. Werk de steel van de basis omhoog naar de bloem. Gebruik linnen- en netslag om de bladeren te klossen.

Faites d'abord la fleur du milieu, puis exécutez les pétales extérieurs en grille. Travaillez la tige du bas vers la fleur, et les feuilles en mat et en grille.

43
Dahlia (2)

Fig. 43-a right side photograph

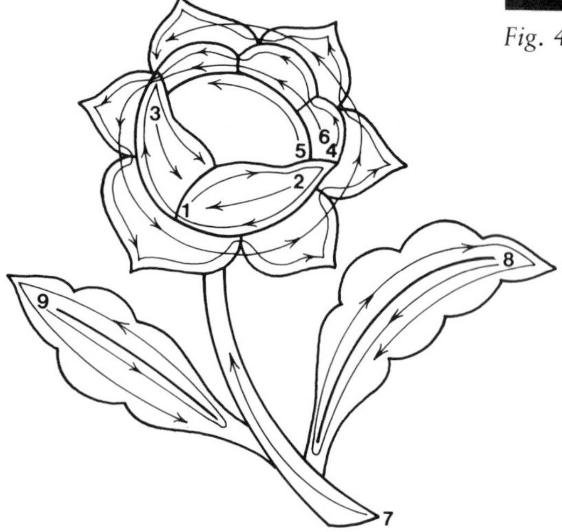

Fig. 43-c working order

Rib to form the outline of the petals and fill with whole and half stitch. The leaves have a centre rib.

Rippe für die Umrandung der Blütenblätter klöppeln. Füllung in Ganz- und Halbschlag. Die Blätter werden durch eine Ader geteilt.

Klos met een rib de omtrek van de bloemblaadjes n vul ze in met linnen- en netslag. De bladeren hebben een middennerf.

Exécutez le lacet pour former le contour des pétales que vous remplirez avec du mat et de la grille. Les feuilles ont un lacet central.

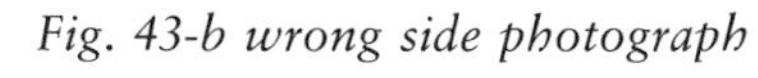

Fig. 43-b wrong side photograph

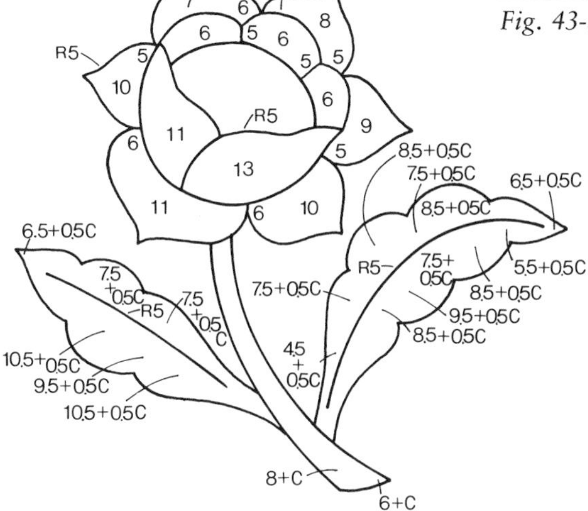

Fig. 43-d number of pairs

R5 = 5 pairs rib
6.5 = 6 pairs and a single thread
0.5C = a single coarse thread

Filling: swing and a pin

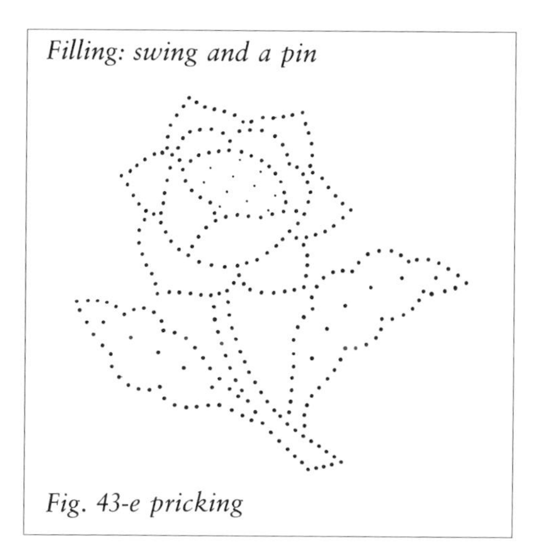

Fig. 43-e pricking

44
Water Lily

Fig. 44-c working order

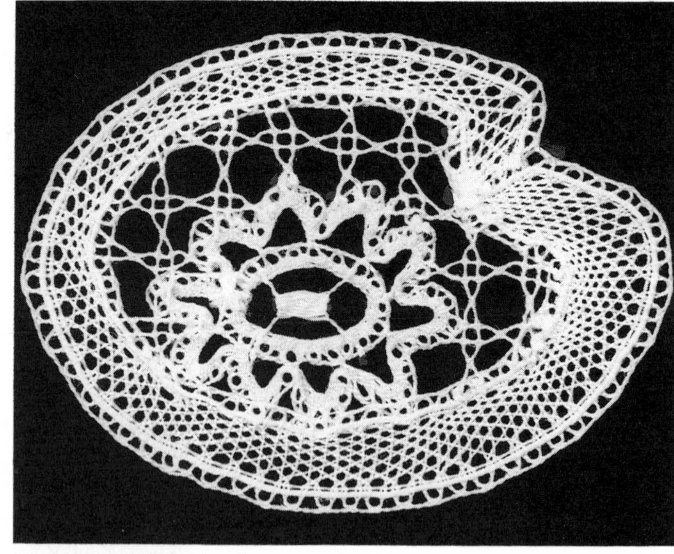

Fig. 44-a right side photograph

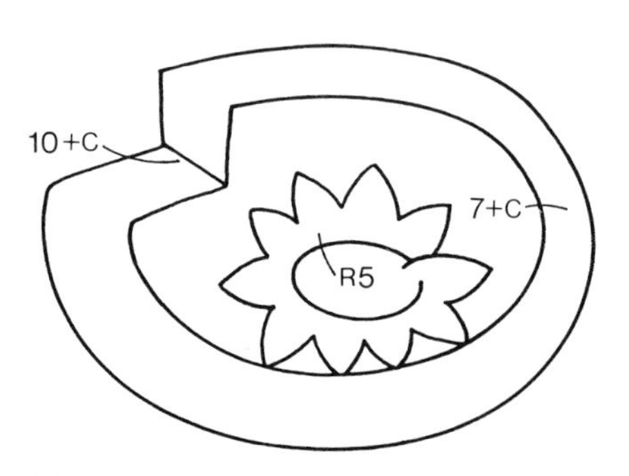

Fig. 44-d number of pairs R5 = 5 pairs rib

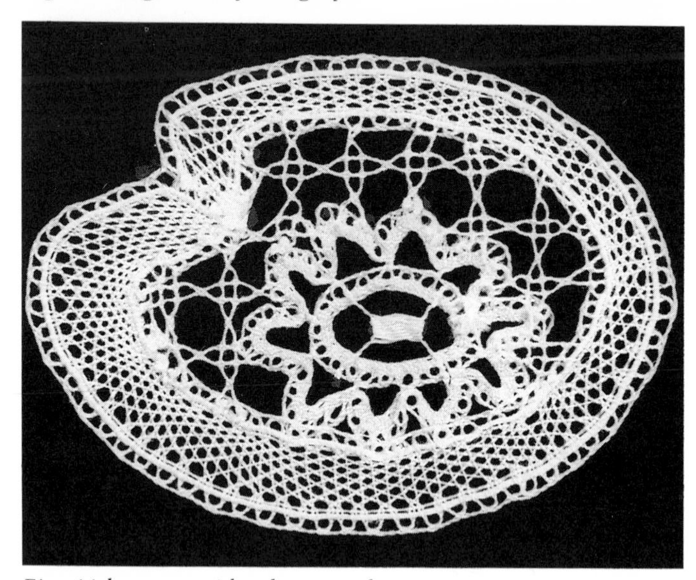

Fig. 44-b wrong side photograph

Fillings: four pin, swing leadworks

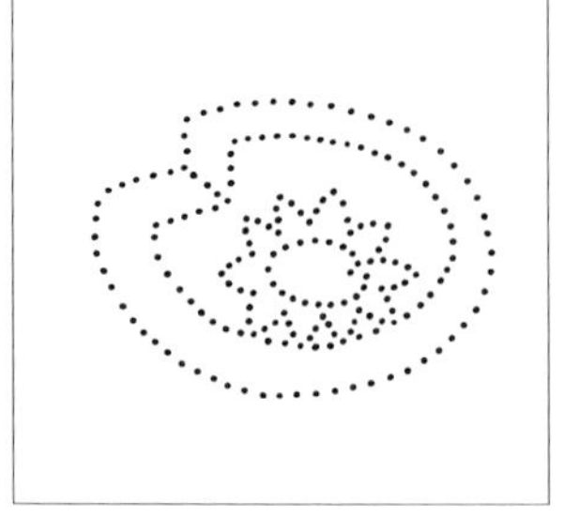

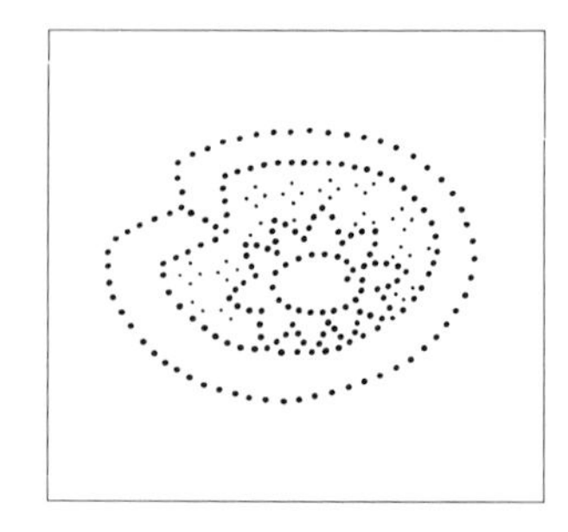

Fig. 44-e prickings

Flat work – a beginners' pattern suitable to set into a brooch. Work the centre circle of the flower first and bring in the rib to form the petals.

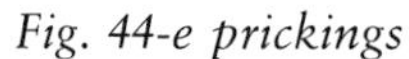

Flache Arbeit. Für Anfänger. Geeignet für eine Brosche. Zürst die Mitte der Blume arbeiten und mit der Rippe die Blütenblätter bilden.

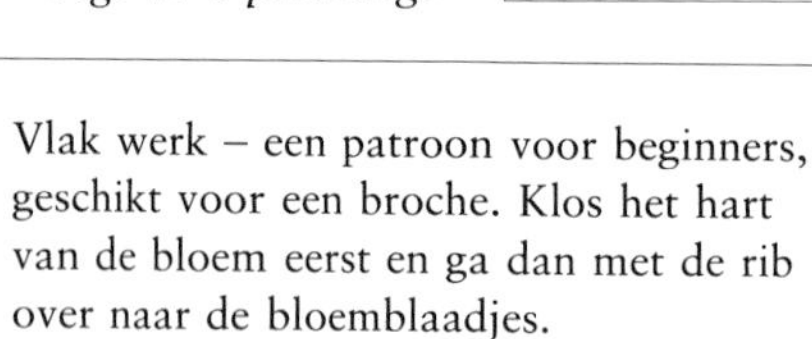

Vlak werk – een patroon voor beginners, geschikt voor een broche. Klos het hart van de bloem eerst en ga dan met de rib over naar de bloemblaadjes.

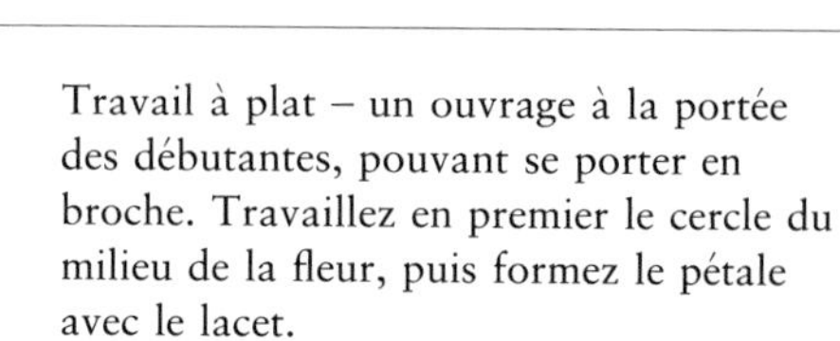

Travail à plat – un ouvrage à la portée des débutantes, pouvant se porter en broche. Travaillez en premier le cercle du milieu de la fleur, puis formez le pétale avec le lacet.

45
Flower Festival

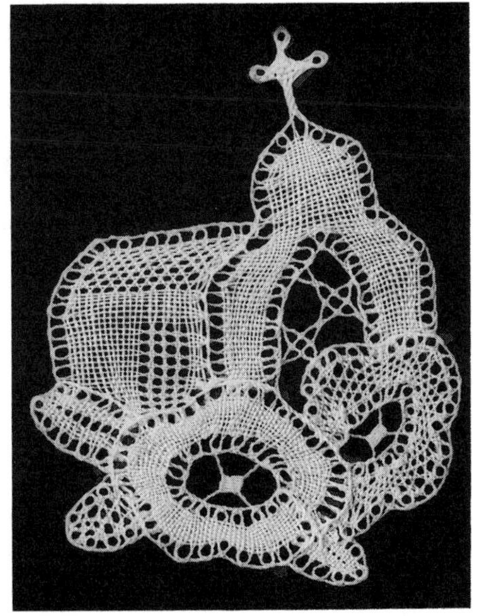
Fig. 45-a right side photograph

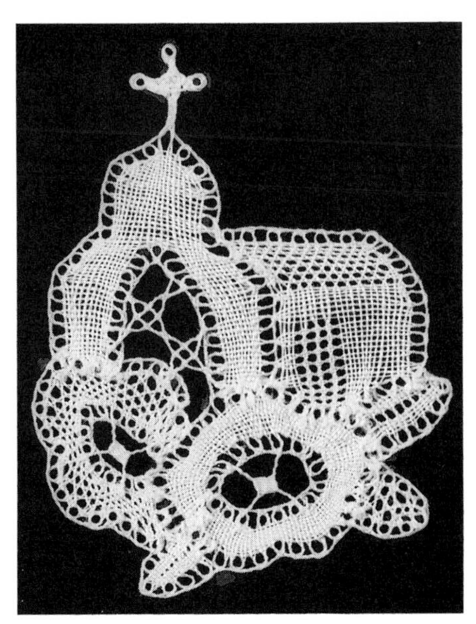
Fig. 45-b wrong side photograph

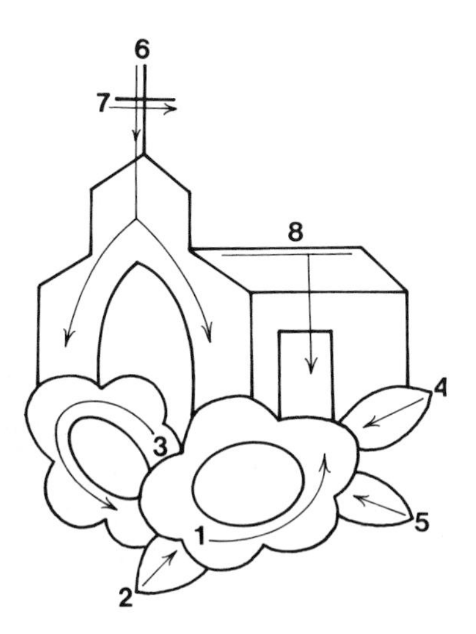

Fig. 45-c working order

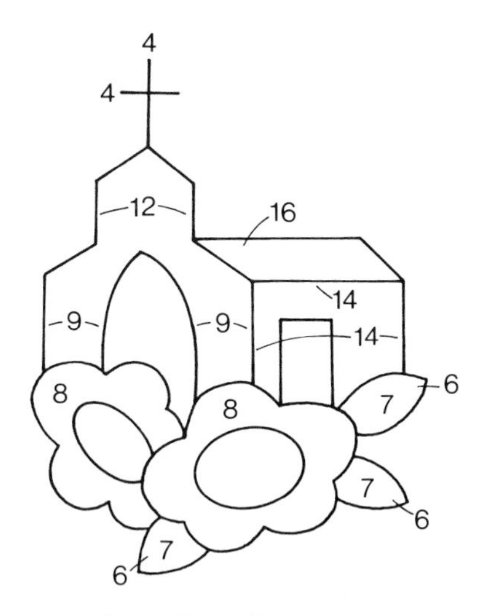

Fig. 45-d number of pairs

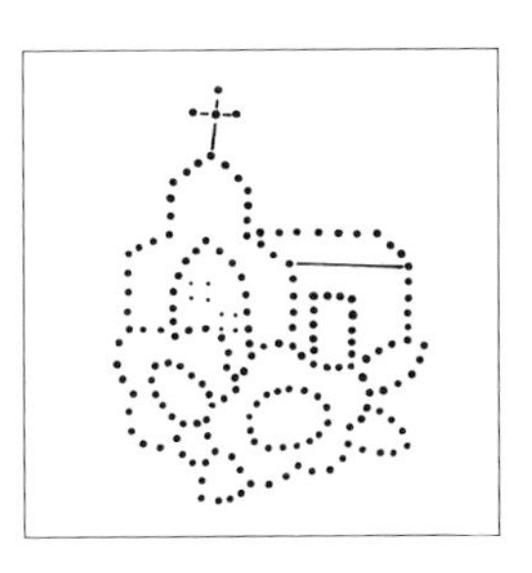
Fig. 45-e pricking

Fillings: four pin, swing leadworks

Flat work – a suitable pattern for a brooch. Work the front flower first in whole stitch, then the side flower in half stitch.

Flache Arbeit. Geeignetes Motiv für eine Brosche. Zuerst die vordere Blume in Ganzschlag, dann die seitliche Blume in Halbschlag arbeiten.

Vlak werk – een patroon geschikt voor een broche. Klos eerst de voorste bloem in linnenslag, dan de bloem ernaast in netslag.

Travail à plat – pouvant se porter en broche. Faites d'abord la fleur au premier plan en mat, puis celle sur le côté en grille.

46
Flower Motif (1)

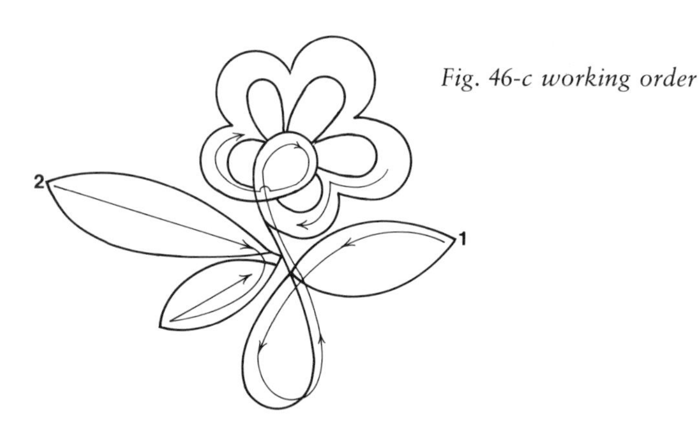

Fig. 46-c working order

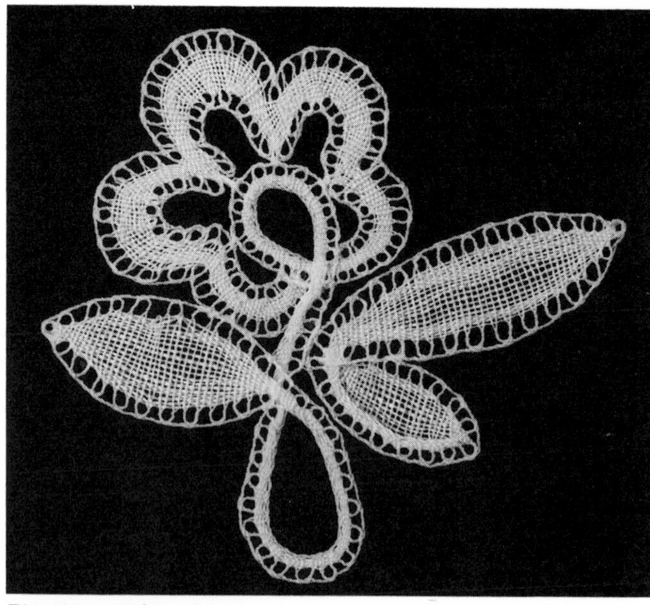

Fig. 46-a right side photograph

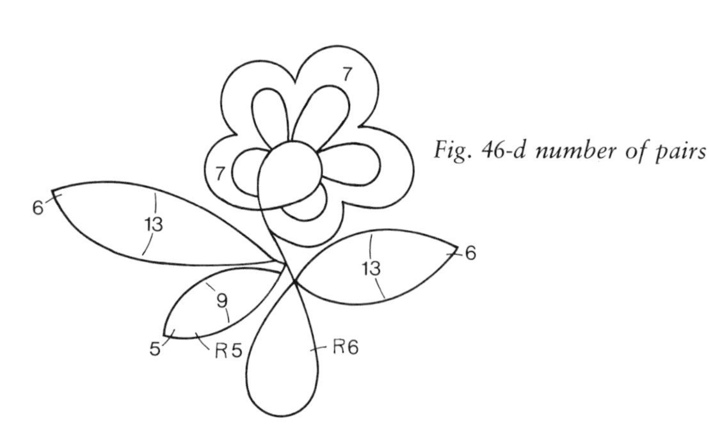

Fig. 46-d number of pairs

R6 = 6 pairs rib

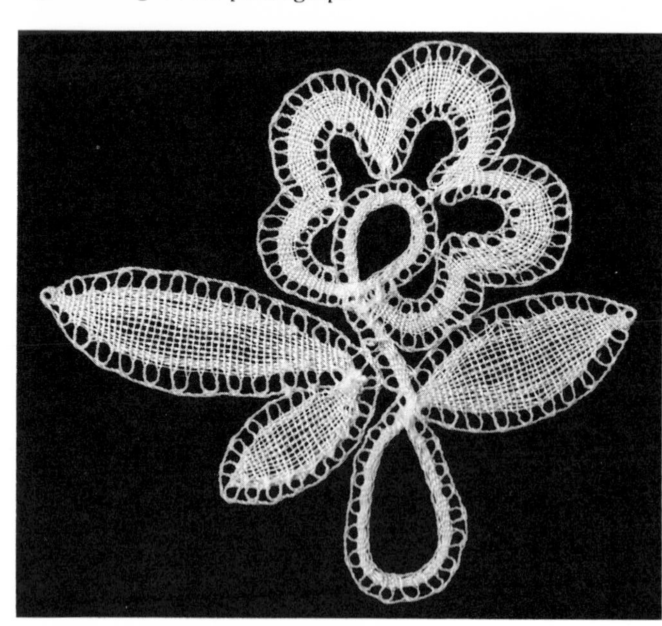

Fig. 46-b wrong side photograph

Fig. 46-e pricking

This beginners' pattern is adapted from a traditional Honiton lace design and is ideal to fit into a brooch.

Dieses Muster für Anfänger wurde einem traditionellen Honitonentwurf nachempfunden und eignet sich hervorragend für eine Brosche.

Dit patroon voor beginners is een variatie op een oud Honiton patroon en past goed in een broche.

Ce patron destiné particulièrement aux débutantes, est une adaptation d'un dessin traditionnel de dentelle Honiton et peut se porter en broche.

47
Flower Motif (2)

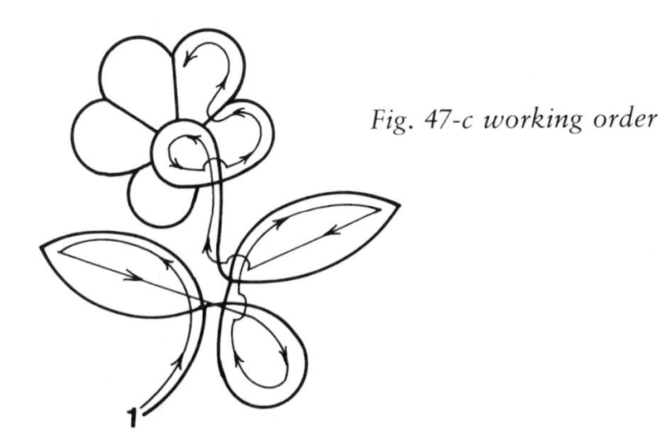

Fig. 47-c working order

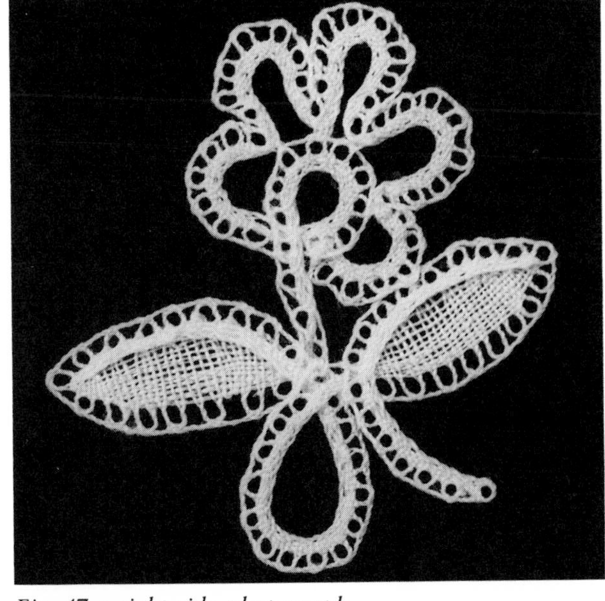

Fig. 47-a right side photograph

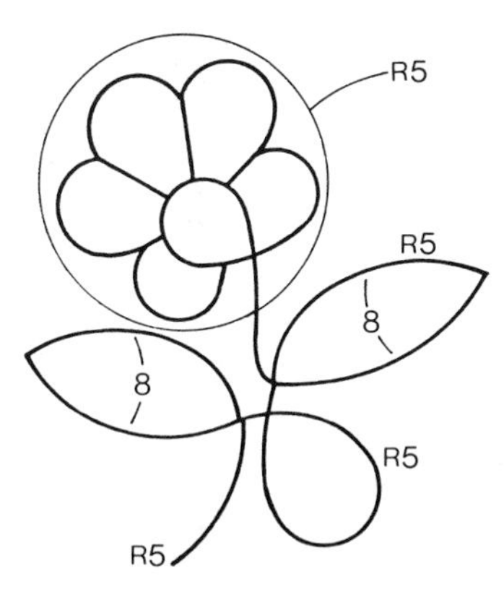

Fig. 47-d number of pairs

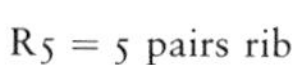

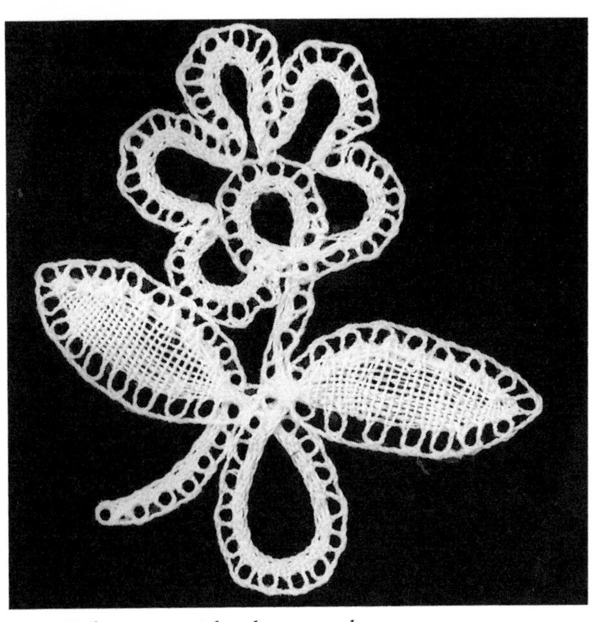

Fig. 47-b wrong side photograph

This beginners' pattern is adapted from a traditional Honiton lace design and is ideal to fit into a brooch. Start the motif at the bottom, and work up to the leaves and flowers.

Fig. 47-e pricking

Dieses Muster für Anfänger wurde einem traditionellen Honitonentwurf nachempfunden und eignet sich hervorragend für eine Brosche. Man beginnt das Motiv unten und arbeitet aufwärts zu den Blüten und Blättern.

Dit patroon voor beginners is een variatie op een oud Honiton patroon en past goed in een broche. Begin het motief aan de onderkant en werk omhoog naar de bladeren en de bloem.

Ce patron pour débutantes est adapté d'un dessin traditionnel de dentelle Honiton et est idéal pour une broche. Commencez le motif en bas et exécutez ensuite les feuilles et les fleurs.

48
Rose (3)

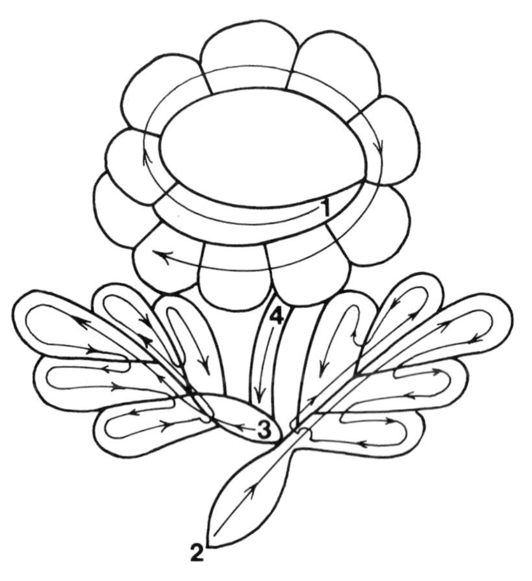

Fig. 48-c working order

Fig. 48-a right side photograph

This is adapted from a traditional Honiton lace design, with a flat flower and raised leaves. Work the flower petals first with whole and half stitch. Work the rib, forming the centre vein first and then make the highest central leaf segment. Roll the threads and work the rib, then form the second leaf segment with whole stitch, until each section of the leaf is finished.

Dieses Muster mit flacher Blüte und erhabenen Blättern wurde einem traditionellen Honitonentwurf nachempfunden. Zuerst die Blütenblütter in Ganz- und Halbschlag arbeiten. Die Rippe ausführen, indem die Ader zuerst und danach das oberste Blattsegment gearbeitet wird. Die Fäden werden gerollt und die Rippe gearbeitet, dann das zweite Blattsegment in Ganzschlag arbeiten, bis alle Teile des Blattes fertiggestellt sind.

Dit is een variatie op een oud Honiton patroon, met een vlakke bloem en raised bladeren. Klos eerst de bloemblaadjes in linnen- en netslag. Klos de rib die de middennerf vormt eerst en maak dan het hoogste midden bladdeel. Rol de draden en werk de rib. Klos daarna het tweede bladdeel in linnenslag tot alle delen van het blad klaar zijn.

Voici une adaptation d'un dessin traditionnel de dentelle Honiton, avec une fleur à plat et des feuilles en relief. Travaillez d'abord les pétales en mat et en grille. Faites le lacet pour former la nervure en premier, puis exécutez la partie supérieure de la feuille centrale. Roulez les fils, puis faites le lacet et exécutez la partie en mat de la deuxième feuille; continuez ainsi jusqu'à la fin de chaque feuille.

Fig. 48-b wrong side photograph

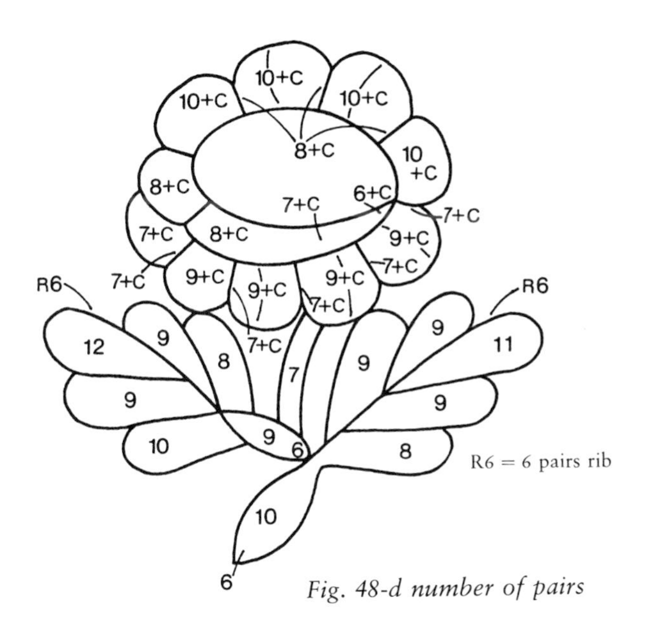

Fig. 48-d number of pairs

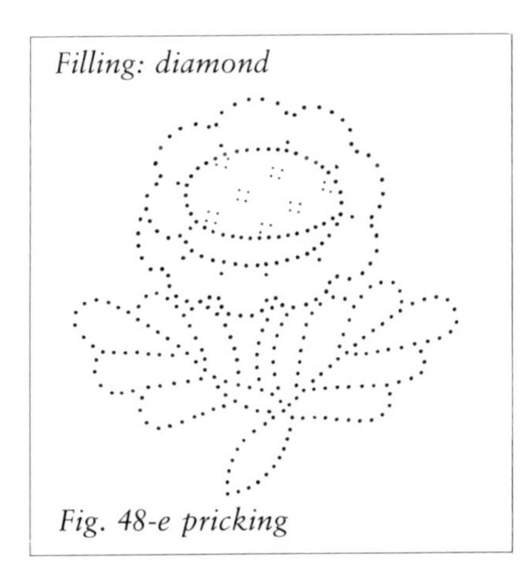

Fig. 48-e pricking

Appendix 1: Fillings

The great variety of fillings is one of the characteristic features of Honiton lace. Many Honiton lacemakers prick their fillings by eye, without the aid of graph paper, sometimes using a ruler as a guide. This makes it possible to fit a filling into a given shape in such a way that the groups of holes are complete at the edges and matching at both sides. An example of such filling worked into a curved space and a round space can be seen in Pattern 36. However, to give the student some idea of the size the fillings should be, they are shown here on a grid and should be pricked on *one millimetre graph paper*.

The pairs for the fillings are sewn into the completed braid above and as near as possible to the groups of holes where they will be required, and often more than one pair will need to be sewn into the same hole. When sewing out pairs which have worked a row of filling, they are either tied three times and laid back to be cut off later, or they are brought in again to be used in a subsequent row if they are needed to fill in a widening space.

When a filling has been completed, and all the pairs have been sewn out and tied, the bobbins must be cut off and the ends of the thread trimmed before the pins are removed from the filling. Take out all the pins from the filling.

It often happens that the groups of holes of which many fillings consist are not complete at the edges of the space to be filled. When this happens, work the incomplete group as nearly as possible to the instructions given for these fillings – it is often possible to make a sewing into the edge of the braid to replace any missing holes.

1. Füllungen kann man mit Hilfe eines Lineals oder nach Augenmass vorstechen. So ist es möglich, komplette Gruppen von Löchern in unregelmäßige Formen einzupassen (z.B. Muster 36).
2. Werden Gitter benutzt, sticht man auf 1 mm-Papier.
3. Bei den Füllungen werden je nach Bedarf ein oder mehrere Paare (P) in die geklöppelten Bänder so dicht wie möglich an den Lochgruppierungen angehäkelt.
4. Paare für eine Anzahl von Füllungen werden in das Bändchen eingehäkelt, 3 x geknotet, später abgeschnitten oder für die nächste Füllung benutzt.
5. Ist die Füllung beendet, abhäkeln und die übrigen Fäden 3 x knoten. Fäden kurz abschneiden, Nadeln entfernen.
6. Wird ein vorgestochenes Gitter benutzt, kann es vorkommen, daß Lochgruppierungen unvollständig sind. Soweit wie moeglich arbeiten, in die Bändchen einhäkeln, um ein evtl. fehlendes Loch zu ersetzen.

1. Vullingen kunnen met behulp van een lineaal worden geprikt of 'op het oog', zodat complete groepen van gaatjes in onregelmatige vormen gepast kunnen worden (bv. zie patroon 39).
2. Prik, als U 'grids' gebruikt, op 1 mm ruitjespapier.
3. Hang voor vullingen het gewenste aantal paren (pr of prn) zo dicht mogelijk bij de gaatjesgroepjes in aan voltooide bandjes.
4. Paren die voor rijen vullingen gebruikt zijn, worden in een bandje aangehaakt, dan 3 maal geknoopt om later te worden afgeknipt, of opnieuw gebruikt voor de volgende rij van de vulling.
5. Haak, als een vulling klaar is, aan en knoop alle overblijvende paren 3 maal. Knip de draden netjes bij en verwijder daarna de spelden uit de vulling.
6. Bij gebruik van een geprikte 'grid', kan het voorkomen dat een groepje gaatjes niet compleet is. Klos dan zoveel mogelijk en haak aan in een bandje als U een gaatje moet vervangen.

1. Le piquage des fonds peut être fait à l'aide d'une règle ou à main levée; ceci permet de loger des groupes entiers de trous dans des formes irrégulières (*voir* par exemple l'ouvrage 36).
2. Si vous utilisez un gabarit, faites le piquage sur du papier millimétrique.
3. Pour les fonds, crochetez une ou plusieurs paires (prs), autant que nécessaire, dans les bandes terminées, aussi près que possible des groupes de trous.
4. Les prs utilisées pour les rangées de fond sont crochetées dans la bande, puis nouées 3 fois pour être coupées ensuite ou réutilisées pour la rangée suivante du fond.
5. Une fois le fond terminé, crochetez et nouez 3 fois toutes les prs restantes. Coupes les fils, puis enlevez les épingles du fond.
6. Si vous utilisez un gabarit perforé, certains groupes de trous peuvent être incomplets. Travaillez le plus loin possible en crochetant dans une bande si vous devez mettre en place un trou supplémentaire.

How to prick

Transfer the dots for the chosen filling onto tracing paper, lay this over the pricking, and prick through into the space to be filled. Another method is to prick a block of the filling onto a piece of acetate, or a used and washed X-ray plate; this is laid over the pricking and pricked through onto the pattern. These pricked 'templates' can be used again and again, providing that the pricking is done carefully, so as not to enlarge the holes in the template.

1. Das gewuenschte Pricking nachzeichnen, auf das Muster legen und auf die zu oder füllende Fläche stechen.
2. Die gewünschte Fläche des Pricking auf transparenten Film stechen. Als Schablone benutzen und vorsichtig auf das Muster stechen, damit man die Schablone mehrmals verwenden kann.

1. Neem de gekozen 'gridpricking' over, leg die op het patroon en prik hem door in de te vullen ruimte.
2. Prik een gedeelte van 'grid pricking' over op een vel stevig doorzichtig plastic. Gebruik dit als model en prik dan zorgvuldig (zodat het model vaker kan worden gebruikt) op het patroon.

1. Tracez le gabarit choisi, posez-le sur le dessin et perforez l'espace à remplir.
2. Perforez une surface du gabarit sur un film transparent. Utilisez-le comme modèle et perforez le carton soigneusement (afin de pouvoir le réutiliser).

grid pricking

Diamond

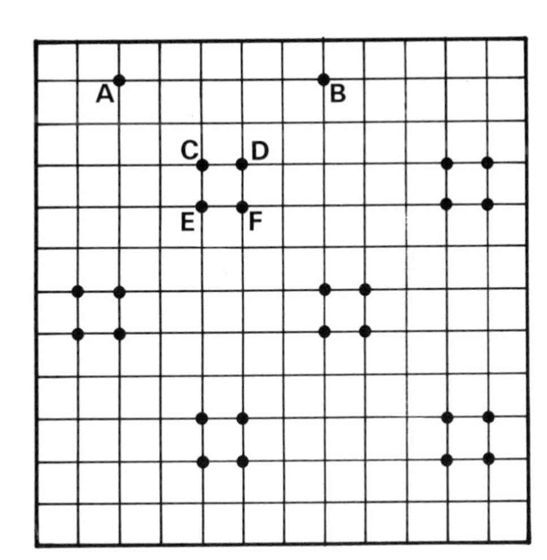

Diagram 1

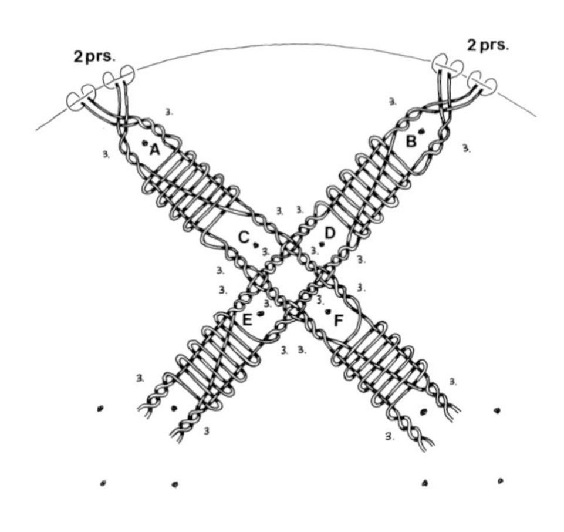

(Refer to diagram 1, 1a, and Pattern 2, Wild Rose.) Sew in two pairs above A and two pairs above B. These may be sewn into adjacent pin holes of the completed braid. With the two pairs above A, work a whole stitch and twist both pairs three times. Add pin A between the two pairs. Repeat for hole B.

With each set of two pairs make a narrow leadwork to reach as far as C and D. When both leadworks are complete, twist all four pairs three times and set pins C and D between each two pairs. With the two centre pairs work a whole stitch (No Pin). Twist both these pairs three times. With the two left-hand pairs work a whole stitch, twist both pairs three times and set pin E between them. With the two right-hand pairs work a whole stitch, twist both pairs three times and set pin F between them. With the two centre pairs work a whole stitch and twist both pairs three times (No Pin). Each two pairs now work another leadwork to the group of holes diagonally below, where they are joined by two pairs coming in from the opposite direction.

1. 2 P. über A einhäkeln, Ganzschlag, beide P.3 x drehen, Nadel A dazwischen stecken.
2. Wiederholen für Nadel B.
3. Schmalen Formenschlag von A nach C, beide P. 3 x drehen, Nadel C dazwischen stecken.
4. Wiederhole (3) von B nach D
5. Mit den 2 mittleren P. Ganzschlag, beide 3 x drehen (keine Nadel)
6. Mit den beiden linken P. Ganzschlag, beide 3 x drehen, Nadel E dazwischen stecken
7. Mit den beiden rechten P. Ganzschlag, beide 3 x drehen, Nadel F dazwischen stecken
8. Wiederhole (5)
9. Schmaler Formenschlag von Nadel E und F in diagonaler Richtung.

1. Hang 2 pr in boven A, klos linnenslag (lsl), draai (dr) beide paren (prn) 3 keer, speld (sp) A ertussen.
2. Herhaal voor sp B.
3. Klos smalle moes ('leadwork') van A naar C, dr beide prn 3 keer, sp C ertussen.
4. Herhaal (3) van B naar D
5. Lsl met 2 midden prn, dr beide 3 keer (geen sp)
6. Linker 2 pr lsl, dr beide 3 keer, sp E ertussen
7. Rechter 2 pr lsl, dr beide 3 keer, sp F ertussen
8. Herhaal (5)
9. Klos smalle moes van sp E en F in diagonale richting.

1. Crochetez 2 paires (prs) au-dessus de A, faites une passée (mat) et tordez (t) 3 fois, piquez l'épingle dans A entre les 2 prs.
2. Répétez pour l'épingle B.
3. Faites un point d'esprit étroit de A à C, t les prs 3 fois, piquez l'épingle à C au milieu.
4. Répétez (3) entre B et D.
5. Mat avec les 2 prs centrales, t 3 fois les 2 prs (sans épingle)
6. Mat avec les 2 prs de gauche, t 3 fois, épingle E au milieu.
7. Mat sur les 2 prs de droite, t 3 fois, épingle F au milieu.
8. Répétez (5).
9. Faites un point d'esprit de E à F en diagonale.

No Pin

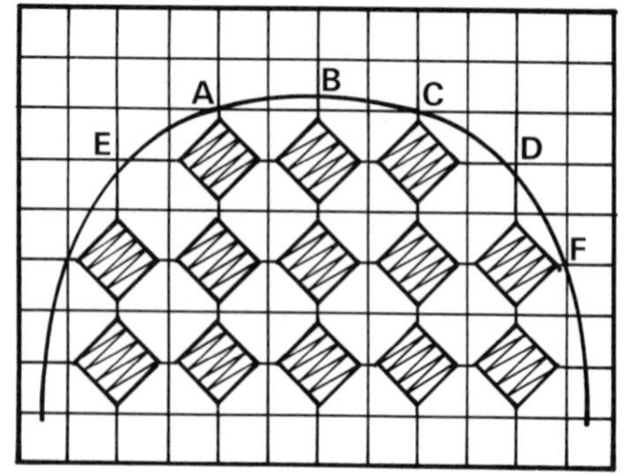

Diagram 2

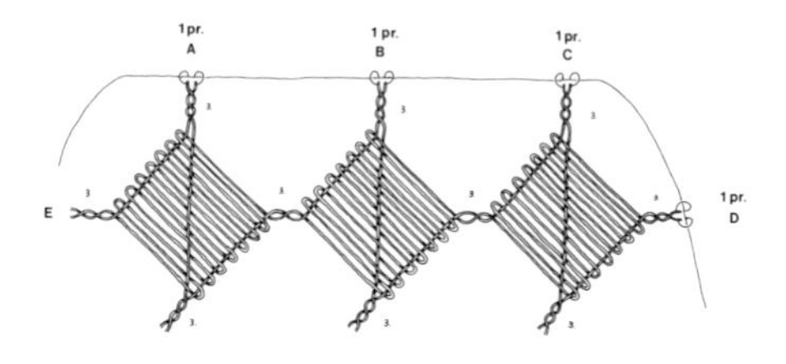

(Refer to diagram 2, 2a, and Pattern 10, Dahlia.) No pricking is needed for this filling, as the name suggests. It consists of rows of small square leadworks.

Sew one pair into each hole (or if the holes are very close together, into every other hole) in a straight line across the top of the space to be filled, and one pair on the right-hand side (at D on the diagram, usually the next hole slightly below C). Twist all pairs three times. Use the left-hand bobbin from D as the weaver for the first leadwork and take it under, over and back under the next two bobbins (from C).* It is now in the right position to weave the leadwork. When this has been completed, the weaver is again the second bobbin from the left. Twist both pairs three times. This brings the weaver to lie as the outer bobbin on the left. Leave the right-hand pair and work the next leadwork with the left-hand pair and the pair from B, *again using the same weaver*, which is first passed under, over and back under the two bobbins from B. Repeat from * across the row and after working the last leadwork, sew out the left-hand pair (containing the runner) at E. If the shape being filled curves, as in the diagram, sew in a new pair at D and one at F. Twist both pairs three times and work another row of leadworks. The pair sewn out at E may also be brought in again and twisted three times to make an extra leadwork if needed.

1. Über den für Formenschlag vorgesehenen Punkten (A, B & C) je 1 P. einhäkeln
2. 1 P. bei D einhäkeln
3. Jedes P. 3 x drehen
4. Linker Klöppel von D wird Läufer vom ersten Formenschlag, für den 1 P. von C dient.
5. Formenschlag mit 2. Klöppel links als Läufer beenden
6. Beide P. 3 x drehen
7. Mit dem gleichen Läufer wie zuvor wird ein neuer Formenschlag mit dem linken P. des vorherigen Formenschlags und einem P. von B ausgeführt.
8. Wiederhole (7) für 3. Formenschlag mit P. von A
9. Paar einschliesslich Läufer von E abhäkeln. Dieses Paar kann bei Bedarf für einen anderen Formenschlag der Füllung benutzt werden
10. Ein neues P. bei D und F für die nächste Reihe der Füllung einhäkeln.

1. Hang 1 pr in boven iedere plaats waar een moes ('leadwork') gemaakt moet worden (A, B & C)
2. Hang 1 pr in bij D
3. Draai (dr) elk pr 3 keer
4. Gebruik linker klos van D als loper voor de eerste moes met pr v an C
5. Eindig moes met loper als 2e klos van links
6. Dr beide prn 3 keer
7. Gebruik dezelfde loper, maak nieuwe moes met linker pr van eerste moes en pr van B
8. Herhaal (7) voor 3e moes met pr van A
9. Haak pr met loper aan bij E. Dit pr kan waar nodig opnieuw worden gebruikt voor een andere moes in de vulling.
10. Bij D en F wordt 1 nieuw pr ingehangen voor de volgende rij van de vulling

1. Crochetez 1 paire (pr) au-dessus de chaque départ de point d'esprit (A, B et C).
2. Crochetez une pr en D.
3. Tordez (t) chaque pr 3 fois.
4. Utilisez le fuseau de gauche de D comme meneur pour le premier point d'esprit, avec 1 pr de C.
5. Terminez le point d'esprit avec le meneur en 2è position en partant de la gauche.
6. T les 2 prs 3 fois.
7. Avec le même meneur que précédemment, faites un nouveau point d'esprit, avec la pr venant du premier point d'esprit et 1 pr de B.
8. Répétez (7) pour faire le 3è point d'esprit avec 1 pr venant de A.
9. Crochetez en prenant le meneur en E. Cette pr peut être réutilisée pour un autre point d'esprit dans le fond, si nécessaire.
10. Une nouvelle pr est crochetée à D et à F pour la rangée suivante du fond.

Four Pin

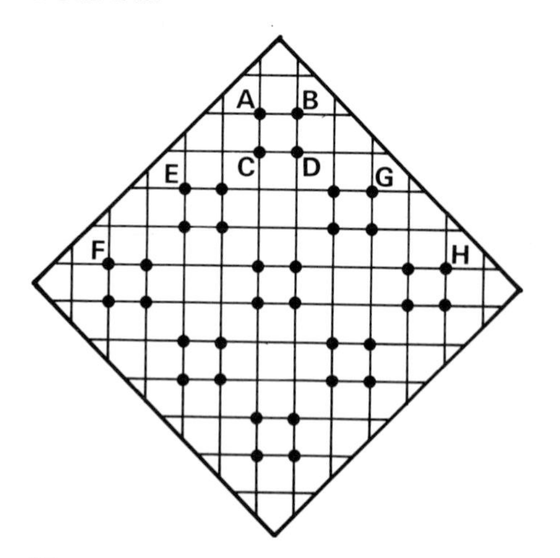

Diagram 3

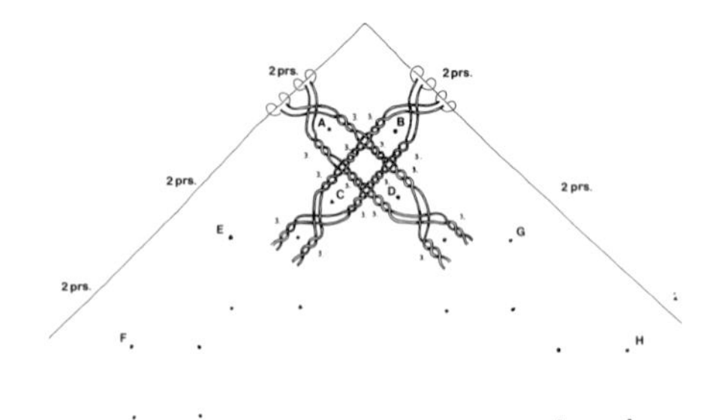

(Refer to diagram 3, 3a, and Pattern 31, Kotobuki.) Sew in two pairs above each hole A, B, E, F, G and H. The four pairs from the above A and B work the first group of four holes as follows. * With the two left-hand pairs work a whole stitch, twist both pairs three times, and set pin A between them. With the two right-hand pairs work a whole stitch, twist both pairs three times and set pin B between them. With the two middle pairs work a whole stitch and twist both pairs three times (No Pin). With the two left-hand pairs work a whole stitch, twist both pairs three times and set pin C between them. With the two right-hand pairs work a whole stitch, twist both pairs three times and set pin D between them. With the two middle pairs work a whole stitch and twist both pairs three times (No Pin). * The two left hand pairs and the two pairs from above E now work the next group of four holes * to *, and at the end of the two left-hand pairs from this group meet the two pairs from above F to work the next group of four holes. Continue down this diagonal line until the row is complete; at the end, sew out the left-hand two pairs. Return to the top and work the next group of holes with the two pairs from above G and the two pairs from D. Continue down this diagonal line, using the two left-hand pairs of each group with the pairs left from the previous line of four pins.

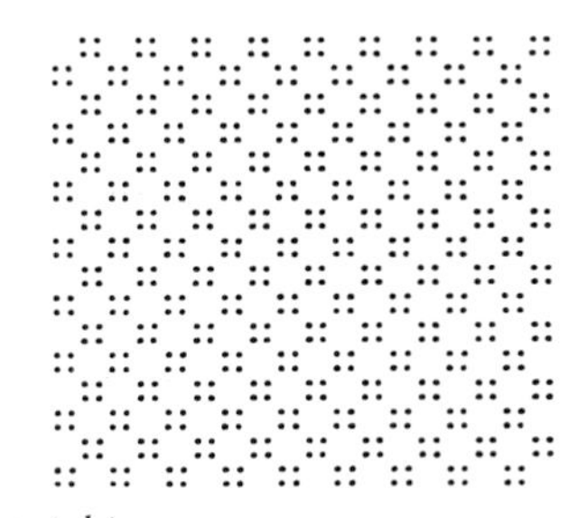

grid pricking

1. Je 2 P. über den Nadelpunkten A, B, E, F, G und H einhäkeln
2. Mit 2 P. über A Ganzschlag, beide 3 x drehen. Nadel zwischen beide P. bei A
3. Wiederhole (2) mit 2 P. über B für Nadel B
4. Mittlere 2 P. Ganzschlag, beide P. 3 x drehen (keine Nadel)
5. 2 linke P. Ganzschlag, beide 3 x drehen, Nadel C dazwischen stecken
6. 2 rechte P Ganzschlag, beide 3 x drehen, Nadel D dazwischen stecken
7. Wiederhole (4)
8. 2 P. von C und 2 P. über E arbeiten, die folgende Gruppe von 4 Löchern links.

1. Hang 2 pr in boven A, B, E, F, G & H
2. Klos linnenslag (lsl) met 2 pr boven A, draai (dr) beide 3 keer, sp tussen beide prn bij A
3. Herhaal (2) met 2 pr boven B, voor sp B
4. Met 2 midden prn lsl, dr beide 3 keer (geen sp)
5. Met 2 linker prn lsl, dr beide 3 keer, sp C ertussen
6. Met 2 rechter prn lsl, dr beide 3 keer, sp D ertussen
7. Herhaal (4)
8. De 2 pr van C en 2 pr boven E maken de volgende groep van 4 gaatjes aan de linkerkant

1. Crochetez 2 paires (prs) au-dessus de chaque trou A, B, E, F, G et H.
2. Avec les 2 prs au-dessus de A, travaillez en passée (mat), tordez (t) 3 fois ces 2 prs. Piquez l'épingle entre les 2 prs de A.
3. Répétez (2) avec les 2 prs au-dessus de B, piquez l'épingle B.
4. Travaillez les 2 prs du centre en mat, t 3 fois (sans épingle).
5. Mat sur les 2 prs de gauche, t 3 fois, épingle C au milieu.
6. Mat sur les 2 prs de droite, t 3 fois, piquez l'épingle D au milieu.
7. Répétez (4).
8. Les 2 prs de C et les 2 prs au-dessus de E font le groupe de 4 trous suivant la gauche.

Whole Stitch Block Variation

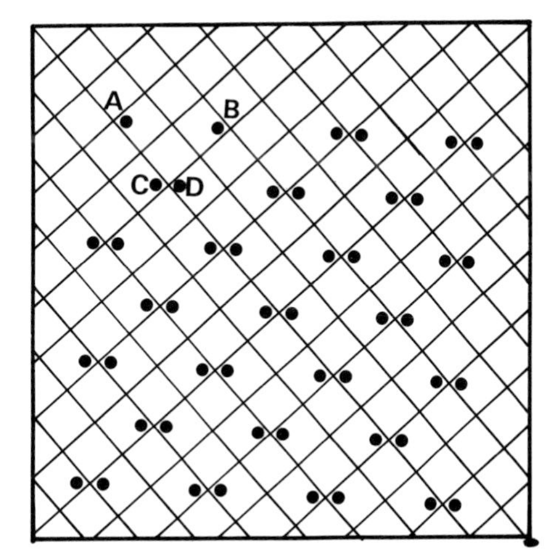

Diagram 4

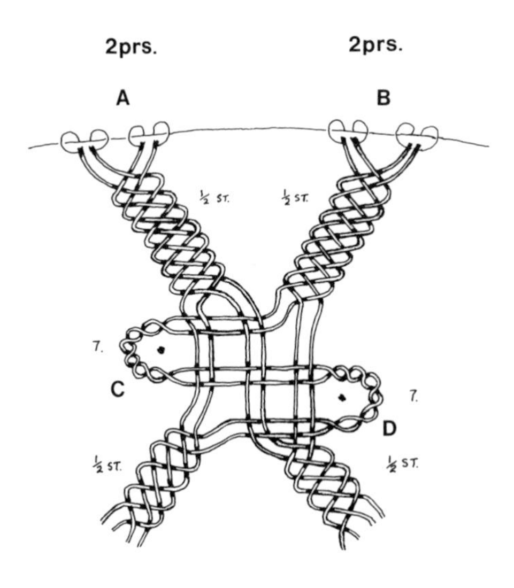

(Refer to diagram 4, 4a, and Pattern 23, Magnolia.) Four pairs are required to work each group of two holes. Sew in two pairs at A and B. Work a half stitch plait with each two pairs to reach to just above C and D. * Use the second pair from the right of these four pairs as runners and take them in whole stitch through two pairs to the left. Twist the runners seven times and set pin C under them. Work the runners through three pairs to the right, twist them seven times and set pin D under them. Work the runners through two pairs to the left and leave. With each two pairs work a half stitch plait to the group diagonally below (four half stitches should be enough), where they repeat the procedure from *, together with two pairs coming from the other side.

grid pricking

1. Je 2 P. bei A und B einhäkeln
2. Halbschlag-Flechte A nach C und B nach D
3. 2 P. von rechts Ganzschlag durch 2 P. nach links
4. 7x drehen um Nadel C

5. Ganzschlag 3 P. nach rechts
6. 7x drehen um Nadel D
7. Ganzschlag 2 P. nach links
8. Halbschlag-Flechte diagonal zur nächsten Gruppe von Nadelpunkten

1. Hang telkens 2 pr in bij A & B
2. Klos vlechten (vl) van A naar C en van B naar D
3. Gebruik 2e pr van rechts, klos linnenslag (lsl) door 2 pr naar links
4. Draai (dr) 7 keer rond sp C
5. Lsl 3 pr naar rechts
6. Dr 7 keer rond sp D
7. Lsl 2 pr naar links
8. Nsl vl diagonaal naar volgende groep gaatjes

1. Crochetez 2 paires (prs) en A et en B.
2. Faites des cordes en grille (demi-point : dp) de A à C et de B à D.
3. Avec la 2è pr venant de droite, traversez en mat les 2 prs de gauche.
4. Tordez (t) 7 fois autour de l'épingle C.
5. Traversez 3 prs en mat vers la droite.
6. T 7 fois autour de l'épingle D.
7. Traversez en mat 2 prs vers la gauche.
8. Dp en diagonale vers les groupes suivants de trous.

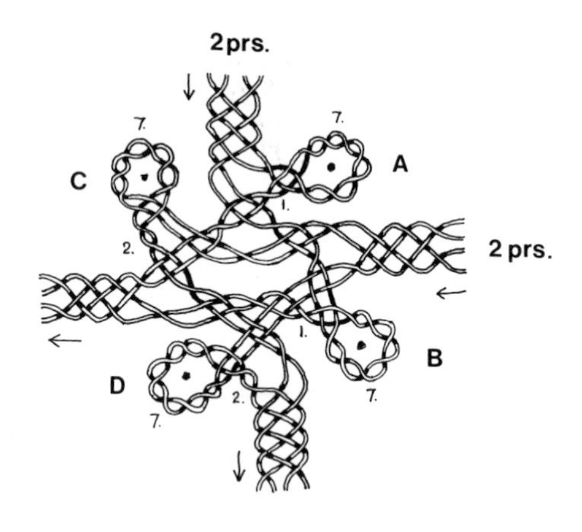

Blossom

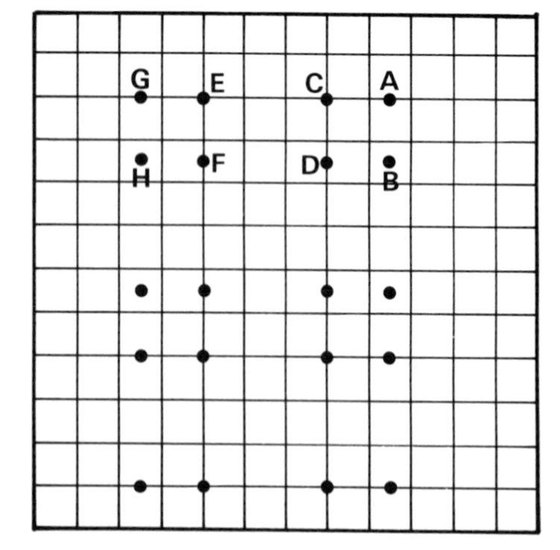

Diagram 5

(Refer to diagram 5, 5a and Pattern 13, Poinsettia.) Sew two pairs into the edge of the braid half-way between and above C and A. Sew in two pairs half-way between and to the right of A and B. Work a half stitch plait with each set of two pairs just to reach as far as the group of four holes. The four holes of each group are used to make purls as follows.

Use the right-hand pair of the left-hand plait to make a purl in hole A, * twisting this pair seven times using the right-hand bobbin to make the loop, and placing the pin under the right-hand thread, pointing to the left, twisting the point over the thread towards you and down into the hole. Lift the other thread round the pin from right to left. Twist the pair once. * Make a whole stitch with the two left-hand pairs and twist both pairs once. With the two centre pairs make a whole stitch and twist both pairs once. With the two right-hand pairs make a whole stitch and use the right of these two pairs to make a purl in hole B * to *.

Make a whole stitch with the two right-hand pairs. With the two left-hand pairs make a whole stitch and use the left of these pairs to make a purl in hole C, ** twisting this pair seven times. Place the pin under the left-hand bobbin, pointing towards the right. Twist the point over the thread towards you and down into the hole. Lift the other thread round the pin from left to right. Twist the pair twice (left over right). ** Work a whole stitch with the two left-hand pairs. Twist the two centre pairs once and make a whole stitch with them. Work a whole stitch with the two right-hand pairs. Use the left of these two pairs to make a purl at D, repeating ** to **. This completes one group of holes.

The two pairs between C and D now make a half stitch plait to reach as far as E, where they work the next group of four holes together with the two pairs sewn in above G and E. Put aside the two pairs between D and B. Continue along this row from right to left and after the last group of holes work a half stitch plait to reach the edge, where these two pairs are sewn out. With the two pairs put aside and left hanging below each group of holes, work half stitch plaits to reach the group of holes below. Sew two more pairs in on the right-hand side, and work a half stitch plait to the next set of holes.

grid pricking

1. 2 P. über und zwischen A und C einhäkeln, Halbschlag-Flechte bis zu den Nadelpunkten
2. 2 P. rechts und zwischen den Nadeln A und B einhäkeln
3. Mit R Paar der linken Flechte Picot bei Nadelpunkt A, zuvor 7x drehen, nach jeder Nadel 1 x drehen
4. Ganzschlag, 2 linke P. drehen
5. Ganzschlag, mit 2 mittleren P. drehen
6. Ganzschlag 2 rechte P., Picot bei Nadelpunkt B, zuvor 7x drehen, nach der Nadel 1 x drehen
7. Ganzschlag 2 rechte P.
8. Ganzschlag 2 li P., Picot bei Nadelpunkt C, zuvor 7 x drehen, nach der Nadel 2 x drehen
9. Ganzschlag 2 linke P.

10. Drehen und Ganzschlag mit 2 mittleren P.
11. Ganzschlag 2 rechte P.
12. Mit linkem P. Picot in Nadelpunkt D, zuvor 7 x drehen, nach der Nadel 2 x drehen
13. Mit 2 P. zwischen C und D Halbschlag-Flechte zu E
14. 2 P. über und zwischen G und E fuer die nähcste Gruppe von vier Nadelpunkten einhäkeln

1. Hang 2 pr in boven en tussen A & C, maak vlecht (vl) tot de speldegaatjes
2. Hang 2 pr in aan de rechterkant en tussen sp A & B
3. Maak met rechter pr van linker vl een picot bij A, dr 7 keer vóór en 1 keer ná iedere sp
4. Linnenslag (lsl) 2 keer dr met twee linker prn
5. Lsl dr met 2 midden prn
6. Lsl met 2 rechter prn, picot in C, 7 keer dr vóór, 2 keer ná sp
7. Lsl met 2 rechter prn
8. Lsl met 2 linker prn, picot in C, 7 keer dr vóór, 2 keer ná sp
9. Lsl met twee linker prn
10. Dr 2 midden prn en klos er lsl mee
11. Lsl 2 rechter prn
12. Maak met linker van deze 2 prn picot in D, 7 keer dr vóór, 2 keer ná sp
13. Met 2 pr tussen C & D vl naar E
14. Hang 2 pr in boven en tussen G & E om de volgende groep gaatjes af te maken

1. Crochetez 2 paires (prs) au-dessus et entre A et C et travaillez en grille jusqu'aux trous d'épingles
2. Crochetez 2 prs à droite et entre les épingles A et B
3. Avec la pr de droite de la bande gauche faites une épingle au trou A, 7 torsions (t) avant et 1 t après chaque épingle
4. Traversez en mat les 2 prs de gauche
5. Mat sur les 2 prs centrales
6. Travaillez en mat les 2 prs de gauche, faites un pointon tourné au trou B, 7 t avant et 1 t après l'épingle
7. Travaillez en mat les 2 prs de droite
8. Mat sur les 2 prs de gauche, faites un pointon tourné au trou C, 7 t avant et 2 t après l'épingle
9. Travaillez en mat les 2 prs de gauche
10. T les 2 prs du centre et travaillez-les en mat
11. Travaillez en mat les 2 prs à droite
12. Avec la pr gauche de ces 2 prs faites un pointon tourné au trou D, 7 t avant et 2 t après l'épingle
13. Avec les 2 prs entre C et D faites une corde en grille jusqu'à E
14. Crochetez 2 prs au-dessus et entre G et E pour compléter le groupe suivant de 4 trous

Italian

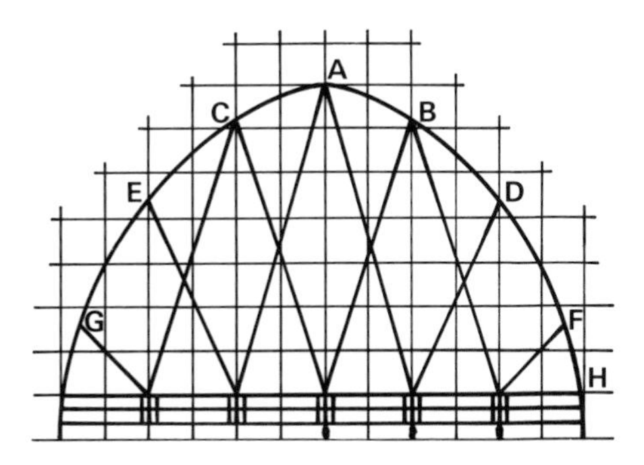

Diagram 6

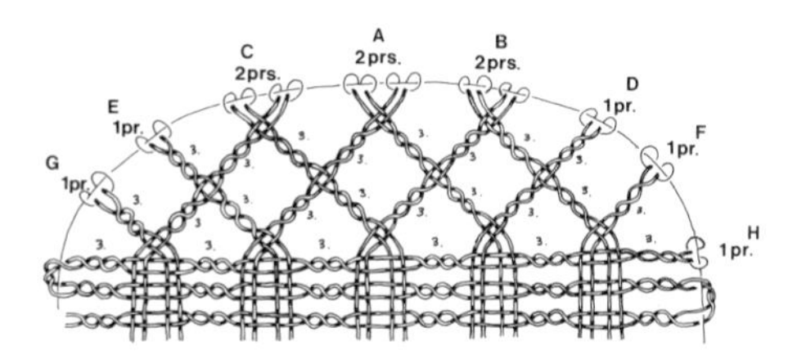

(Refer to diagram 6, 6a, and Pattern 25, Gloxinia.) This is worked without a pricking. Sew in pairs as indicated in the diagram. The pairs across the top are sewn in at every hole, or if the holes are very close together at every other hole. Make a whole stitch and three twists with each two pairs from A, B and C. With the right-hand pair from A and the left-hand pair from B work a whole stitch and three twists. With the left-hand pair from A and the right-hand pair from C work a whole stitch and three twists. Twist the pair from D three times and use it with the right-hand pair from B to work a whole stitch and three twists. Twist the pair from E three times and use it with the left-hand pair from C to work a whole stitch and three twists. Twist the pair from F three times and use it with the next pair on the left to work a whole stitch. Do not twist. Work a whole stitch with the next two pairs on the left; leave these, work another whole stitch with the next two pairs on the left, and so on across the row. The odd pair at the end is joined by the pair from G which has first been twisted three times.

There are now complete sets of four bobbins across the row and complete diamonds have been formed above these. The pair sewn in at H now becomes the runner pair for the horizontal rows dividing the diamonds. Twist this pair three times, * work it in whole stitch through the next set of two pairs, twist the runners three times and repeat from * across the row, sewing the runner pair into the braid at the other side, after pulling it up well. Ensure the line is horizontal and the pairs through which the runners pass are not twisted.

After sewing, tie the runners once, twist them three times and work a return row as above, again sewing the runners in at the right-hand side into hole H. Occasionally, if the first line is not quite straight, the second sewing may be made into the next hole below H. Again, twist the runners three times and work another row as the first, sewing them out at the end and into the same hole as the first sewing on that side. This completes one repeat of the pattern. The runners may be needed for the twisted diamond work, otherwise they are tied three times and laid back to be cut off later.

The next set of diamonds is worked as above and is started by working a whole stitch and three twists with each set of four bobbins hanging below the last horizontal bar. The diamond work at the sides will vary according to the shape of the space; the odd pairs at the sides will either be sewn in at the sides, twisted three times, and brought back again to work with any odd pairs, or an extra pair may need to be sewn in, to use with the odd pair at the sides to form extra diamonds in a widening space. There must be complete sets of four bobbins ready before the horizontal line is worked.

1. 2 P. ueber A, B und C einhäkeln
2. 1 P. bei D, E, F, G und H einhäkeln
3. Bei A Ganzschlag, jedes P. 3 x drehen
4. Wiederhole (3) für B und C
5. Mit P. von D und rechtem P. von B Ganzschlag, jedes P. 3 x drehen
6. Mit nächsten 2 P. nach links Ganzschlag, jedes P. 3 x drehen
7. Wiederhole (6) zweimal
8. Mit P. von G und erstem P. rechts Ganschlag
9. Ganzschlag mit nächsten 2 P. nach rechts
10. Wiederhole (9) bis zum Ende der Reihe
11. Mit P. von H, 3 x drehen, * Ganzschlag mit nächsten 2 P., Laufpaar 3 x drehen. Wiederholen * zum Ende der Reihe
12. Laufpaar in Bändchen einhäkeln, die Reihe horizontal halten
13. Wiederhole (11 und 12) um zur rechten Seite zurückzukehren
14. Wiederhole (11 und 12) um zur linken Seite zurückzukehren
15. Abschluß eines Musterrapports. Der folgende Satz 'Diamonds' wird wie oben gearbeitet, man beginnt mit Ganzschlag und 3 x drehen mit jedem Satz von 2 P. über eine Reihe

1. Hang 2 pr in boven A, B & C
2. Hang 1 pr in bij D, E, F, G & H
3. Klos bij A linnenslag (lsl), draai (dr) elk pr 3 keer
4. Herhaal (3) voor B & C
5. Klos met pr van D en rechter pr van B lsl, dr elk pr 3 keer
6. Met volgende 2 prn lsl naar links, dr elk pr 3 keer
7. Herhaal (6) nog 2 keer
8. Met pr van G en eerste pr naar rechts lsl
9. Klos lsl met volgende 2 prn naar rechts
10. Herhaal (9) langs hele rij
11. Met pr van H, 3 keer dr, *lsl door volgende 2 prn, dr lopers 3 keer. Herhaal van * langs hele rij
12. Hang looppaar in aan bandje, houd de kloslijn horizontaal
13. Herhaal (11 & 12) om naar de rechterkant terug te keren
14. Herhaal (11 & 12) om naar linkerkant terug te keren
15. Dit is één rapport van het patroon. De volgende serie diamonds wordt net zo geklost, en begonnen met lsl en 3 keer dr met ieder stel van 2 pr langs de rij

1. Crochetez 2 paires (prs) au-dessus de A, B et C
2. Crochetez 1 pr près D, E, F, G et H
3. En A travaillez en mat, tordez (t) chaque pr 3 fois
4. Répétez (3) à A et C
5. Avec 1 pr de D et la pr droite de B faites 1 passée (mat) et 3 torsions (t) sur chaque pr
6. Mat avec les 2 prs suivant de gauche, 3 t sur chaque pr
7. Répétez (6) encore 2 fois
8. Travaillez en mat une pr de G et la première pr à droite
9. Traversez en mat les 2 prs suivantes à droite
10. Répétez (9) sur tout le rang
11. Tordez (t) 3 fois 1 pr de H, * traversez en mat les 2 prs suivantes et t les meneurs 3 fois. Répétez à partir de * sur tout le rang
12. Crochetez les meneurs dans la bande, en respectant l'horizontale
13. Répétez (11) et (12) pour revenir vers la droite
14. Répétez (11) et (12) pour revenir vers la gauche
15. Un rapport du dessin est terminé. Le groupe suivant de diamants est exécuté comme le précédent en commençant avec 1 mat et 3 t sur chaque groupe de 2 prs sur tout le rang

Swing and a Pin

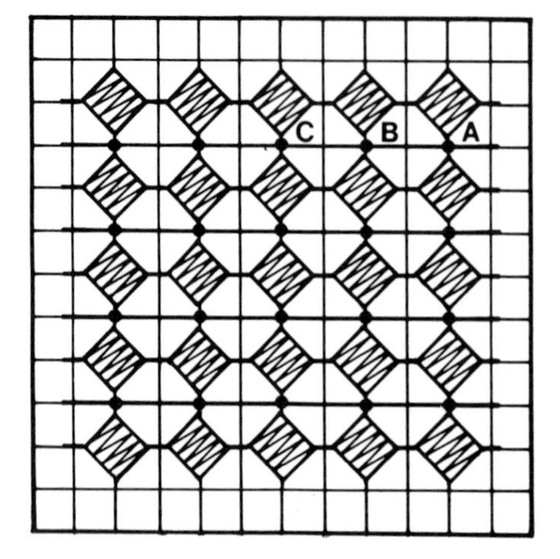

Diagram 7

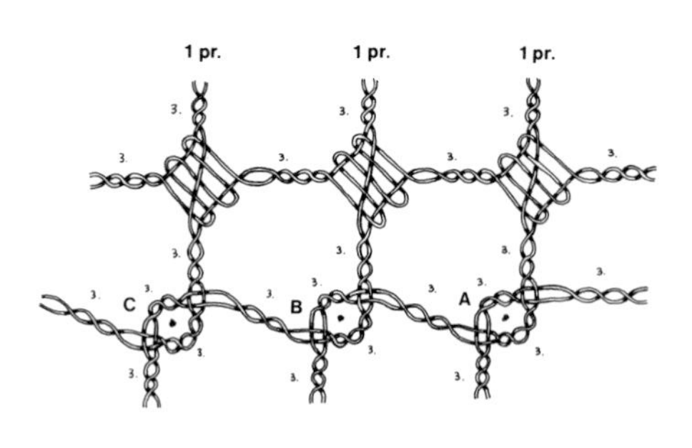

(Refer to diagram 7, 7a and Pattern 1, Daisy (1).) The holes needed for this filling are pricked in as the filling progresses. The first row consists of leadworks, which are sewn in and made in exactly the same way as described for No Pin (page 110).

The rows of leadworks alternate with rows in which a twisted pair is worked through the leadwork pairs and pinholes are made, as follows. Sew in one pair at the right-hand edge immediately below the level of the leadworks. Twist this pair three times and work a whole stitch with the pair from the nearest leadwork. Twist both pairs three times. * Prick a hole immediately below the leadwork and set a pin into it between these two pairs. Enclose the pin with a whole stitch and three twists. Leave the right-hand pair, and with the left-hand pair and the next pair on the left, work a whole stitch and three twists. Repeat from * across the row. Ensure that the pinholes are pricked in a straight line. Sew out the left-hand pairs at the left side. The next row is a leadwork row.

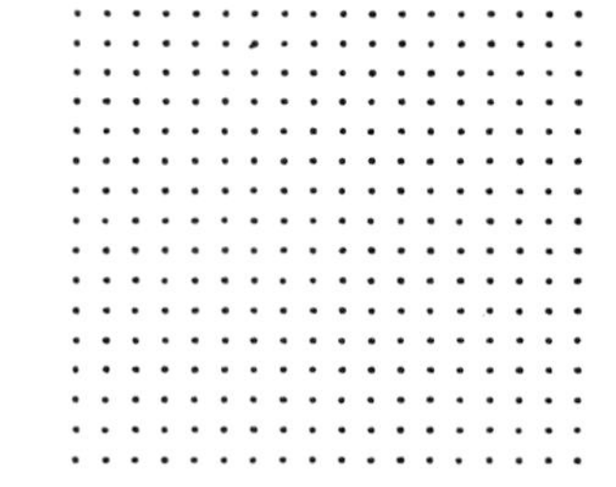

grid pricking

1. Die erste Reihe Formenschlag gemäss 'No Pin', Seite 110 arbeiten
2. Rechts 1 P. in Höhe der Nadelpunkte

unter jedem Formenschlag einhäkeln, 3 x drehen
3. Mit dem P. des ersten Formenschlags Ganzschlag, 3 x drehen, Nadel A, Ganzschlag, beide 3 x drehen
4. Mit dem linken der beiden P. und dem P. vom nächsten Formenschlag Ganzschlag, beide 3 x drehen, Nadel B, Ganzschlag, beide 3 x drehen
5. Wiederhole (4) für C und jede Nadel über die Reihe
6. Es folgt eine Reihe Formenschlag
7. Diese Fuellung kann nach Augenmaß geprickt werden, die Nadelpunkte müssen geradlinig verlaufen

1. Klos eerste rij 'leadwork' als in No Pin, p. 110
2. Hang rechts 1 pr in ter hoogte van de speldegaatjes onder iedere moes ('leadwork'). Draai (dr) 3 keer
3. Met pr van 1e moes linnenslag (lsl) dr beide 3 keer, sp A, lsl dr beide 3 keer
4. Met linker van deze 2 prn en pr van volgende moes, lsl dr beide 3 keer, sp B, lsl dr beide 3 keer
5. Herhaal (4) voor C en elke sp van de rij
6. De volgende rij is een moezenrij
7. Deze vulling kan tijdens het klossen 'op het oog' geprikt worden. Zorg dat de speldegaatjes op een rechte lijn staan

1. Travaillez le premier rang de points d'esprit comme pour le No Pin, page 110.
2. Crochetez 1 paire (pr) à droite à la même hauteur que les trous faits en-dessous de chaque point d'esprit. Tordez (t) 3 fois.
3. Avec 1 pr du premier point d'esprit travaillez 1 mat et t 3 fois; piquez l'épingle en A, mat, t 3 fois chacune des prs.
4. Avec la pr gauche de ces 2 prs et 1 pr du point d'esprit suivant, travaillez 1 mat, t 3 fois, épingle B, mat, t 3 fois.
5. Répétez (4) en C et à chaque épingle sur le rang.
6. Le rang suivant se fait en points d'esprit.
7. Ce fond peut être piqué à main levée au fur et à mesure que le travail avance; veillez à ce que les trous se trouvent sur une ligne droite

Pin and a Stitch

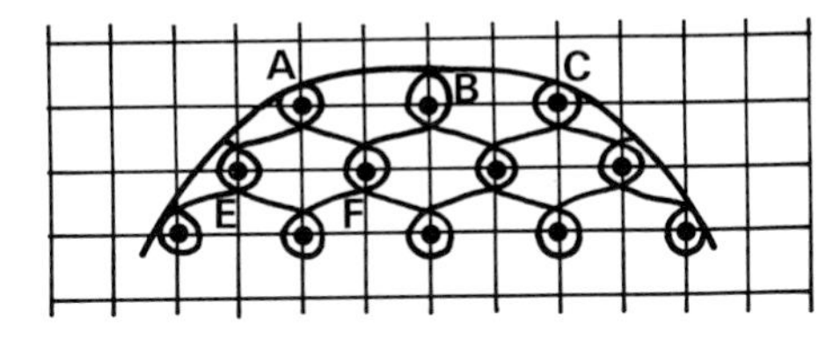

Diagram 8

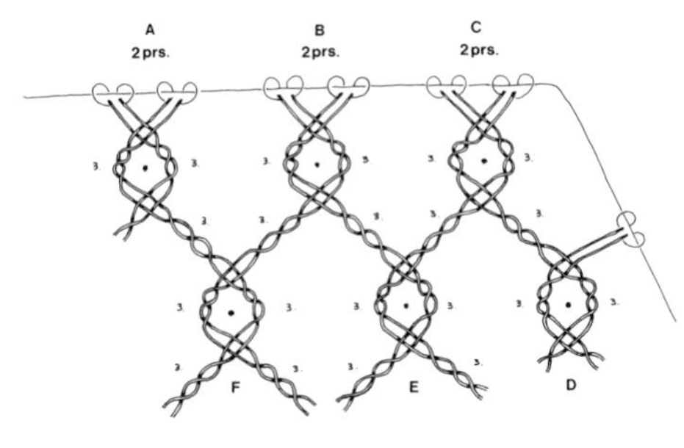

(Refer to diagram 8, 8a, and Pattern 29, Hana.) Sew in two pairs above each hole along the top line. With each two pairs, work a whole stitch and three twists and set pins between them, enclosing the pins with a whole stitch and three twists. The pairs now divide to work the holes diagonally below them, the right-hand pair from A and the left-hand pair from B working hole F, etc., as above. The left-hand pair from A meets a new pair sewn in at the edge and twisted three times, to work hole E.

grid pricking

1. 2 P. in jeden Nadelpunkt der oberen Reihe (A, B und C) einhäkeln
2. Ganzschlag, 3 x drehen, Nadel, Ganzschlag, mit je 2 P. 3 x drehen
3. Mit rechtem P von A und linkem P. von B Nadelpunkt F wie unter (2) beschrieben arbeiten

1. Hang 2 pr in boven elke speld langs bovenkant (A, B & C)
2. Klos linnenslag (lsl), draai (dr) 3 keer, sp, lsl, dr 3 keer met elke 2 pr
3. Gebruik rechter pr van A en linker pr van B, werk sp F als boven (2)

1. Crochetez 2 paires (prs) au-dessus de chaque trou en haut (A, B et C)
2. Travaillez en mat, tordez (t) 3 fois, piquez l'épingle, mat et t 3 fois chacune des prs
3. Avec la pr de droite de A et la pr de gauche de B, travaillez l'épingle comme précédemment

Pin and a Chain

Diagram 9

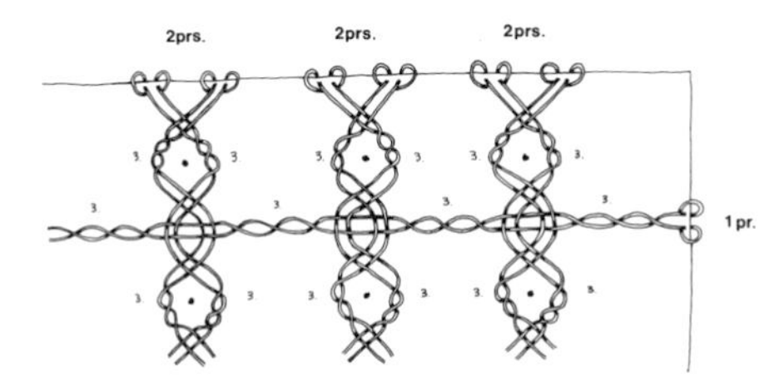

(Refer to diagram 9, 9a, and Pattern 36, Chrysanthemum.) This consists of a pinhole row and a row made with a twisted pair alternating. Sew in two pairs above each hole along the top. With each two pairs work a whole stitch, twist both pairs three times, set a pin between them and enclose the pin with a whole stitch. Do not twist. This completes the first horizontal row of holes.

Sew in a new pair at the right-hand side, between the row of holes just worked and the next row. Twist this pair three times, and use it as a runner pair to work in whole stitch through the two pairs which enclosed the nearest pin. * Twist the runners three times and work them through the next two pairs in whole stitch, repeat from * across the row and sew out the runners at the end after twisting them three times and pulling up well. The next row is a pinhole row and is worked like the first.

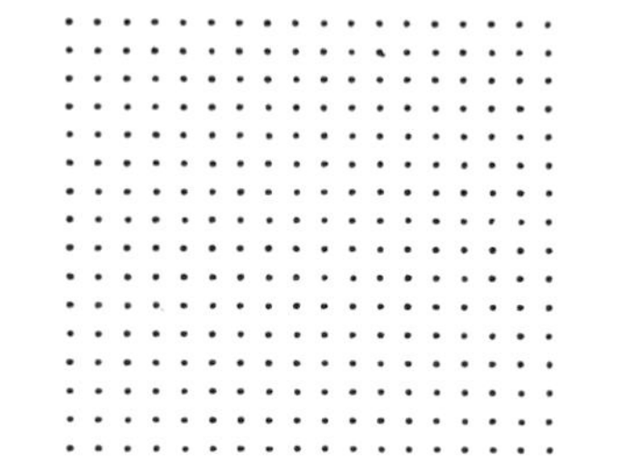

grid pricking

1. 2 P. über jeden Nadelpunkt der oberen Reihe einhäkeln
2. Ganzschlag, beide 3 x drehen, Nadel, Ganzschlag
3. Rechts 1 P. einhäkeln, 3 x drehen
4. Ganzschlag durch 2 P., 3 x drehen
5. Wiederhole (4) zum Ende der Reihe Läufer 3 x drehen, abhäkeln
6. Wiederhole (2) für die Nadelpunktreihe

1. Hang 2 pr in boven elk gat langs de bovenste rij
2. Klos linnenslag (lsl), draai (dr) beide 3 keer, sp, lsl
3. Hang rechts 1 pr in, dr 3 keer
4. Klos lsl door 2 pr, dr 3 keer
5. Herhaal (4) tot eind van rij, dr looppaar 3 keer, haak aan
6. Herhaal (2) voor speldenrij

1. Crochetez 2 paires (prs) au-dessus de chaque trou sur le rang en haut.
2. Faites une passée (mat), tordez (t) 3 fois, épingle, mat.
3. Crochetez 1 pr à droite, t 3 fois.
4. Traversez 2 prs en mat, t 3 fois.
5. Répétez (4) jusqu'à la fin du rang, t les meneurs 3 fois, sortez-les.
6. Répétez (2) pour la rangée des trous.

Swing and a Stitch

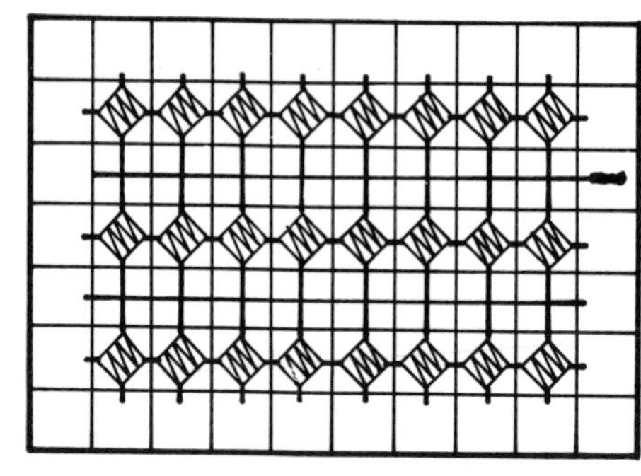

Diagram 10

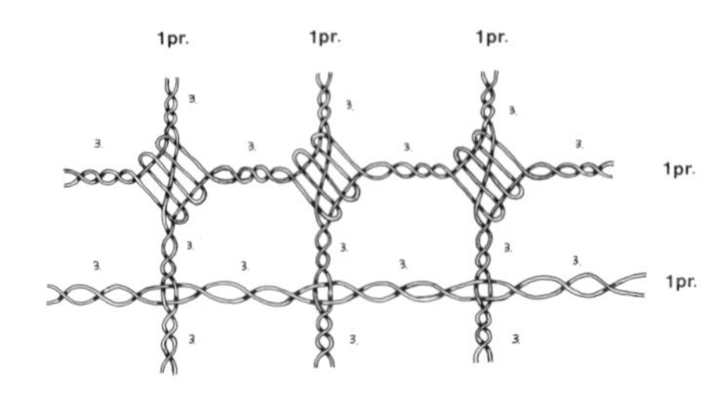

(Refer to diagram 10, 10a and Pattern 22, Prickly Poppy.) This filling needs no pricking and is similar to Swing and a Pin (page 114). It consists of rows of leadworks and rows made with a twisted pair alternating. Work the first row of leadworks as explained in No Pin (page 110). Sew in a new pair at the right-hand edge immediately below the level of the leadworks. Twist this pair three times and work a whole stitch with the nearest leadwork pair, * twist both pairs three times, leave the right-hand pair and, with the left-hand pair and the next leadwork pair, work a whole stitch. Repeat from * across the row and sew out the left-hand pair at the end of the row, after pulling it as much as possible into a straight line below the leadworks.

1. Erste Reihe Formenschlag gemäss 'No Pin' Seite 110 arbeiten
2. 1 P. rechts direkt unter Formenschlägen einhäkeln, 3 x drehen
3. Mit erstem P. von Formenschlag Ganzschlag, beide 3 x drehen
4. Über die Reihe Ganzschlag, beide P. 3 x drehen. In das Bändchen links abhäkeln
5. Neue Reihe beginnt mit Formenschlag

1. Klos eerste rij 'leadwork' als in No Pin, p. 110
2. Hang rechts een pr in, net onder de moezen en draai (dr) 3 keer
3. Met eerste pr van moes, linnenslag (lsl), dr beide prn 3 keer
4. Vervolg de rij in lsl, beide prn 3 keer dr. Haak aan in bandje links
5. Volgende rij weer 'leadwork'

1. Faites le premier rang des points d'esprit comme pour le No Pin, page 110
2. Crochetez 1 paire (pr) à droite, juste en-dessous des points d'esprit et tordez-la (t) 3 fois
3. Traversez en mat la première pr venant du point d'esprit, t 3 fois les 2 prs
4. Mat, t 3 fois sur tout le rang. Crochetez une pr pour l'incorporer ã' la bande sur la gauche
5. Le nouveau rang commence avec des points d'esprit

Trolly Net

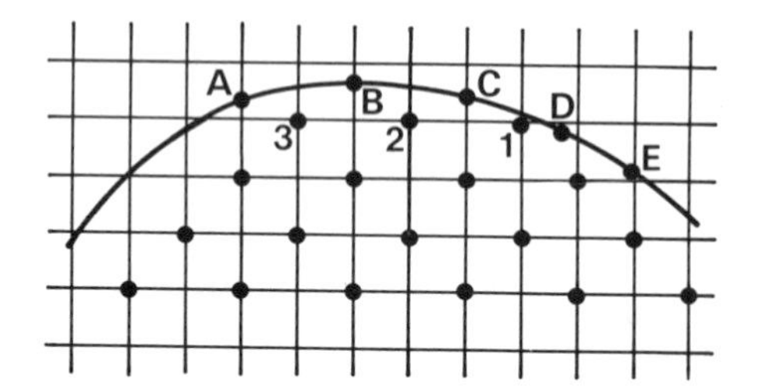

Diagram 11

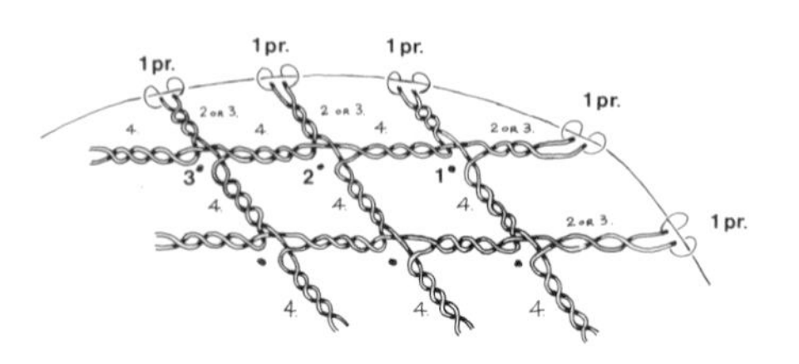

(Refer to diagram 11, 11a, and Pattern 36, Chrysanthemum.) This filling is worked in horizontal rows. (Prick diagonally for a smaller mesh.) Sew in one pair at A, B and C above and between each two holes of the filling. Sew in one pair at D on the right-hand side level with the first row of holes. Twist all pairs two or three times, according to the distance between the pinholes and the edge of the braid. With the pairs from D and

C work a half stitch, twist both pairs four times and set pin 1 between them. * Leave the right-hand pair, and with the left-hand pair and the pair from B work another half stitch and four twists. Set a pin between these pairs. Repeat from * across the row, using the next pair on the left for each stitch. Sew out the left-hand pair at the end of the row. Sew in a new pair at E, twist it and use it with the pair from 1 to work a half stitch and four twists. Set a pin between these pairs. Repeat from * above. The threads run in a diagonal line from top left to bottom right.

grid pricking

1. 1 P. bei A, B, C, D und E einhäkeln
2. Jedes P. 2–3 x zum Nadelpunkt drehen
3. Mit Paaren von D und C Halbschlag, beide 4 x drehen, Nadel 1
4. Linkes P. und nächstes P. links Halbschlag, beide 4 x drehen, Nadel zwischen die Paare stecken
5. Wiederhole (4) zum Reihenende, in das Baendchen abhäkeln
6. Paar von E und Paar von Nadel 1 Halbschlag, beide 4 x drehen, Nadel zwischen die Paare
7. Wiederhole (5)

1. Hang 1 pr in bij A, B, C, D, & E
2. Draai (dr) elk pr 2 of 3 keer tot speldegat
3. Met prn van D & C, netslag (nsl), dr beide 4 keer, sp 1
4. Met linker pr en volgende pr links, lsl, dr beide 4 keer, sp tussen de prn
5. Herhaal (4) tot eind van rij en haak aan in bandje
6. Met pr van E en pr van sp 1, lsl, dr beide 4 keer, sp tussen prn
7. Herhaal (5)

1. Crochetez une paire (pr) en A, B, C, D et E
2. Tordez (t) chaque pr 2 ou 3 fois pour rejoindre le trou de l'épingle
3. Avec une pr de D et C faites une demi-passée (croisez, tordez), tordez (t) les 2 prs 4 fois, piquez l'épingle à 1
4. Une demi-passée sur la pr gauche et la pr suivante à gauche, t 4 fois les 2 prs, épingle au milieu
5. Répétez (4) jusqu'à la fin du rang, crochetez 1 pr pour l'incorporer dans la bande
6. Avec 1 pr venant de E et 1 pr venant de l'épingle 1, faites une demi-passée, t les 2 prs 4 fois, épingle au milieu
7. Répétez (5)

Straight Pin

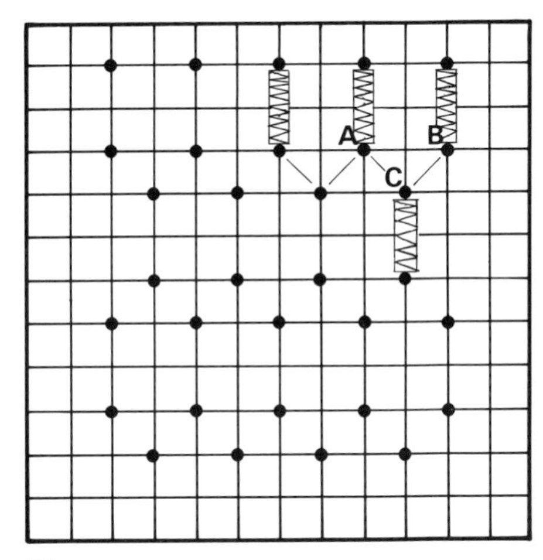

Diagram 12

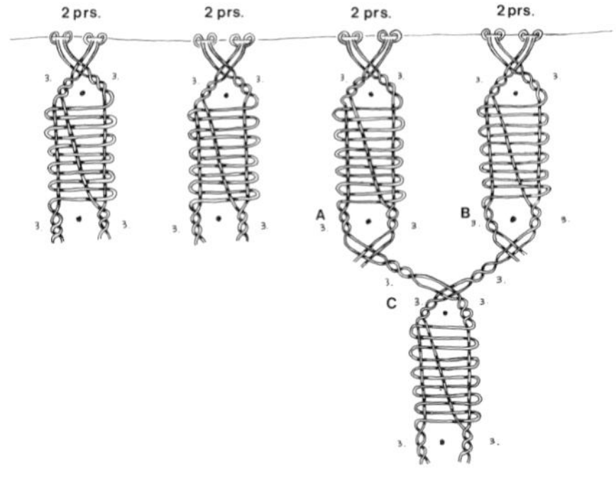

(Refer to diagram 12, 12a, and Pattern 3, Rose (1).) Sew two pairs above each hole across the top of the pattern; with each two pairs make a whole stitch, twist both pairs three times and set pins into the holes between them. With each two pairs work a narrow leadwork to reach the pinholes in the next row. Twist the pairs three times and set a pin between the pairs of each leadwork. Enclose the pins with a whole stitch and twist both pairs three times. The right-hand pair from A and the left-hand pair from B now meet and repeat the pattern (i.e. make a whole stitch and three twists, set pin C between them and use them to make another leadwork). The remaining pairs from A and B meet a pair coming from each side.

grid pricking

1. 2 P. in jeden Nadelpunkt der oberen Linie einhäkeln
2. Mit je 2 P. Ganzschlag, beide 3 x drehen, Nadel zwischen jeweils 2 P.
3. Schmalen Formenschlag zu Nadelpunkten direkt unter den ersten Nadeln
4. Beide P. 3 x drehen, Nadel, Ganzschlag, beide 3 x drehen
5. Mit rechtem P. von A und linkem P. von B Ganzschlag. Schmalen Formenschlag bei C beginnend wie unter (2) beschrieben arbeiten

1. Hang 2 pr in boven elk gat langs bovenkant
2. Met elke 2 pr, linnenslag (lsl), draai (dr) beide 3 keer, sp telkens tussen 2 pr
3. Klos smalle moezen naar spelden vlak onder eerste sp
4. Dr beide prn 3 keer, sp, lsl, dr beide 3 keer
5. Met rechter pr van A en linker pr van B lsl. Maak den smalle moes vanaf C, zoals boven (2)

1. Crochetez 2 paires (prs) au-dessus de chaque trou en haut
2. Travaillez chaque groupe de 2 prs en mat, tordez (t) 3 fois, épingle au milieu
3. Faites des points d'esprit jusqu'aux épingles situées directement en-dessous des premières épingles
4. Tordez (t) les 2 prs 3 fois, piquez l'épingle, mat, t 3 fois
5. Travaillez en mat la pr de droite venant de A et la paire de gauche venant de B. Faites ensuite un point d'esprit en commençant à C, comme (2)

Whole Stitch Block

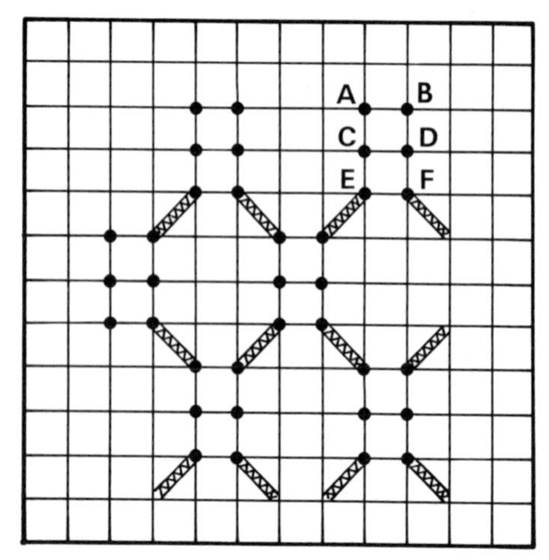

Diagram 13

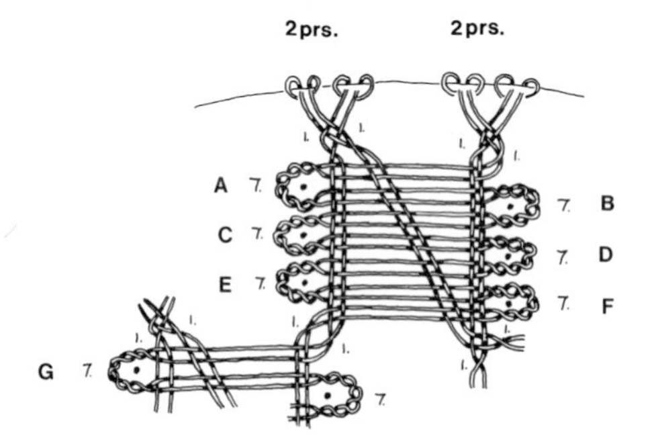

(Refer to diagram 13, 13a, and Pattern 38, Gentian.) Four pairs are sewn in above each snatch hole and a whole stitch and one twist is made with each two pairs before beginning to work the snatch. To work the group of six holes or snatch (as it is called in Devon), use the right hand pair of the four as runners and work through these pairs to the left in the whole stitch. Twist the runners seven times and add a pin in the first hole. Continue back and forth until all six holes are worked. After the last pin of the snatch has been set, work the runners through to the outer side once more, twist them and the last pair they passed through once and leave them. The other two pairs make a whole stitch and twist once. The right-hand pair of the two from E becomes the runner pair for the next snatch diagonally below and works through three pairs to the left, then twists round pin G.

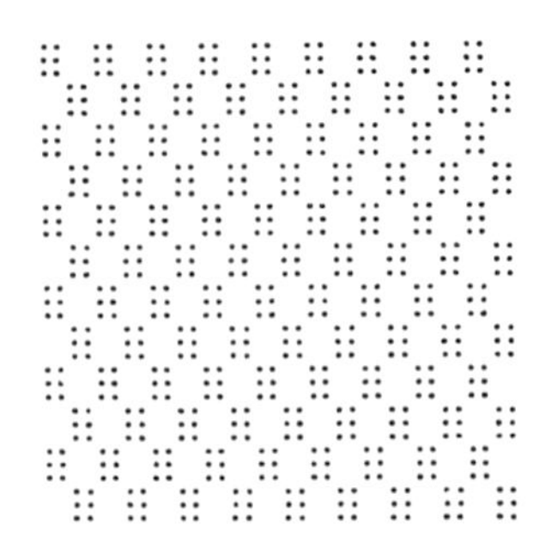

grid pricking

1. 2 P. über jeden Nadelpunkt der oberen Reihe (a und B) einhäkeln
2. Mit je 2 P. Ganzschlag, drehen
3. Mit rechtem P. Ganzschlag durch 3 P. nach links, 7 x drehen, Nadel A
4. Block in Ganzschlag bis F arbeiten, 7 x um jede Nadel drehen
5. Ganzschlag durch 2 P. nach links, Ganzschlag, drehen mit letztem P. links
6. Ganzschlag, drehen, mit restlichen 2 P. rechts
7. Das rechte P. der beiden von E wird Laufpaar durch 3. P. nach links und Nadelpunkt G für den nächsten Block.

1. Hang 2 pr in boven elk gat langs bovenkant (A & B)
2. Klos met iedere 2 pr, linnenslag draaien (lsl dr)
3. Met rechter pr in lsl door 3 pr naar links, dr 7 keer en zet sp
4. Maak 'Block' in lsl tot sp F, dr 7 keer rond iedere sp
5. Lsl door 2 pr naar links, dan lsl dr met laatste pr links
6. Met laatste 2 rechter prn lsl dr
7. Het rechter pr van de 2 bij E wordt looppaar door 3 pr naar links en G om nieuw 'Block' te beginnen

1. Crochetez 2 paires (prs) au-dessus de chaque trou en haut (A et B)
2. Mat sur chaque groupe de 2 prs, tordez (t)
3. Avec la pr de droite, traversez en mat 3 prs à gauche, t 7 fois et piquez l'épingle en A
4. Complétez le 'bloc' en mat jusqu'à l'épingle F avec 7 torsions autour de chaque épingle
5. Traversez 2 prs en mat à gauche, travaillez en mat la dernière pr à gauche, t.
6. Travaillez en mat et t les 2 prs restantes à droite
7. La pr droite des 2 prs venant de E traverse comme meneurs 3 prs à gauche, faites le trou G et commencez le 'bloc' suivant

Devonshire Cutwork Variation

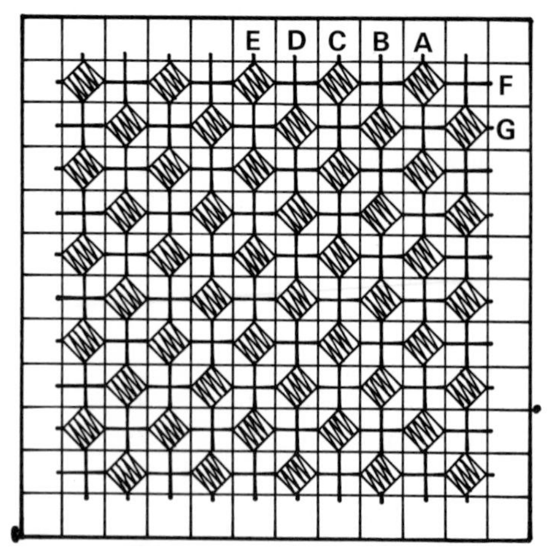

Diagram 14

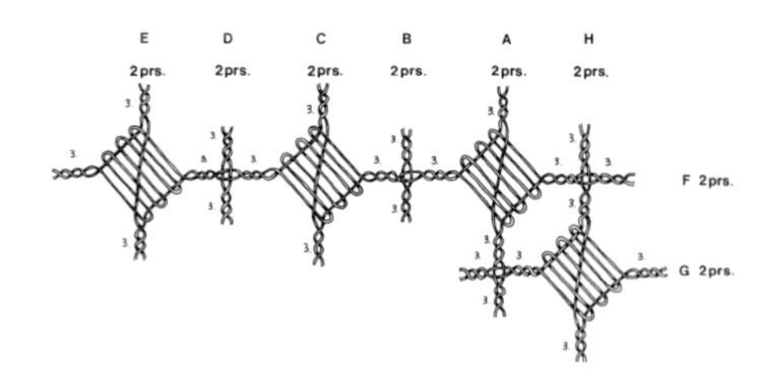

(Refer to diagram 14, 14a, and Pattern 19, Helleborus.) No pricking is needed. Sew in one pair at every hole or, if the holes are close together, at every other hole, across the top of the space, and one pair on the right side at F, one hole below A. Twist all pairs three times. The left-hand bobbin of the pair from F is the weaver for the leadwork. * It is taken under the next thread on the left and over and back under the next thread, to bring it into the right position to begin weaving a small square leadwork. When this is finished and both pairs have been twisted three times, the weaver is the outer thread on the left of these four. Leave the right-hand pair and with the left-hand pair and the pair from B, work a whole stitch and three twists. Pull up the stitch carefully. Leave the right-hand pair and with the left-hand pair and one pair from C make another leadwork, using the same weaver as for the previous leadwork; this is the second thread from the right of these four. Repeat from * across the row, sewing in the pair which has woven across at the end. For the next row a new pair is sewn in at G, and in this row the leadworks are made with the pair that made the whole stitch, so that they come in alternate spaces, with a whole stitch made between the leadworks. Repeat these two rows to fill the space.

Pricking ist nicht erforderlich
1. 2 P. über den jeweiligen Punkt für Formenschlag (A, B, C, D, usw.) einhäkeln
2. Jedes P. 3 x drehen
3. Mit P. von H und F Ganzschlag, beide 3 x drehen
4. Mit dem linken dieser 2 P. und dem nächsten P. links (A) schmalen Formenschlag arbeiten, beide P. 3 x drehen
5. Mit dem linken dieser 2 P. und dem nächsten P. links (B) Ganzschlag, beide 3 x drehen
6. Wiederhole (4 und 5) zum Ende der Reihe
7. Mit Paaren von G und H Formenschlag als Anfang der nächsten Reihe
8. Wiederhole (5) für P. von A

Geen prikking nodig
1. Hang 2 pr in boven iedere te klossen moes ('leadwork') (A, B, C, D enz.)
2. Draai (dr) elk pr 3 keer
3. Klos met prn van H & F linnenslag (lsl), dr beide 3 keer
4. Maak met linker van deze 2 pr en volgende pr links (A) smalle moes, dr beide prn 3 keer
5. Met linker van deze 2 prn en volgende pr links (B), lsl, dr beide 3 keer
6. Herhaal (4 & 5) langs hele rij
7. Maak met prn van G & H moes aan begin van volgende rij
8. Herhaal (5) voor pr van A

Ne demande pas de piquage
1. Accrochez 2 paires (prs) au-dessus de chaque point d'esprit à exécuter (A, B, C, D, etc.)
2. Tordez (t) chaque pr 3 fois
3. Travaillez en mat les prs de H et F, tordez-les (t) 3 fois
4. Avec la pr de gauche de ces 2 prs et la pr suivante à gauche (A), faites un point d'esprit et t les 2 prs 3 fois
5. La pr gauche de ces 2 prs traverse en mat la pr suivante à gauche (B), t 3 fois
6. Répétez (4) et (5) sur tout le rang
7. Avec des prs de G et de H faites un point d'esprit au début du rang suivant
8. Répétez (5) avec la pr de A

Four Pin and Leadwork

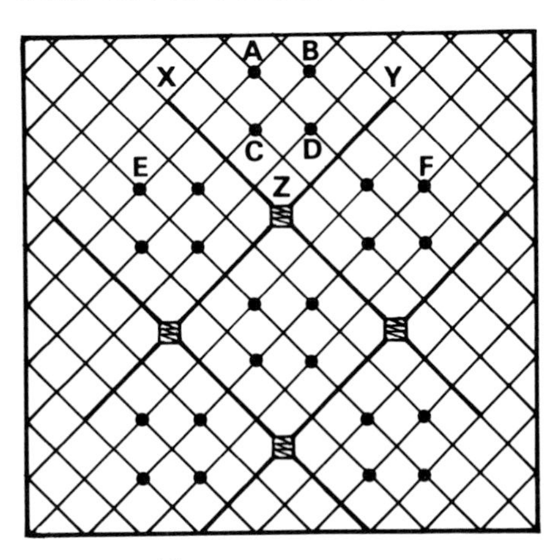

Diagram 15

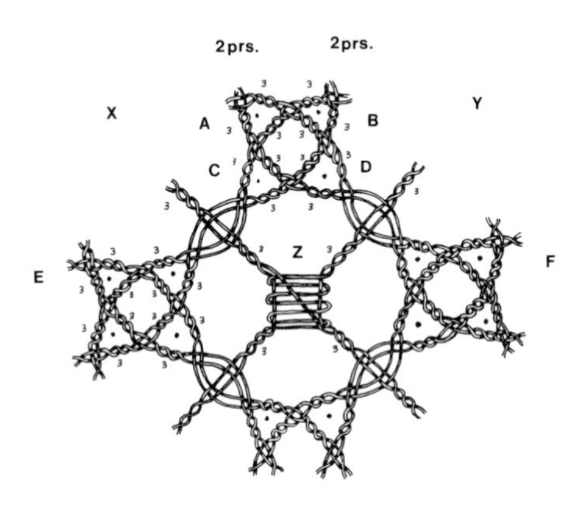

(Refer to diagram 15, 15a, and Pattern 39, Sunflower.) Sew in two pairs above each hole A, B, E and F and one pair at each point X. Using the four pairs above A and B, work the first group of four holes as follows. * With the two left-hand pairs work a whole stitch, twist both pairs three times and set pin A between them. With the two right-hand pairs work a whole stitch, twist both pairs three times and set pin B between them. With the two middle pairs work a whole stitch and twist both pairs three times (No Pin). With the two left-hand pairs work a whole stitch, twist both pairs three times and set pin C between them. With the two right-hand pairs work a whole stitch, twist both pairs three times and set pin D between them. With the two middle pairs work a whole stitch and twist both pairs three times (No Pin). * Now enclose pins C and D with a whole stitch. Twist the pairs from X three times and work them in whole stitch through the pairs from C and D, so that they meet in the space below the first group of holes, where they are twisted three times and work a square leadwork. Twist both pairs three times after the leadwork and leave them. The pairs from C and E work the next four pin group from * to *, after which the two lower pairs are enclosed with a whole stitch, and the left-hand pair of the leadwork is worked in whole stitch through the two right-hand pairs of this group.

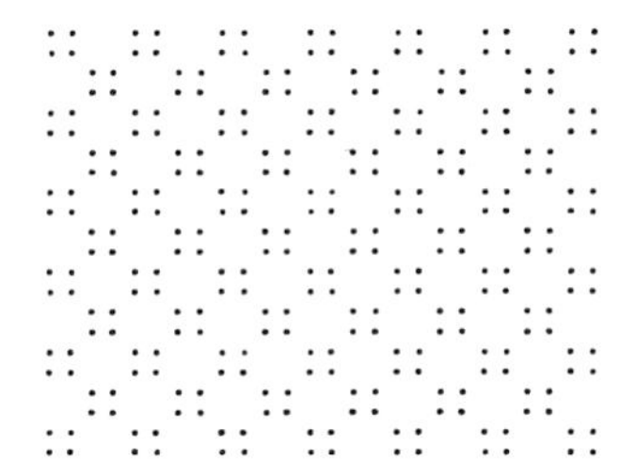

grid pricking

1. Arbeite Nadel A, B, C und D wie bei 'Four Pin', Seite 110 beschrieben
2. 2 P. bei X und Y anhängen, 3 x drehen
3. Mit P. von X Ganzschlag durch 2 P. von C, beide 3 x drehen
4. Mit P. von Y Ganzschlag durch 2 P. von D, beide 3 x drehen
5. Formenschlag bei Z, beide P. 3 x drehen
6. Paare von C und E bilden nächste 'Four Pin' Gruppe links
7. Paare von D und F bilden nächste 'Four Pin' Gruppe rechts

1. Bewerk spelden A, B, C & D als in Four Pin, p. 110
2. Hang 2 pr bij X & Y, draai (dr) 3 keer
3. Met pr van X, lsl door 2 pr van C, dr beide 3 keer
4. Met pr van Y, lsl door 2 pr van D, dr beide 3 keer
5. Klos moes bij Z, dr beide prn 3 keer
6. Prn van C & E vormen volgende Four

Pin groep aan linkerkant
7. Prn van D & F vormen volgende Four Pin groep aan rechterkant

1. Travaillez les épingles A, B, C et D comme pour le Four Pin, page 110
2. Accrochez 2 prs à X et Y, tordez-les (t) 3 fois
3. Avec la paire (pr) venant de X, traversez en mat 2 prs de C, t 3 fois les 2 prs
4. Avec la pr venant de Y, traversez en mat 2 prs de D, t 3 fois
5. Faites un point d'esprit à Z et t les 2 prs 3 fs
6. Des prs de C et E font le groupe suivant de Quatre Épingles à gauche
7. Des prs de D et F font le groupe suivant de Quatre Épingles à droite

Leadwork Bars

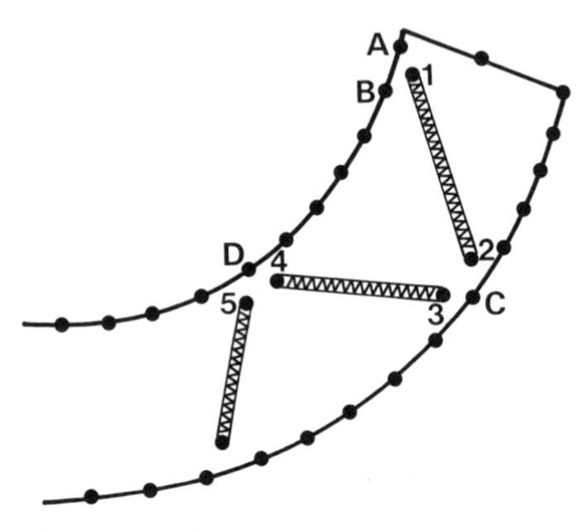

Diagram 16

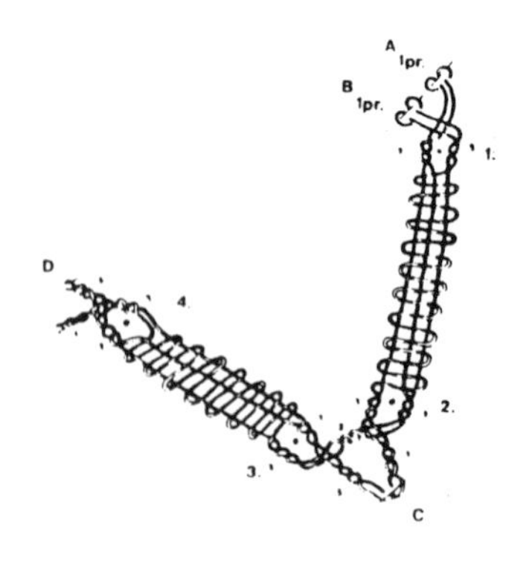

(Refer to diagram 16, 16a, and Pattern 8, Clarkia.) Sew a pair into the braid at pinholes A and B. Make a whole stitch and twist each pair three times. Put a pin into the single pinhole 1. Work a leadwork towards pinhole C. Twist the pairs three times. Set a pin in hole 2, make a whole stitch, and twist each pair three times on the pin. Sew the outer pair into pinhole C, tie once, make a whole stitch, twist three times and put a pin into hole 3. Make the leadwork from hole 3 to hole 4 and repeat from 4 to 5 as from 2 to 3, until the last pinhole is reached. At the last pinhole, twist each pair three times and put a pin in the single pinhole; make a whole stitch, twist each pair three times and sew out each pair into the nearest two holes of the braid.

1. Je 1 P. bei A und B einhäkeln
2. Ganzschlag, beide 3 x drehen, Nadel 1 dazwischen stecken
3. Schmalen Formenschlag zu Nadelpunkt 2
4. Beide P. 3 x drehen, Nadel 2, Ganzschlag, beide 3 x drehen
5. Rechtes P. bei C einhäkeln, knoten, 3 x drehen
6. Ganzschlag, beide 3 x drehen, Nadel 3 dazwischen stecken
7. Schmalen Formenschlag zu Nadelpunkt 4. Wiederholen wie fuer Nadel 2 und 3

1. Hang bij A & B ieder 1 pr in
2. Klos linnenslag (lsl), draai (dr) beide 3 keer, zet sp ertussen
3. Maak smalle moes naar sp 2
4. Dr beide prn 3 keer, sp 2, lsl, dr beide 3 keer
5. Haak rechter pr aan bij C, knoop, dr dan 3 keer
6. Lsl, dr beide 3 keer, zet sp 3 ertussen
7. Maak smalle moes naar sp 4. Herhaal als bij sp 2 & 3

1. Crochetez une paire en A et B
2. Travaillez en mat, tordez (t) 3 fois, épingle au milieu
3. Faites un point d'esprit jusqu'au trou 2
4. Tordez les 2 prs 3 fois, piquez l'épingle à (2), mat, t 3 fois
5. Crochetez la pr droite en C, nouez-la et t 3 fois
6. Mat, t 3 fois, épingle 3 au milieu
7. Faites un point d'esprit étroit jusqu'au trou 4. Répétez le travail des épingles 2 et 3

Swing Leadworks

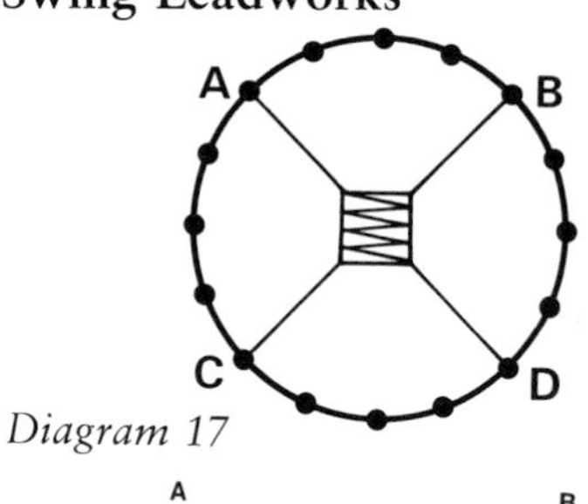

Diagram 17

A B
1pr. 1pr.
3 or more
3 or more
3 or more
3 or more
C D

(Refer to diagram 17, 17a, and Pattern 5, Primrose.) Sew one pair at holes A and B and tie each pair once. Twist each pair three times (depending upon the size of the space to be filled, more twists may be necessary so that the single leadwork will lie in the central position). Work a small square leadwork. Twist the pairs three times and sew out at C and D, taking care not to pull the weaver thread. Tie each pair three times. These Swing Leadworks are only suitable to fill small spaces.

1. Je ein P. bei A und B einhäkeln
2. Jedes P. drei oder mehrmals bis zum Anfang des Formenschlags drehen
3. Schmalen Formenschlag in der Mitte
4. Jedes P. wie zuvor bis zu C und D drehen
5. Paare bei C und D abhäkeln, jedes P. 3 x knoten

1. Hang bij A & B ieder 1 pr in
2. Draai (dr) elk pr 3 of meer keer tot aan de moes ('leadwork')
3. Maak kleine moes in midden
4. Dr Elk pr als hiervoor, tot C & D
5. Haak prn aan bij C & D. Knoop elk pr 3 keer

1. Crochetez une paire (pr) à A et B
2. Tordez (t) chaque pr 3 fois ou davantage pour rejoindre le début des points d'esprit
3. Faites un petit point d'esprit au centre
4. T chaque pr comme précédemment, jusqu'à C et D
5. Crochetez les prs en C et D. Nouez chaque pr 3 fois

Appendix II: Working threads from one section to another

First method

Work to 1 and make a back stitch at this hole. Work to 2 and sew the runner pair and the edge pairs at this hole. Tie the edge pair three times at this hole and lay aside to be cut off later. With the sewn runners work through one pair. Tie the runners once and work them through two more pairs. * Leave the runners and with the last pair they worked through, work back to hole 3. Sew the runners here. Take the two bobbins inside the coarse bobbin or, if a coarse thread is not being used, inside the first bobbin, tie them three times and cut them out. Work the sewn runners again through three pairs, and repeat from * twice (holes 4 and 5). From 5 the sewn runners are taken through all downrights to 1, to make up the back stitch there. Work to 6 and sew the runners there. Tie the runners once, twist them three times and leave them to become an edge pair. The threads are now in position to work the adjoining section. Take the edge pairs left at 1 as runners out to the outer edge and work the next pin hole there. Continue the next section taking sewings on the inner side.

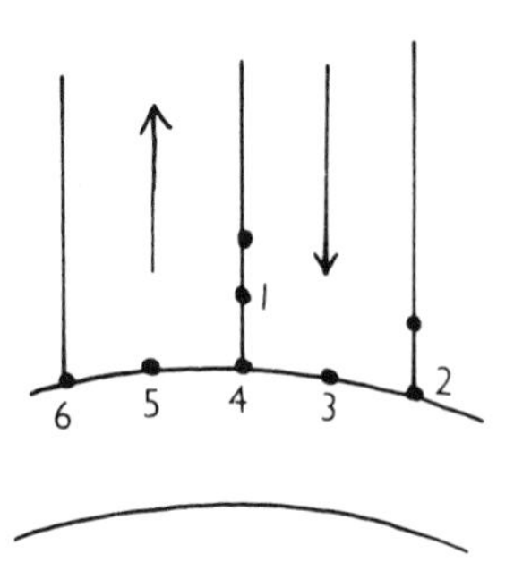

Second method

Sometimes the two sections are not joined as above. In this case, work as above until the runners have been sewn at 6. Work the sewn runners to 7 and make the edge stitch there. Before returning, sew a new pair at 6, twist it three times and use it as the new edge pair on this side.

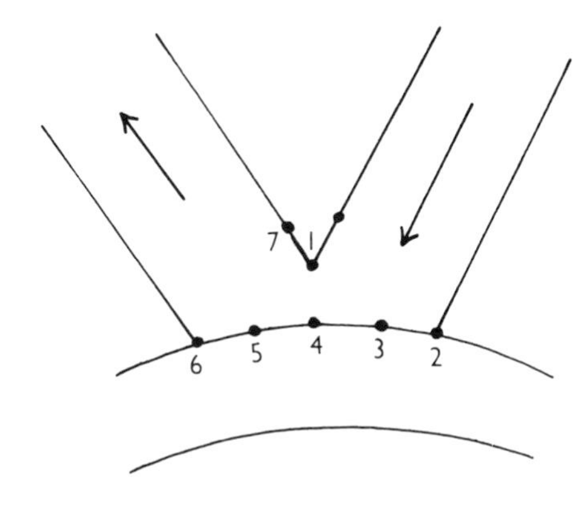

Third method

In this turning there is no completed edge to which the runners can be sewn and the lower edge 2–6 must be made at the same time as the turn. Work to 1 and make a backstitch at this hole. Work to 2 and make the edge stitch. Work through the coarse pair, tie the runners and work through two more pairs. ** Leave the runners and use the last pair they worked through as new runners to work to 3, where they make the edge stitch. Take the two bobbins inside the coarse thread, tie them three times and cut them off. Work back through three pairs and repeat from ** for holes 4 and 5 (do not take out a pair at 5). From 5 the runners work through to 1 to make up the back stitch there. Work to 6. Untwist the inner edge pair and weave the coarse thread between these two bobbins to lie as the thread next to the sewing edge. Continue the next section, after tying the runners at 6, and take sewings on the inner side.

These are general methods and must be adapted to suit each individual pattern. The number of pin holes along the base line may vary according to the width of the piece being turned and there may not be enough pairs to enable one to throw out a pair at the last hole or two of the turn. On the other hand, if there are too many pairs, making the clothwork too thick round the back stitch, one or two extra pairs may be taken out before the back stitch is made up.

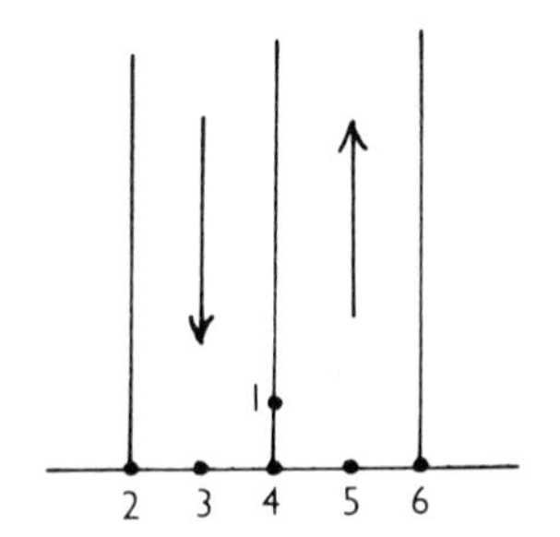

Appendix III: Book suppliers

ENGLAND
The following are stockists of the complete Batsford/Dryad Press range:

AVON
Bridge Bookshop
7 Bridge Street
Bath BA2 4AS

Waterstone & Co.
4–5 Milsom Street
Bath BA1 1DA

BEDFORDSHIRE
Arthur Sells
Lane Cover
49 Pedley Lane
Clifton
Shefford SG17 5QT

BERKSHIRE
Loricraft
4 Big Lane
Lambourn

West End Lace Supplies
Ravensworth Court Road
Mortimer West End
Reading RG7 3UD

BUCKINGHAMSHIRE
J. S. Sear
Lacecraft Supplies
8 Hillview
Sherington MK16 9NJ

CAMBRIDGESHIRE
Dillons the Bookstore
Sidney Street
Cambridge

CHESHIRE
Lynn Turner
Church Meadow Crafts
15 Carisbrooke Drive
Winsford CW7 1LN

CORNWALL
Creative Books
22A River Street
Truro TR1 2SJ

DEVON
Creative Crafts & Needlework
18 High Street
Totnes TQ9 5NP

Honiton Lace Shop
44 High Street
Honiton EX14 8PJ

DORSET
F. Herring & Sons
27 High West Street
Dorchester DT1 1UP

Tim Parker (mail order)
124 Corhampton Road
Boscombe East
Bournemouth BH6 5NZ

Christopher Williams
19 Morrison Avenue
Parkstone
Poole BH17 4AD

DURHAM
Lacemaid
6, 10 & 15 Stoneybeck
Bishop Middleham DL17 9BL

GLOUCESTERSHIRE
Southgate Handicrafts
63 Southgate Street
Gloucester GL1 1TX

Waterstone & Company
89–90 The Promenade
Cheltenham GL50 1NB

HAMPSHIRE
Creative Crafts
11 The Square
Winchester SO23 9ES

Doreen Gill
14 Barnfield Road
Petersfield GU31 4DR

Larkfield Crafts
4 Island Cottages
Mapledurwell
Basingstoke RG23 2LU

Needlestyle
24–26 West Street
Alresford

Ruskins
27 Bell Street
Romsey

ISLE OF WIGHT
Busy Bobbins
Unit 7
Scarrots Lane
Newport PO30 1JD

KENT
The Handicraft Shop
47 Northgate
Canterbury CT1 1BE

Hatchards
The Great Hall
Mount Pleasant Road
Tunbridge Wells

LONDON
W. & G. Foyle Ltd.
113–119 Charing Cross Road
WC2H 0EB

Hatchards
187 Piccadilly W1V 9DA

MIDDLESEX
Redburn Crafts
Squires Garden Centre
Halliford Road
Upper Halliford
Shepperton TW17 8RU

NORFOLK
Alby Lace Museum
Cromer Road
Alby
Norwich NR11 7QE

Jane's Pincushions
Taverham Craft Unit 4
Taverham Nursery Centre
Fir Covert Road
Taverham
Norwich NR8 6HT

Waterstone & Company Ltd
30 London Street
Norwich NR2 1LD

NORTHAMPTONSHIRE
Denis Hornsby
149 High Street
Burton Latimer
Kettering NN15 5RL

SOMERSET
Bridge Bookshop
62 Bridge Street
Taunton TA1 1UD

STAFFORDSHIRE
J. & J. Ford
October Hill
65 Upper Way
Upper Longdon
Rugeley WS16 1QB

SUSSEX
Waterstone & Company Ltd.
120 Terminus Road
Eastbourne

WARWICKSHIRE
Christine & David Springett
21 Hillmorton Road
Rugby CV22 6DF

WILTSHIRE
Everyman Bookshop
5 Bridge Street
Salisbury SP1 2ND

NORTH YORKSHIRE
Craft Basics
9 Gillygate
York

Shireburn Lace
Finkle Court
Finkle Hill
Sherburn in Elmet LS25 6EB

The Craft House
23 Bar Street
Scarborough YO13 9QE

WEST MIDLANDS
Needlewoman
21 Needles Alley
off New Street
Birmingham B2 5AG

WEST YORKSHIRE
Sebalace
Waterloo Mill
Howden Road
Silsden BD20 0HA

George White Lacemaking Supplies
40 Heath Drive
Boston Spa LS23 6PB

Jo Firth
58 Kent Crescent
Lowtown, Pudsey
Leeds LS28 9EB

SCOTLAND
Embroidery Shop
51 William Street
Edinburgh
Lothian EH3 7LW

Waterstone & Company Ltd.
236 Union Street
Aberdeen AB1 1TN

WALES
Bryncraft Bobbins (*mail order*)
B. J. Phillips
Pantglas
Cellan
Lampeter
Dyfed SA48 8JD

Appendix IV: Equipment suppliers

UNITED KINGDOM
General equipment

Alby Lace Museum
Cromer Road
Alby
Norwich
Norfolk NR11 7QE

Busy Bobbins
Unit 7
Scarrots Lane
Newport
IOW PO30 1JD

Central Scotland Lace Supplies
3 Strude Howe
Alva
Clack's FK12 5JU

Chosen Crafts Centre
46 Winchcombe Street
Cheltenham
Glos GL52 2ND

Jo Firth
Lace Marketing & Needlecraft Supplies
58 Kent Crescent
Lowtown
Pudsey
W Yorks LS28 9EB

J. & J. Ford
October Hill
Upper Way
Upper Longdon
Rugeley
Staffs WS16 1QB

Framecraft
83 Hamstead Road
Handsworth Wood
Birmingham B2 1JA

R. Gravestock
Highwood
Crews Hill
Alfrick
Worcs WR6 5HG

The Handicraft Shop
47 Northgate
Canterbury
Kent CT1 1BE

Frank Herring & Sons
27 High West Street
Dorchester
Dorset DT1 1UP

Honiton Lace Shop
44 High Street
Honiton
Devon EX14 8PJ

Denis Hornsby
149 High Street
Burton Latimer
Kettering
Northants NN15 5RL
also at:
25 Manwood Avenue
Canterbury
Kent CT2 7AH

Frances Iles
73 High Street
Rochester
Kent ME1 1LX

Jane's Pincushions
Taverham Craft Unit 4
Taverham Nursery Centre
Fir Covert Road
Taverham
Norwich NR8 6HT

Just Lace
Lacemaker Supplies
14 Ashwood Gardens
Gildersome
Leeds LS27 7AS

Loricraft
4 Big Lane
Lambourn
Berks

Needlestyle
5 The Woolmead
Farnham
Surrey GU9 7TX

Needlestyle
24–26 West Street
Alresford
Hants

Needlework
Ann Bartleet
Bucklers Farm
Coggeshall
Essex CO6 1SB

Needle and Thread
80 High Street
Horsell
Woking
Surrey GU21 4SZ

The Needlewoman
21 Needles Alley
off New Street
Birmingham B2 5AE

Tim Parker (*mail order*)
124 Corhampton Road
Boscombe East
Bournemouth
Dorset BH6 5NZ

Jane Playford
North Lodge
Church Close
West Runton
Norfolk NR27 9QY

Redburn Crafts
Squires Garden Centre
Halliford Road
Upper Halliford
Shepperton
Middx TW17 8RU

Christine Riley
53 Barclay Street
Stonehaven
Kincardineshire
Scotland

Peter & Beverley Scarlett
Strupak
Hill Head
Cold Wells, Ellon
Grampian
Scotland

Ken & Pat Schultz
134 Wisbech Road
Thornley
Peterborough
Cambs

J. S. Sears
Lacecraft Supplies
8 Hillview
Sherington
Bucks MK16 9NJ

Sebalace
Waterloo Mills
Howden Road
Silsden
W Yorks BD2 0NA

A. Sells
49 Pedley Lane
Clifton
Shefford
Beds SG17 5QT

Shireburn Lace
Finkle Court
Finkle Hill
Sherburn in Elmet
N Yorks LS25 6EB

SMP
4 Garners Close
Chalfont St Peter
Bucks SL9 0HB

Southern Handicrafts
20 Kensington Gardens
Brighton
Sussex BN1 4AC

Spangles
Carole Morris
Cashburn Lane
Burwell
Cambs CB5 0ED

Stitches
Dovehouse Shopping Parade
Warwick Road
Olton, Solihull
W Midlands

Teazle Embroideries
35 Boothferry Road
Hull
N Humberside

Lynn Turner
Church Meadow Crafts
15 Carisbrooke Drive
Winsford
Cheshire CW7 1LN

The Craft House
23 Bar Street
Scarborough
N Yorks

George Walker
The Corner Shop
Rickinghall, Diss
Norfolk

West End Lace Supplies
Ravensworth Court Road
Mortimer West End
Reading
Berks RG7 3UD

George White Lacemaking Supplies
40 Heath Drive
Boston Spa
W Yorks LS23 6PB

Bobbins

A. R. Archer
The Poplars
Shetland
near Stowmarket
Suffolk IP14 3DE

Bartlett, Caesar and Partners
12 Creslow Court
Stony Stratford
Milton Keynes MK11 1NN
also at:
The Glen
Shorefield Road
Downton
Lymington
Hants SO41 0LH

T. Brown
Temple Lane Cottage
Littledean
Cinderford
Glos

Bryncraft Bobbins
B.J. Phillips
Pantglas, Cellan
Lampeter
Dyfed SA48 8JD

Chrisken Bobbins
26 Cedar Drive
Kingsclere
Bucks RG15 8TD

Malcolm J. Fielding
2 Northern Terrace
Moss Lane
Silverdale
Lancs LA5 0ST

Richard Gravestock
Highwood
Crews Hill
Alfrick
Worcs WR6 5HF

Itsa Bobbins
G. & R. Downs
2 Ryll Close
Exmouth
Devon EX8 1TY

Larkfield Crafts
Hilary Ricketts
4 Island Cottages
Mapledurwell
Basingstoke
Hants RG25 2LU

Loricraft
4 Big Lane
Lambourn
Berks

Tim Parker (*mail order*)
124 Corhampton Road
Boscombe East
Bournemouth
Dorset BH6 5NZ

D. H. Shaw
47 Lamor Crescent
Thrushcroft
Rotherham
S Yorks S66 9QD

Christine & David Springett
21 Hillmorton Road
Rugby
War CV22 5DF

Richard Viney
Unit 7
Port Royal Street
Southsea
Hants PO5 3UD

West End Lace Suppliers
Ravensworth Court Road
Mortimer West End
Reading
Berks RG7 3UD

Winslow Bobbins
70 Magpie Way
Winslow
Bucks MK18 3PZ

Lace pillows
Newnham Lace Equipment
15 Marlowe Close
Basingstoke
Hants RG24 9DD

Bartlett, Caesar and Partners
12 Creslow Court
Stony Stratford
Milton Keynes MK11 1NN
also at:
The Glen
Shorefield Road
Downton
Lymington
Hants SO41 0LH

Silk embroidery and lace thread
E. & J. Piper
Silverlea
Flax Lane, Glemsford
Suffolk CO10 7RS

Silk weaving yarn
Hilary Chetwynd
Kipping Cottage
Cheriton, Alresford
Hants SO24 0PW

Frames and mounts
Doreen Campbell
Highcliff
Bremilham Road
Malmesbury
Wilts SN16 0DQ

Framecraft Miniatures Ltd
148–150 High Street
Aston
Birmingham B6 4US

Matt coloured transparent adhesive film
Heffers Graphic Shop
26 King Street
Cambridge CB1 1LN

Linen by the metre (yard) and made up articles of church linen
Mary Collins
Church Furnishings
St Andrews Hall
Humber Doucy Lane
Ipswich
Suffolk IP4 3BP

Hayes & Finch
Head Office & Factory
Hanson Road
Aintree
Liverpool L9 9BP

UNITED STATES OF AMERICA

Arbor House
22 Arbor Lane
Roslyn Hights
NY 11577

Baltazor Inc.
3262 Severn Avenue
Metairie
LA 7002

Beggars' Lace
P.O. Box 17263
Denver
Colo 80217

Berga Ullman Inc.
P.O. Box 918
North Adams
MA 01247

Frederick J. Fawcett
129 South Street
Boston
MA 02130

Frivolité
15526 Densmore N.
Seattle
WA 98113

Happy Hands
3007 S. W. Marshall
Pendleton
Oreg 97180

International Old Lacers
P.O. Box 1029
Westminster
Colo 80030

Lace Place de Belgique
800 S. W. 17th Street
Boca Raton
FL 33432

Lacis
2150 Stuart Street
Berkeley
CA 9470

Robin's Bobbins
RTL Box 1736
Mineral Bluff
GA 30559

Robin and Russ
Handweavers
533 North Adams Street
McMinnvills
Oreg 97128

Some Place
2990 Adline Street
Berkeley
CA 94703

Osma G. Todd Studio
319 Mendoza Avenue
Coral Gables
FL 33134

The Unique And Art Lace Cleaners
5926 Delman Boulevard
St Louis
MO 63112

Van Scriver Bobbin Lace
130 Cascadilla Park
Ithaca
NY 14850

The World in Stitches
82 South Street
Milford
N.H. 03055

AUSTRALIA

***Australian Lace* magazine**
P.O. Box 1291
Toowong
Queensland 4066

Dentelles Lace Supplies
c/o Betty Franks
39 Lang Terrace
Northgate 4013
Brisbane
Queensland

The Lacemaker
94 Fordham Avenue
Hartwell
Victoria 3124

Spindle and Loom
Arcade 83
Longueville Road
Lane Cove
NSW 2066

Tulis Crafts
201 Avoca Street
Randwick
NSW 2031

BELGIUM

't Handwerkhuisje
Katelijnestraat 23
8000 Bruges

Kantcentrum
Balstraat 14
8000 Bruges

Manufacture Belge de Dentelle
6 Galerie de la Reine
Galeries Royales St Hubert
1000 Bruxelles

Orchidée
Mariastraat 18
8000 Bruges

Ann Thys
't Apostelientje
Balstraat 11
8000 Bruges

FRANCE

Centre d'Initiations à la Dentelle du Puy
2 Rue Duguesclin
43000 Le Puy en Velay

A L'Econome
Anne-Marie Deydier
Ecole de Dentelle aux Fuseaux
10 rue Paul Chenavard
69001 Lyon

Rougier and Plé
13-15 bd des Filles de Calvaire
75003 Paris

GERMANY

Der Fenster Laden
Berliner Str. 8
D 6483 Bad Soden
Salmünster

P. P. Hempel
Ortolanweg 34
1000 Berlin 47

Heikona De Ruijter
Klöppelgrosshandel
Langer Steinweg 38
D4933 Blomberg

HOLLAND

Blokker's Boektiek
Bronsteeweg 4/4a
2101 AC Heemstede

Theo Brejaart
Dordtselaan 146-148
P.O. Box 5199
3008 AD Rotterdam

Magazijn ***De Vlijt***
Lijnmarkt 48
Utrecht

SWITZERLAND

Fadehax
Inh. Irene Solca
4105 Biel-Benken
Basel

NEW ZEALAND

Peter McLeavey
P.O. Box 69.007
Auckland 8

Appendix V: Sources of information

UNITED KINGDOM

The Lace Guild
The Hollies
53 Audnam
Stourbridge
West Midlands DY8 4AE

The Lacemakers' Circle
49 Wardwick
Derby DE1 1HY

The Lace Society
Linwood
Stratford Road
Oversley
Alcester
War BY9 6PG

The British College of Lace
21 Hillmorton Road
Rugby
War CV22 5DF

The English Lace School
Oak House
Church Stile
Woodbury
Nr Exeter
Devon

Ring of Tatters
Miss B. Netherwood
269 Oregon Way
Chaddesden
Derby DE2 6UR

United Kingdom Director of International Old Lacers
S. Hurst
4 Dollis Road
London N3 1RG

USA

International Old Lacers
Gunvor Jorgensen (Pres.)
366 Bradley Avenue
Northvale
NR 076647

***Lace & Crafts* magazine**
3201 East Lakeshore Drive
Tallahassee
FL 32312-2034

Further reading

DEVONIA, *The Honiton Lace Book* (The Bazaar Office, London, 1873; reprinted by Paul Minet, London, 1972).

LUXTON, ELSIE, *Honiton Lace Patterns* (B.T. Batsford Ltd, London, 1983)

LUXTON, ELSIE, *The Technique of Honiton Lace* (B.T. Batsford Ltd, London, 1979, 1990)

LUXTON, ELSIE and FUKUYAMA, YUSAI, *Honiton Lace: The Visual Approach* (B.T. Batsford Ltd, London, 1988)

LUXTON, ELSIE and FUKUYAMA, YUSAI, *Royal Honiton Lace* (B.T. Batsford Ltd, London, 1988)

MAIDMENT, MARGARET, *A Manual of Hand-Made Bobbin Lace* (B.T. Batsford Ltd, London, 1931, 1983)

PALLISER, *The History of Lace* (E.P. Publishing Ltd, 1902)

PENDERALL MOODY, A., *Devon Pillow Lace* (Cassell & Co. Ltd, London, 1907)

TAKANO, SAIKOH, *Birds and Animals in Honiton Lace* (B.T. Batsford Ltd, London, 1992)

THOMPSON, SUSANNE, *Introduction to Honiton Lace*, (B.T. Batsford Ltd, London, 1985, 1988)

TREADWIN, *Antique Point and Honiton Lace* (Ward Lock & Tyler, London, 1874)